# Strategic Cost Red[uction]

## Cutting Costs without Killing your Business

## Second Edition

Tim McCormick and Dermot Duff

Chartered Accountants Ireland

Published by
Chartered Accountants Ireland
Chartered Accountants House
47–49 Pearse Street
Dublin 2
www.charteredaccountants.ie

© The Institute of Chartered Accountants in Ireland, 2012.

Copyright in this publication is owned by the Institute of Chartered Accountants in Ireland. All rights reserved. No part of this text may be reproduced or transmitted or communicated to the public in any form or by any means, including photocopying, Internet or e-mail dissemination, without the written permission of the Institute of Chartered Accountants in Ireland. Such written permission must also be obtained before any part of this document is stored in a retrieval system of any nature.

This publication is designed to provide accurate and authoritative information in regard to the subject matter covered. It is provided on the understanding that the Institute of Chartered Accountants in Ireland is not engaged in rendering professional services. The Institute of Chartered Accountants in Ireland disclaims all liability for any reliance placed on the information contained within this publication and recommends that if professional advice or other expert assistance is required, the services of a competent professional should be sought.

ISBN: 978-1-908199-34-8

Typeset by Datapage
Printed by Turners Printing Company, Longford

# Table of Contents

*Foreword to the first edition*   xi
*Acknowledgements*   xiii
*Introduction*   xvii

### Part I   Evaluating budgeting and other traditional approaches to cost reduction to assess the health of the business and the need for cost reduction

**1. Budgeting challenges**   3
   Different approaches to budgeting   4
   The role of budgeting and cost reduction   5
   Budgeting in practice   6
   Zero-based budgeting   8
   Priority-based budgeting   10
   Beyond budgeting   11
   Conclusions   12
   Management checklist   12

**2. Effective control**   13
   Organisational prerequisites   13
   The principles of effective budgeting   15
   The usual budgetary problems   17
   Prioritisation of costs for reduction   18
   Reducing individual costs through the '3 Es'   20
   Conclusions   23
   Management checklist   24

**3. The role of the functions in traditional cost reduction**   25
   Financial control   26
   Operations   27
   Procurement or purchasing   28
   Engineering   30

| | |
|---|---|
| Human resources (HR) | 31 |
| Information technology (IT) | 33 |
| Logistics | 34 |
| Sales and marketing | 35 |
| Internal audit/organisation and methods | 35 |
| Management by objectives (MBO) | 36 |
| The most likely areas for cost reduction | 37 |
| A holistic or piecemeal approach? | 37 |
| Conclusions | 38 |
| Management checklist | 39 |

**4. Is there a problem with current performance?**     **40**

| | |
|---|---|
| Health check | 41 |
| Worrying symptoms | 41 |
| The health objective: shareholder value | 42 |
| Return on invested capital (ROIC) | 44 |
| Benchmarking ROIC | 44 |
| Setting a target ROIC | 45 |
| The drivers of ROIC | 46 |
| Setting a cost reduction target | 46 |
| Limitations of ROIC | 47 |
| Prognosis without intervention | 48 |
| Conclusions | 49 |
| Management checklist | 49 |

**5. Emergency cost reduction in a cash crisis**     **50**

| | |
|---|---|
| The cashflow model of business | 51 |
| Working capital management | 52 |
| Short-term cash generation | 54 |
| The credit crunch | 55 |
| Initial reactions to the credit crunch | 57 |
| Addressing the credit crunch | 58 |
| Consequences of emergency cost reduction | 59 |
| Conclusions | 59 |
| Management checklist | 60 |

## Part II Approaching cost reduction strategically to fit the cost reduction programme into the wider framework and values

6. **Preliminary strategic considerations**     63
   Cost reduction failures     63
   The strategic framework     64
   Memo from the chairman     65
   Issues for the board     67
   Overall cost leadership and the alternatives     67
   Core values     69
   Key issues for the CEO: style and participation     70
   Use of external resources: consultants and mentors     72
   Conclusions     73
   Management checklist     74

7. **Critical functional considerations**     75
   Memo from the CEO     75
   Issues for the sales and marketing director     77
   Issues for the finance director     78
   Issues for the operations director     82
   Issues for the human resources director     84
   Issues for other disciplines     86
   Reconciling functional imperatives     87
   Conclusions     87
   Management checklist     88

8. **Discovering the strategic drivers of cost**     89
   Size and growth cost drivers     89
   Situational cost drivers     92
   Relationship cost drivers     93
   Discretionary cost drivers     96
   An example from the printing industry     97
   Service industry applications     98
   Conclusions     101
   Management checklist     102

## 9. Exploiting the value chain — 103
The value chain — 103
Ryanair — 105
Ryanair and the value chain — 108
Conclusions — 114
Management checklist — 115

## 10. Deciding on size — 116
An optimal size? — 116
Economies of scale — 118
Diseconomies of scale — 120
Franchising — 121
Impact of globalisation — 122
Impact of technology — 124
The choice to remain small — 125
Conclusions — 126
Management checklist — 127

### Part III  Using modern operational aids to analyse and manage costs, providing a path to 'leanness' and continuous improvement

## 11. World class and lean manufacturing — 131
Introduction — 132
WCM techniques — 133
Core principles of WCM — 133
WCM – getting started — 134
WCM roadmap — 135
Continuous improvement — 136
The 7 steps sequence of problem-solving — 137
Aids to each of the steps — 139
'Lean thinking' — 140
Service industry example – specialist legal practice — 142
Combining 'lean' with activity-based budgeting: a North American example — 144
Conclusions — 145
Management checklist — 145

## 12. Radical improvement — 146
Continuous v. radical improvement — 146
WCM: 'The Toyota Way' –Total Production System — 147
The Toyota Way: guiding principles — 148
Applying the principles to reducing cost and improving quality — 149
Responding to the recall crisis — 153
WCM: The Motorola Way – Six Sigma — 154
Six Sigma and the need for reliability in operations — 155
WCM (lean and Six Sigma) cost reductions and financial data — 156
Example: medical devices manufacturer — 157
Example: national service provider — 158
Conclusions — 160
Management checklist — 160

## 13. Business process re-engineering — 161
Introduction — 161
Designing cost efficiency into the business model — 163
Planning and implementing BPR — 163
Phases in BPR — 164
Waste — 165
BPR in a life assurance company — 166
BPR in a pharmaceutical plant — 168
Conclusions — 169
Management checklist — 169

## 14. Benchmarking — 170
Approaching benchmarking — 170
Benchmarking procedure — 172
Costs of benchmarking — 175
Example – newspaper industry — 175
Conclusions — 179
Management checklist — 179

## 15. Outsourcing — 180
The development of outsourcing — 181
The decision to outsource (why?) — 182

| | |
|---|---|
| Deciding which activities to outsource (What?) | 183 |
| On-shoring or offshoring? (Where?) | 185 |
| 10 Steps to outsourcing (how?) | 188 |
| Dos and don'ts of outsourcing | 191 |
| Conclusions | 191 |
| Management checklist | 191 |

## Part IV  Implementing cost reduction successfully in a strategic manner, while preserving core values and avoiding financial failure

**16. Structuring and rewarding the labour force** — **195**

| | |
|---|---|
| Hidden costs of the labour force | 195 |
| The 'Shamrock Organisation' | 196 |
| Five approaches to reduce labour costs | 198 |
| Redundancy | 201 |
| Example from the electronics assembly industry | 202 |
| Influence of the rewards system | 203 |
| The rewards system and the sub-prime lending crisis | 206 |
| Wipro: an Indian IT model | 211 |
| Conclusions | 211 |
| Management checklist | 212 |

**17. Strategic cost reduction – the critical links** — **213**

| | |
|---|---|
| Budgeting and costing systems | 213 |
| Head office | 215 |
| Strategy, values and quality | 217 |
| The 'balanced scorecard' | 220 |
| Loss of values – Irish bank property lending | 222 |
| Conclusions | 230 |
| Management checklist | 230 |

**18. The fundamental causes underlying business failure** — **231**

| | |
|---|---|
| The seven deadly sins | 232 |
| An SME example | 234 |
| Lehman Brothers | 235 |
| Anglo Irish Bank | 238 |
| Early warning signs | 243 |

|  |  |
|---|---|
| The public sector | 244 |
| Conclusions | 248 |
| Management checklist | 248 |

**19. Managing the change process** — **249**
| | |
|---|---|
| Project management | 249 |
| Force field analysis | 251 |
| Managing change | 252 |
| Communications and negotiation | 253 |
| Monitoring progress and continuous improvement | 254 |
| Eight steps in leading change | 255 |
| Application in the public sector | 257 |
| Conclusions | 263 |
| Management checklist | 263 |

**20. Planning the journey** — **264**
| | |
|---|---|
| The current scenario | 264 |
| The fitness challenge | 268 |
| Planning the journey | 269 |
| Getting started | 272 |
| Conclusions | 273 |
| Management checklist | 273 |

| | |
|---|---|
| **Appendix 1: Companies addressing IMI SCR conferences 23 June 2004, 26 May 2006 and 28 April 2009** | **275** |
| **Appendix 2: Approaching Six Sigma** | **277** |
| **References** | **281** |
| **Selected Further Reading** | **295** |
| **Index** | **301** |

# Foreword to the first edition

George Soros is somebody to be admired for his clear thinking on business matters. In a recent book, he postulated that the market tends to extremes rather than to the equilibrium of Adam Smith.

That same tendency is to be seen in many aspects of business. In days of plenty the head office grows in size, the corporate entertainment flows and 'courtiers' around the Chairman of a growing organisation appear to multiply in number.

On the other hand, when we experience turmoil such as that arising from the current international banking crisis, the sudden impact on business brings home to everybody the absolute necessity of getting their business lean and trim. The danger lies in the rush to slash and burn where the cuts themselves may become the problem.

We all know, inherently, that both approaches are fundamentally flawed, but from the perspective of one who over the years has worked in the area of insolvency and corporate recovery I have had the experience of dealing with both the cost bloated entity and the carcass of a once fine business where ill-advised cost cutting has caused terminal damage.

I have long been of the view that one of the major differences between successful and unsuccessful companies is that the former take decisions, (some right/some wrong) while the unsuccessful ones tend to ignore the problem. If you are in the latter type of organisation, and do not change, I look forward to meeting you professionally.

If on the other hand you want to improve the quality of your decisions and you want to reduce your cost base in a focused way, read on. The key word in the title is 'Strategic' – see what you are doing in its proper context.

This book is written for the player and not the financial spectator. In these very difficult times it is both a welcome handbook for the person taking their first tentative, and necessary, steps in this difficult area and a reminder for those of us who have faced the issue over the years.

We should be grateful to Tim and Dermot that they saw the need for this book even if, perhaps to our cost, we too did not see the signs that were apparent to them given the appropriateness of their timing.

John McStay, FCA
McStay Luby
Dublin

# Acknowledgements

We are grateful to many people who provided assistance whether directly or indirectly with the production of this book.

First, we wish to acknowledge the help provided by leading academics and authors whose models and ideas we have freely borrowed. In this context we would particularly mention Alfred Rappaport, Leonard Spacek Professor Emeritus of the Kellogg Graduate School of Management at North West University, whose shareholder value model is central to **Chapter 4**; Professor Michael Porter, Bishop William Lawrence University Professor at Harvard Business School, whose generic strategies model is used in **Chapter 6**, whose work on strategic cost drivers is fundamental to **Chapter 8** and whose value chain model is employed in **Chapter 9**; Dermot McAleese, Emeritus Whately Professor of Political Economy at Trinity College, Dublin, whose analysis of economies and diseconomies of scale provides the basis of **Chapter 10**; Jeffery Liker, Professor of Industrial and Operations Engineering at the University of Michigan, whose writing on Toyota underpins **Chapters 11 and 12**, Charles Handy, author and former Professor at the London Business School, whose 'Shamrock organisation' forms the groundwork for **Chapter 16**; and Robert Kaplan, Marvin Bower Professor of Leadership at Harvard Business School, whose original work on activity-based costing and subsequent development with David Norton of the balanced scorecard provides important contributions to **Chapter 17**. In this edition, for the causes of corporate failure in **Chapter 18**, reliance is placed on the framework of John Argenti and Irish research by Edward Cahill, Professor of Accounting and Dean of the faculty of Commerce at University College Cork. The models of the psychologist Kurt Lewin and the methodology of John Kotter, Konosuke Matsushita Professor of Leadership Emeritus at Harvard Business School, were used as a foundation for **Chapter 19**.

Secondly, our thanks to those practitioners whose approach to cost reduction stimulated us to write this book. These included the speakers at the Irish Management Institute (IMI) Cost Reduction Conferences held in 2004, 2006 and 2009. It also includes the graduates of the TCD/IMI MSc in Business Practice, with whom we worked over the years in an 'action learning' mode.

Thirdly, we especially appreciate all those who read the text of the first edition and provided invaluable initial advice and insights. These were Dr Chris Horn, Vice-Chairman of IONA Technology plc; Professor Dermot McAleese of Trinity College, Dublin; Geoff Meagher, President of the Institute of

Certified Public Accountants in Ireland and formerly Deputy Group Managing Director and Group Finance Director of Glanbia plc; Dr Klaus Oesch, Chairman of Orell Fuessli Holding AG; Frank O'Regan, Global Vice-President of Bausch & Lomb; and Horst Schneider, Chairman of IPAG AG and RayTools AG.

Fourthly, we wish to pay tribute to all those who provided ideas on individual aspects of the first edition. In this context we appreciate all the early help of our former colleague in the IMI, Frank Scott Lennon, who provided numerous suggestions to the early drafts. Ray Murphy, director of Strategic Computing, advised on procurement. Our former IMI colleague, Martin Farrelly, generated much useful information on HR. Niall English, director of Futura Design, assisted on outsourcing. Nelson Loane, former CEO of Adare Printing provided details for that example. Ciaron Brady helped on Six Sigma. The late inclusion of **Chapter 5**, Emergency Cost Reduction, is entirely due to conversations with Geoffrey Stirling, who advises numerous SMEs. Others who read the later drafts were John McStay of McStay Luby, Chartered Accountants and specialists in corporate recovery, who kindly wrote the forward to the first edition of this book; Dr Ronan O'Connor, Head of Risk, National Pension Reserve Fund at the National Treasury Management Authority; solicitor Simon McCormick; journalist Stephen Ryan; and our former colleagues in the IMI, Tony Dromgoole and Moira Creedon.

For this edition we wish to thank all who provided additional material. In particular we must mention Daisy Downes, editor of *Accountancy Ireland*, who in the last three years has published 17 articles by Tim on the subjects of cost reduction and banking, allowing him to test out a range of ideas. Several of these articles were reproduced in *GAA Accounting*, the journal of the Global Accounting Alliance, which provided access to a wider international readership. The New Zealand Institute of Chartered Accountants made numerous useful suggestions for the edition of the book adapted to their market, many of which have been retained in this edition. The speakers at the third IMI cost reduction conference in 2009 provided other new ideas. Many people who provided ideas for the first edition did so again for this edition. Others who provided helpful advice on banking matters include Mike Soden, former CEO of Bank of Ireland; John Carroll, former investment banker; and Maurice O'Brien, founder of Flagstone Consultants. Our former IMI colleagues, Ruth Handy and Andrew McLaughlin, provided ideas on human resources and public sector issues, respectively. Christopher Kitchin provided an engineering perspective. Professor Bill Lawler of Babson

College, Boston provided interesting North American material. Others who provided useful ideas and suggestions have chosen to do so anonymously.

In particular, we wish to thank Professor Dermot McAleese and Dr Ronan O'Connor, who read the entire text, providing numerous insights and suggestions. Also, we are indebted to Michael Diviney and Jennifer Thompson of Chartered Accountants Ireland, who painstakingly edited the final draft and provided many useful amendments.

Finally, we wish to thank again our respective families for their tolerance while we took time to write this book. In Tim's case, thanks are due to his four children, Myles, Conor, Patrick and Tara, while Dermot is indebted to his wife, Mary, and son, Seán.

To all of the above we offer our gratitude. Any remaining flaws and mistakes are, of course, totally our own responsibility.

# Introduction

"What is a cynic? A man who knows the price of everything and the value of nothing."

*Oscar Wilde*

## The origins

In 2003, the Irish Management Institute (IMI) surveyed 100 chief executives to establish the most important issues that they faced.[1] The single biggest challenge proved in the majority of cases to be cost reduction, perhaps a surprising finding in a time of economic prosperity.

Yet, despite its perceived importance, there was little available on the topic in management literature. Certainly there were books on budgeting and on current operational subjects, such as Six Sigma, re-engineering and outsourcing, as well as broader works on total quality management, just-in-time and 'lean' manufacturing. They provided useful ideas, but were sometimes written by consultants, presenting their approach as a universal panacea. There were the war stories of individuals, usually chief executives, related to a specific business in a particular set of circumstances and constraints. What was missing, however, was a comprehensive, holistic approach. Cost reduction appeared to be a missing chapter in management literature.

For many companies, cost reduction is, of course, only one route to competitiveness. Quality, innovation and service may also be vital to attract and retain customers. Mindless or cynical cost cutting may sever a corporate artery, while persistent draconian cost reduction can lead to corporate anorexia. Random cost cutting may achieve short-term success, but the costs have a habit of bouncing back before long like a rubber ball. The challenge is how to radically reduce costs, while still surviving and prospering. Effective cost reduction needs to be fitted into a wider strategic framework.

To address these complex issues, the two authors of this book, with backgrounds in finance and operations respectively, decided to run a conference where a range of leading practitioners could explain how they set about major cost reduction. The first conference was held in 2004 and a second one in 2006.

Companies addressing the IMI Cost Reduction conferences in 2004 and 2006 (see **Appendix 1**) were comprised as follows:

- 5 Manufacturing
- 5 Consultancy
- 2 High Technology
- 2 Financial Services
- 1 Low Fares Airline (twice)
- 1 Brewing
- 1 Clothes Retailing

The companies chosen to address the topic were diverse. They were all Irish-based businesses from the private sector. Nevertheless, they had an international orientation. There were manufacturing companies that had adopted world class manufacturing, but were facing global competition and possibly closure of Irish operations. There were technology companies suffering from the fallout of the dotcom boom. There were suppliers to supermarkets under constant margin pressure. There was a low cost airline, determined to be the lowest cost provider in the industry. A few were consultants with particular case studies to relate. Some businesses were highly unionised, others were not. But they all had one feature in common: they were all in the private sector and had all significantly reduced unit costs, typically by 15% or more. The experience of these companies provided the stimulus to guide senior management, chief executives and their boards, who want to reduce their costs to a significant extent in a strategic way.

A further conference in April 2009 provided additional ideas for this edition.

## Action learning

Another significant influence on the book was both authors' involvement with a wide range of companies over more than a decade in 'action learning', a methodology, and its application at the IMI, which finds favour with the eminent business academic, Henry Minzberg.[2] Throughout more than a decade we acted as tutors or mentors constantly over a period of 18 months each to senior managers tasked with the creation and implementation of a strategy for their company or business unit. Our role was to point them in the direction of the relevant literature, constantly challenge their ideas and review with them their action plans.

For many of these companies cost management was an important issue. In some cases, there were pressures from group headquarters to meet performance targets, while for others it was direct shareholder requirements for change. Usually, the task entailed a new strategy and the management of significant change. Cost reduction, when it was needed, had to be linked into the overall strategy, rather than simply comply with short-term budgetary requirements.

## The approach

This book is intended to provide assistance to anyone embarking on a course of cost reduction. It cannot be comprehensive, but it attempts to set out some of the tools used by businesses which have undertaken major cost reduction. We have broadened the scope well beyond the original companies which addressed the conferences, and have used tools employed by the public as well as the private sectors. We have discussed our ideas with a wide range of companies to ascertain their experience. This has involved managers at different levels, but usually at a high level. Sometimes we have included advice from companies with which we have not worked when published information has been available to us that we considered to be relevant to the topic.

We have attempted to present the issues relevant to all companies, irrespective of size. To this end, we have included advice from leading companies and sometimes anecdotal illustrations. While drawing on the literature where appropriate, our main aim is to provide managers with a practical roadmap to applying strategic cost reduction in practice.

Our intended reader is anyone who is in a position to plan, implement or influence strategy, whether in the private or public sectors. Inevitably, in most organisations this will be senior management, essentially board members and general managers. In larger organisations it will be business unit managers. In smaller organisations it will be owner–managers. Where we address budgeting issues, the readership should include the departmental or functional managers. MBA students should also find it a useful text.

Since every strategy is unique to a particular company, so too should be the route to achieve cost reduction in a strategic manner. Each business must craft its approach to fit its own strategy and values. We are not advocates of any one tool, panacea or 'magic bullet' which purports to address any given situation. It is up to the reader to choose whether or not to adopt any given approach. We have not included detailed checklists, since we believe that they need to be tailored to the chosen course of action. Nevertheless, there are questions which any company should find useful to consider, even if the answers are different in most cases.

To highlight common issues and in an effort to meet the goals of a diverse audience we have included a brief checklist on which the practising manager may choose to reflect at the end of each chapter. Frequently, managers think that these are not issues relevant to their organisation. In that case, they should pass on. In other cases, they may choose to dwell on the topic and consider how it could be applied in their organisation.

Finally, we have tried to be as concise as possible about what is a broad subject. It is our belief that cost reduction is most effective when it is conducted by practising managers, rather than delegated to external consultants. There are many demands on the time of any manager. Reading wordy tomes is one extra imposition which can be avoided. We hope that the essence of the messages will not be diminished due to the brevity of this book.

## Outline of the book

*Strategic Cost Reduction* is in four parts:

**Part I** assesses the level of corporate fitness necessary for survival, a key theme of this book, while examining conventional ways of tackling the issue. It starts with budgeting and other traditional methods of cost reduction, then addresses issues around the budgetary control and the problems which frequently arise. It also highlights the functional areas where cost reduction usually takes place and raises the question of a target level of costs. Finally, it tackles the issue of emergency cost reduction, where short-term survival is at stake. For those companies which consider that they do not need major surgery, **Part I** should be their major focus of attention.

**Part II** approaches cost reduction from a strategic viewpoint. It places the cost reduction programme into the wider corporate framework and values. Since many major cost reduction programmes fail, we start by confronting the kind of issues that must be considered by the board and functional managers if the programme is to succeed. This is followed by a chapter on the strategic drivers of cost and an analysis of the value chain through the example of a low fares airline. **Part II** finishes with an examination of economies and diseconomies of scale, together with their limitations.

**Part III** outlines the modern operational tools used to analyse and manage costs by contemporary world class companies. It starts by examining world class and 'lean' manufacturing, seeking continuous improvement. It then outlines the more radical approaches of Toyota Production Systems and 'Six Sigma'. It introduces business process re-engineering, explaining how it should be approached and finishes with the challenges of benchmarking and outsourcing, whether onshore or offshore. Throughout, practical tips for implementation are provided, as well as lists of the options available, with copious examples.

**Part IV** addresses issues of successful implementation, while avoiding the pitfalls of corporate failure. It begins by looking at ways of reducing the cost of the labour force and then examines the link between cost reduction with company values and the budgetary system, showing how progress can be monitored effectively. It sketches out the causes of business failure before addressing the challenges arising in project and change management. **Part IV** finishes by examining how to plan the cost reduction journey and where to start.

This second, enlarged edition expands on the material included in the first edition published in 2009. The subsequent cost reduction conference held in April 2009 produced further, more recent examples of cost reduction in a deteriorating economic climate. In particular, this edition emphasises implementation issues and includes many more examples, including two new chapters in **Part IV**, dealing with the causes of business failure and implementing the cost reduction plan, with illustrations from financial services and the public sector.

Readers are encouraged to select the parts of the book and specific chapters relevant to their needs, rather than necessarily reading the book from start to finish. For example, those mainly interested in cost reduction in the public sector might focus on the chapters on budgeting and control in **Part I**, the drivers of cost and economies of scale in **Part II**, the issues around benchmarking and outsourcing in **Part III** and signs of failure and implementing change in **Part IV**.

We have worked together to produce this book. Tim was responsible for the design and integration of the book, writing **Parts I, II** and **IV**, while Dermot wrote most of **Part III**. We hope that the different parts fit together relatively seamlessly.

## The Irish economic background

When we first published this book in 2009, Ireland and the rest of the world were facing a 'recession'. However, many people avoided the word, regarding the issue as a temporary downturn and had to be convinced of the gravity of the problem. Sadly, the recession has proved to be very serious indeed. Ireland was among the first into recession and is likely to be amongst the last to recover, with problems more severe than elsewhere.

Ireland is a small, open economy, which is highly dependent on international trade. In the decade prior to 2007, it achieved phenomenal economic growth. Yet, now it is experiencing increased unemployment, the aftermath of a massive property bubble, a crisis in banking and a credit squeeze. The country faces a major problem with its public finances and a general crisis of confidence. In a remarkably short period, the much admired 'Celtic Tiger' joined a group of Mediterranean countries, Portugal, Italy, Greece and Spain with the less illustrious name of 'PIIGS'.

Ireland's problems were exacerbated by the weakness of its banking system, arising from reckless lending during the property bubble. In 2010/11 the World Economic Forum ranked the Irish banking system as the weakest of the 139 countries surveyed, trailing both Iceland and Zimbabwe, a ranking which failed to improve the following year.[3] The cost of bailing out the banking system imposed enormous strain on the public finances. Facing EU pressure in late 2010, the Irish Government was obliged to seek assistance from the EU and the IMF to address funding difficulties arising from its rapidly rising public deficit.

The Government unveiled a four-year austerity programme to save €15 billion over the period 2011 to 2014, starting with a €6 billion reduction in the first year.[4] Two-thirds of the savings were to be achieved by reducing expenditure in public sector pay, social welfare and general current spending, with the balance provided by increases in taxation. Since the terms of the €85 billion rescue package demanded that the austerity package was adopted, cost reduction was placed top of the political agenda, and the succeeding Irish Government had little option but to continue on a similar track.

By 2012, the uncertainties had increased, with the crisis surrounding the Euro. If the plan for a more centralised European fiscal policy is adopted, austerity will almost certainly be rigorously enforced. In this environment, strategic cost reduction should be undertaken in both the public and private sectors as a matter of urgency. Politicians may have no alternative in the public sector, while negligible growth prospects or possible recession means that most private sector businesses face reduced demand for their goods and services.

## Irish competitiveness

Being part of a small, open economy, maintaining competitiveness is critical for the private sector. While Ireland has benefited enormously from membership of the European Union, it must compete now with new members operating from a lower cost base. While it remains an attractive place to live and in which to do business,[5] costs have been increasing. A 2008 survey moved Ireland up to fourth place out of 23 countries in terms of living costs.[6]

Surveys of multinational corporations in Ireland from 2008 to 2011 showed a worrying concern for competitiveness centred on costs.[7] In addition to wage costs, energy, transport, professional services and telecommunications remain expensive. The years 2010 and 2011 showed some improvement due to the weakness of the Euro and falling construction costs but, nevertheless, Ireland is still considered to be a relatively expensive business location. The National Competitiveness Council in 2012 reported that a further fall in the cost base was needed.[8]

Ireland has attracted substantial overseas investment, especially from the United States, but the country must suffer as planned overseas investment is cancelled by foreign multinationals. Since, for many Irish subsidiaries the major threat comes from sister plants, relative lack of cost competitiveness and continuing rising costs remain a serious concern. Major foreign businesses, such as Dell, have withdrawn manufacturing from Ireland, preferring to locate in centres with lower wages, etc. Several international service businesses, reviewing their options in a global marketplace, have relocated elsewhere. Where costs outside the control of the private sector cause competitive problems, it is crucial that businesses tackle those areas within their control to maintain overall competiveness.

The World Economic Forum Global Competitiveness Index for 2010/11 showed that Ireland slipped a further four places, having already dropped three places the year before to 25th place out of 139 countries, a ranking which stabilised the following year.[9] For a small, open economy, deteriorating competitiveness is a worrying development. The most problematic areas for doing business were identified as access to finance, government bureaucracy, infrastructure supply and restrictive labour regulations. In addition to the weakness of the banks mentioned above, availability of credit, inflexibility of wage determination and the level of Government debt scored particularly poorly.

Few businesses can ignore the challenge of competitiveness. Many small Irish businesses face a collapse in the domestic market, leading to declining sales and a struggle to obtain finance, which is scarce and often expensive. Exporters, no longer so concerned with the strength of the Euro, nevertheless are concerned with the high cost of labour. Unfortunately, constraints on the public sector capital expenditure budget means that little assistance for the private sector can come from that quarter in the foreseeable future. There is little option in these circumstances other than to place cost reduction at the top of the management agenda in the private sector also.

Ireland, being part of the Eurozone, does not have the customary option of restoring competitiveness through devaluation of its currency. There is greater cross-border transparency than in the past, resulting from the introduction of the Euro and the expansion of the Internet, so lack of competiveness is not easily hidden. For many organisations facing loss of revenue, whether in the private, public or indeed the voluntary sector, there is no alternative other than to seek a dramatic reduction in costs under their control.

## Global applications

Although we write from an Irish base, where competiveness poses a particularly strong challenge for business and Government, we believe that the lessons outlined in this book have a much wider application. Some illustrations have been drawn from North America and Asia. Readers of the first edition in mainland Europe have confirmed the relevance of the book to their situation while, further afield, the New Zealand Institute of Chartered Accountants has licensed the book for publication in that market.

Many of the companies that we have studied are multinationals, trying to achieve cost reduction on a global basis. For the Irish business to survive against competition from countries with a much lower wage base, an effective programme of cost reduction is fundamental if the parent company is to be persuaded to remain. Given Ireland's dependence on foreign investment and exporting, the problem may be more acute here than in countries with large domestic markets. But, as ever more companies consider outsourcing their business from Western Europe, America or Australasia, these same issues are being faced elsewhere. Even when with economic recovery, we believe that cost reduction will remain on the agenda of businesses everywhere for the foreseeable future.

It can be argued that cost reduction programmes should be unnecessary. In a well-managed business costs are kept under control all of the time and only small tweaks are needed occasionally to keep them on track. This may be so in an ideal world but, in practice, companies find out quite suddenly that something needs to be done to address the issue. There is little comfort to be had from the old Irish joke: "If you want to get there, you should not be starting from here."

Cost reduction often may not be an easy or pleasant journey. It is not a popular topic, and there are no easy solutions. If revenue is reduced in a lasting market turndown, hard decisions will have to be taken, and jobs will often need to be sacrificed in the short term. There is a very real human aspect, which makes it a most sensitive issue and one which many would prefer to avoid. Employees can be the most important asset in a business, costly to hire and train, but also costly to release. Nevertheless, if businesses are to survive, such realities have to be faced for the ultimate prosperity of all stakeholders.

There are no easy quick fixes. Different situations require different approaches, but all need realistic analysis and practical solutions. We believe that this book provides practical guidance to anyone setting out on this arduous, perilous journey. We also trust that this second edition embodies continuous improvement in practice and will be surprised if readers cannot get the benefit of a significant multiple of the book's price. In any event, your comments will be much appreciated, and can be made at www.timmccormick.ie.

# Part I

# Evaluating budgeting and other traditional approaches to cost reduction to assess the health of the business and the need for cost reduction

# Chapter 1

# Budgeting challenges

> "Not to beat about the bush, but the budgeting process is the most ineffective practice in management. . . . It sucks fun, time and big dreams out of an organisation. It hides opportunities and stunts growth. It brings out the most unproductive behaviours in an organization, from sandbagging to settling for the mediocre. In fact when companies win, in most cases it is despite their budgets, not because of them."
>
> Jack Welch, former CEO of GEC[1]

Andrew Carnegie, the American industrialist and philanthropist, urged businessmen over a century ago to "watch the costs and profits will look after themselves". Many managers since then have heeded his advice and have planned their costs assiduously. With the assistance of computers and accountants, who collect the data on costs, analyse the figures and report the results, managers seek to control costs and maximise profits. The costs (broadly, the resources consumed to generate revenue) of any business, of course, should be produced in a manner that facilitates this process, according to the specific needs of the entity concerned.

Ask most managers how and when cost reduction takes place in their business, however, and the answer is usually "during budgeting," a time when cost targets are set. Clearly, not everyone is enamoured by budgeting, an opinion which has been unequivocally stated by Jack Welch (also known as "Neutron Jack"), the man who oversaw the transformation of many American businesses in the General Electric group during the 20th Century. Nevertheless, an examination of the budgetary system provides a sensible starting point to cost reduction. If the budgetary system is truly effective, then there may be no need to look further than this framework. If, however, budgeting fails to root out inefficiencies and brings out unproductive behaviour, then a different approach may be required.

Any organisational review by management should assess the rigour of the system, the link with strategy and the practical difficulties that arise in the practice of budgeting. Such a review will be undertaken in this chapter under the following headings:

- Different approaches to budgeting
- The role of budgeting and cost reduction
- Budgeting in practice
- Zero-based budgeting
- Priority-based budgeting
- Beyond budgeting

## Different approaches to budgeting

There are certain common features in the way most managers approach the annual budget. Each year, they submit departmental plans for revenue and expenses but, invariably, the early draft is rejected by their bosses with the assistance of the financial controller. Further drafts are then submitted with reduced costs until a satisfactory outcome is achieved. Once the budget has been agreed, it is monitored through management accounts and adverse variances are examined and, where possible, rectified.

This is the standard practice in most organisations of any significant size. It applies not only in the profit-driven private sector, but also in not-for-profit organisations and in the public sector. The actual process of budgeting, of course, varies from business to business and can last for anything between two and six months, or sometimes even longer. A shorter timeframe allows managers to start later with more current trading data, while a longer timeframe allows them to spend more time preparing their inputs and negotiating final figures. Sometimes, the finance director or divisional financial controllers providing 'help' actually 'suggest' cost reduction targets within their budgeting guidelines while, in other cases, they merely reject the submissions until a reduced cost figure appears. Rarely do they accept initial submissions without some proposed change.

Usually, the primary focus of management is on the costs contained in the profit and loss account, both the direct costs of making a product or providing a service, and the indirect costs or overheads. These costs may be broken down by product type, customer groups or particular projects, but the main cost analysis tends to be by departmental responsibility. There will also be a capital budget, where proposed investments are scrutinised and sometimes working capital targets for the reduction of stocks and debtors to contain interest costs.

The rigour with which the budgets are scrutinised varies across different industries and organisations. In industries with tight margins and little room for manoeuvre, costs need to be finely pared, but in high margin businesses, the focus tends to be more on generating revenue than cutting costs. In highly-centralised businesses, particularly if there is good industry data available, there is likely to be a high level of central scrutiny. On the other hand, decentralised organisations tend to permit more local autonomy. In the case of large multinationals with subsidiaries around the world, the ability of the local cost centre subsidiary to produce competitive costs may be fundamental to its survival as a business unit.

## The role of budgeting and cost reduction

It should not be surprising that budgeting is expected to play a major role in cost management. Budgeting should also be the way that organisations implement their strategies. All too often, however, long-term plans, painstakingly prepared in enormous detail and at great length, gather dust because they are not effectively linked to the annual budget. Managers know that if they need to choose between the long-term plan of their organisation and their annual budget, it is the budget that will prevail.

Budgeting, however, is designed to fulfil many functions other than implementing strategy in the short term. It provides the means by which organisations decide on the allocation of resources in terms of people, assets and cash, and is also the occasion when most capital decisions are approved. Organisations without an effective budgetary system can find their costs escalating as managers indulge in empire building, since power in an organisation is linked to the ability to spend. For example, it is always tempting to employ an extra person when a member of staff becomes sick, rather than to manage with fewer resources. In such cases, the easier option may be selected, unless decisions are constrained by the budgetary system.

The essence of budgeting is, thus, motivation and control. If targets are achievable without undue effort, managers may pay little heed to budgeting. Targets should be stretching and a challenging performance standard set that subsequently acts as the basis of performance evaluation. Since budgetary performance forms at least part of most staff evaluations, it tends to get managers' attention. Yet, if a manager is purely rewarded on the budgetary performance of his or her department, it can lead to a 'silo' mentality, which may not be in the wider interests of the business. Where there is no link between budgetary performance and rewards, as is frequently the case in parts of the public sector, budgeting is likely to have much less impact on managers' performance.

Without budgeting, it is hard to see how a large-scale business, let alone a multinational, could continue to exist. If one manager overspends while others stick to their budgets, then the business as a whole overspends. Nevertheless, there is a limit to which any group chief executive can or would want to micro-manage the expenditure of every business unit. Budgeting is the way responsibility is delegated throughout an organisation. If all managers keep to their budgets, then the organisation as a whole will remain within budget. For publicly listed companies, where stock markets punish performance below expectations, this can be a vital requirement. If the chief executive's reputation and future is staked on achieving budget, it is highly likely that there will be a strong budget culture in the organisation.

If budgeting is expected by governing boards to be the essence of motivating managers to contain costs, why are so many organisations dissatisfied with the operation of their budgetary system as a means to reduce costs? All too often, practice diverges from theory, and the intended reductions in cost painstakingly outlined in annual budgets remain elusive.

## Budgeting in practice[2]

Budgeting may be popular with accountants and financial controllers, since it is often fundamental to their existence; however, it can be far less popular with managers who, not surprisingly, often resent the interference. Many detractors of budgeting believe that the controls are too tight and criticisms of the budgeting process are frequently expressed in the following terms:

1. **Budgeting is costly, taking up too much of managers' time:** Modern automated systems may have reduced much of the bureaucratic form-filling of the past but, nevertheless, if managers need to start budget plans six months before the year end and then submit numerous revisions, they are distracted from the day-to-day trading and operational management of their business unit or department.
2. **Budgeting encourages game playing and time wasting:** If a manager wants an overhead budget of €100,000, he or she is unlikely to submit this budget at the outset, since the expectation is that the financial controller will cut the figure. Accordingly, a budget of €150,000 is submitted. The financial controller counters with €50,000 and, after endless haggling, the figure is finally agreed at €100,000. The whole process

is more reminiscent of a traditional oriental bazaar than a 21st Century business.
3. **Budgeting can lead to wasteful expenditure:** In many organisations, and particularly in the public sector, it is not uncommon for managers to make every effort to spend all budgeted costs before the year end: "use it or lose it" is the adage. Fearful that the next year's budget will be cut, managers set out to spend on projects which are unlikely to provide real benefits. (Needless to say, this behaviour is not restricted to the public sector.)
4. **Budgeting can kill initiative:** Most innovation requires some expenditure. If the response to every proposed improvement is, "No – it is not in the budget for this year," most managers will eventually give up. They will be reluctant to defer their initiatives for 12 months only to discover then that the budget remains unavailable. Accepting the status quo normally leads to an easier life.
5. **Budgeting is often de-motivating and can promote inertia:** Many experienced managers try to outwit their financial controllers and set themselves soft targets. Stretch targets may be set in theory, but too often soft targets are the practice. When these targets are achieved, the managers can then relax for the remainder of the year, which can lead to widespread under-performance.
6. **Budgeting can lead to product or service inflexibility:** Customers' needs may change during the year, and businesses should respond to these changes. In some industries, such as the fashion industry, new trends may be difficult to spot far in advance, but industry leaders must respond quickly if they are to be successful. There is little point in continuing to supply goods planned in the budget if the fashion has changed or if the original call was simply wrong. The market is not concerned with the original budget. A strong traditional budgeting culture may inhibit such unpredicted, but necessary changes.
7. **Budgeting can prevent strategic mid-year changes:** Budgets are formulated in an expected economic scenario, but for all sorts of reasons, this may unexpectedly change. For example, budgets in the travel industry needed to change dramatically after the attack on the Twin Towers in 2001, and banks faced a new outlook after the emergence of the sub-prime lending crisis in mid-2007. Equally, sudden spikes in the price of oil may force many businesses to revise their plans. To the extent that budgetary systems discourage such changes, they detract from the efficient running of the business.

## Zero-based budgeting

Many of the flaws of budgeting often experienced in practice derive from its reverence for the past. When preparing a budget, most people start with last year's figures, and add to or subtract from those numbers slightly in the light of current circumstances. For start-ups, such 'incremental budgeting' is not possible, with the result that such budgets can be very wide of the mark. Once a pattern emerges, budgeting becomes simpler. Realistic estimates can be made, particularly in businesses with limited volatility and that are not subject to rapidly changing technology. Repeating past behaviour, however, may simply succeed in papering over the cracks and discourage more radical change.

There are, of course, circumstances where incremental budgeting is inappropriate. If a business takes over another business that is incurring substantial trading losses, there is little point in commencing with figures that are fundamentally unacceptable. The alternative is to reject the incremental approach and start again from scratch, a process which is much easier if the acquirer runs a successful similar business and can apply its own business model and budget system to the acquisition.

Zero-based budgeting takes no cognisance of the previous year, and every cost has to be justified on its own merits. This idea is not new. The technique, generally believed to have originated from Texas Instruments in the 1960s, when Peter Pyrrh attempted to tackle the problems associated with incremental budgeting and burgeoning cost increases. Subsequently, it has been applied in both the public and private sectors for many years, having been popularised by the administration of President Carter in the US some 30 years ago. Over the years, its introduction has met with mixed results.[3]

Advocates of zero-based budgeting stress that it leads to a more efficient allocation of resources, based on a review of needs and benefits. It spreads the load of cost reduction around the organisation and motivates managers to improve cost effectiveness. It is further argued that many organisations using incremental budgeting allow inefficiencies to be built into their systems, because they use the past as a standard, despite the fact that circumstances and technology have changed.

> The story is told of someone who questioned why a piece of modern artillery needed four soldiers to man it. Clearly one loaded, one aimed and one fired. But what was the role of the fourth? After a detailed investigation of the past, it was discovered that the role of the fourth

> soldier was to hold the horses. Zero-based budgeting, by forcing managers to question the basic assumptions around the use of resources, should reveal the waste involved in four soldiers being required to man a gun, which can be efficiently manned by three soldiers.

Zero-based budgeting can also be used to question expense account allowances. In July 2008, the day before Government spending cuts were announced, the tax-free expenses paid to Irish politicians and public servants were increased. The overnight subsistence allowances for politicians living more than 15 miles from Leinster House was set at €144.45, while the allowance to those within the 15 mile radius was set at €61.53 to compensate them for the fact that they don't qualify for subsistence.[4] Zero-based budgeting would question whether the latter allowance should exist.

> *Advantages of zero-based budgeting are:*
> - Every cost needs to be justified
> - Inefficiencies can be pinpointed
> - It involves everyone
> - It can be linked to performance management

Zero-based budgeting does, however, have its disadvantages. The principle issue is one of time. If every year the budgeting process starts anew, it will take far longer than the already substantial amount of time taken up by incremental budgeting. If an organisation has many service departments, there may also be difficulty in defining service level agreements to describe the desired level of output in terms of quality. Some formal systems also entail form filling in minute detail and many layers of bureaucracy. The sceptics of zero-based budgeting advocate that the first cost saving should be the budgeting system itself.

Zero-based budgeting carries the fear that organisational surgery goes too far. Excessive cutting is not healthy, and the patient may not survive the operation. Equally, but more slowly, over years of persistent cost reduction, an unhealthy corporate anorexia may develop. When managers are forced to reduce overheads, they may elect to cut key controls, which may not appear to add value in the customers' eyes. If this does not actually breach regulatory requirements, it most certainly does not constitute best business practice or comply with audit requirements. For example, it would be a foolish financial institution that decided to cut out risk monitoring in pursuit of short-term profit.

---

*Disadvantages of zero-based budgeting are:*

- It involves a lot of time
- Quality can suffer
- Savings can be small if the business is already efficiently run
- It may be non-strategic and short-term in focus

---

Because of the above issues, few businesses use zero-based budgeting to replace their traditional incremental budgeting methods. Nevertheless, zero-based budgeting remains a useful tool that can be employed every few years or in difficult times to hinder or halt the relentless growth of overheads. It must be driven from the top of the organisation, and this may explain why it is not in wider use. Looking at some corporate headquarters, with all the conspicuous luxuries and trappings around the CEO's office, it is not hard to see where cost-cutting could sensibly begin. In practice, of course, employees may lack the courage to make such suggestions, so cost-cutting rarely starts there.

## Priority-based budgeting

A variant of zero-based budgeting can be found in priority-based budgeting, a less radical approach to the problem of locating pockets of inefficiency in organisations. Instead of starting from zero, managers are asked what budget they would submit with, say, 10% or 20% less resources. In this way, they are obliged to order their preferences and effect reductions in spending. In turnaround situations, where businesses are incurring losses, this can be a quick way of reducing overheads with the involvement of the user departments that originate the costs. If properly applied, such an approach should identify abuses of expense claims and areas of mindless waste throughout an organisation. Companies struggling in a market downturn may try to achieve a similar result through head office guidelines. Many organisations could usefully employ priority-based budgeting as a way of reacting to the need to reduce resources in a recession.

## Beyond budgeting

In 1970, Jan Wallander was appointed executive director of Handelsbanken, the largest bank in Sweden. The bank was experiencing some difficulties at the time. Wallander was an eminent professional economist, well aware of the perils of forecasting. He abolished the bank's existing conventional budgetary system, arguing that most forecasts miss changes of direction and that the assumption was that tomorrow would resemble today.[5] When that assumption proved to be incorrect, the explanation offered was usually that variations were only temporary. Thus, fundamental cyclical changes were generally ignored. Detailed forecasting was, according to Wallander, of little value to the organisation. In short, budgeting was an unnecessary evil.

Over the next 25 years, Handelsbanken ranked at or near the top of the Swedish banking league. A profit-sharing scheme was put in place, and management was highly decentralised. The bank had a large number of branches, and the success of any one of its business units could be assessed by comparing it with its peers. In this way, performance was reviewed against the average output of the group rather than against a budget target.

The success of Handelsbanken has persisted to this day.[6] It was the only large Swedish bank not to require external help in the Swedish banking crisis of 1992 and managed to avoid the international banking crisis of 2008. It remains decentralised in style, with 96% of credit decisions made at branch level, rather than head office. Bonuses are equal for all employees, regardless of position, and are only made when performance exceeds the industry average, with payment deferred until retirement. Such a system, based on objective measurement, militates against credit decisions being taken for short-term profits to the detriment of prudent risk management.

Despite the publicity the initiative received in Sweden from 1970 onwards, by 1994 the abolition of budgeting had found no imitators. Since then, however, in Scandanavia at first and subsequently further afield, a number of leading businesses did try to manage without budgetary systems. A 'beyond budgeting' movement was created internationally.

Many readers may share Wallander's scepticism in relation to forecasting. However, few economists foresaw the collapse in global property prices or the advent of the banking crisis in 2008, while others have exaggerated changes, such as the impact of the year 2000 on computer systems.[7] While most businesses still regard the abolition of budgeting to be a step too far, many have found that budgeting is not the best way to produce radical cost reduction. Major cost-reduction programmes may not fit neatly into annual budgetary frameworks and may be approached better independently of the annual budget with a greater focus on strategic cost goals, which span several years, relegating budgeting to a more secondary role. Cost reduction, viewed in this manner, becomes another capital investment project, justified on the basis that the value of the benefits exceeds the costs.

## Conclusions

All industries and all organisations can employ budgeting, although some may have a greater expectation of accuracy than others. Whatever the general merits of budgeting should be as a mechanism for control, in practice serious problems can arise for the organisation when short-term profit targets crowd out longer term development, for example:

- Inefficiencies frequently remain.
- The system may not motivate managers to perform in the desired manner.
- Strategic considerations may be ignored.
- Unnecessary inflexibility may be a consequence.

Nevertheless, budgeting remains the basis of corporate control for most organisations. If it is to remain as such, it is important to ascertain what must be done if the system is to operate effectively and how it can achieve a significant reduction in the cost base.

## Management checklist

1. How effective is budgeting in your organisation?
2. Can budgeting achieve significant cost reduction for you?
3. Does the link between budgeting and the rewards system incentivise managers to run their departments in the desired way?
4. Have you considered zero-based or priority-based budgeting?
5. Could you see your organisation abolishing budgeting or reducing its role?

# Chapter 2

# Effective control

"Annual Income twenty pounds, annual expenditure nineteen pounds, nineteen and six, result Happiness. Annual Income twenty pounds, annual expenditure twenty pounds ought and six, result Misery."

*Mister Micawber in "David Copperfield", by Charles Dickens*

Many organisations take pride in the way in which the budget controls the management of their business. Others may be less satisfied. Some of the difference in effectiveness of budgeting may be attributed to the way in which the budgetary system is organised. Other differences may derive from the rules of engagement by which managers participate in the budgetary process, or the cultural underpinnings of its operation, particularly in dealing with any problems which may emerge. The working of the budget will be tested most severely when managers are obliged to seek savings and make unpalatable choices. The issues surrounding effectiveness will be addressed in this chapter as follows:

- Organisational prerequisites
- The principles of effective budgeting
- The usual budgetary problems
- Prioritisation of costs for reduction
- Reducing individual costs through the '3 Es'

## Organisational prerequisites

If the budgetary system is not properly organised, it is unlikely to influence the cost base seriously. The requirements listed below are common sense, but it is surprising how often they are overlooked:

- **Costs[1] must be categorised into relevant and controllable costs:** The necessity of having a good costing system cannot be overemphasised. Some businesses still labour under legacy systems originally designed to produce financial accounts, broken down into months for management accounting purposes. Such systems rarely provide information properly broken down into departmental reporting systems, since many such costs cross departmental boundaries. If managers are shown costs allocated to them on some arbitrary basis, clearly there is little likelihood that they can come up with ways of reducing them. In such circumstances, central overheads may grow without proper control. Modern enterprise resource planning systems, such as SAP, should address the issues better and often permit managers to drill down into information on a real-time basis to analyse variances. However, such systems are time-consuming and expensive to install.

- **Annual figures must be properly broken down into accounting periods:** If calendar months are the reporting period, figures must allow for different numbers of days, national holidays and so forth. This is rarely a problem. Difficulties can, however, arise in seasonal businesses, particularly those that are weather-dependent. For example, where a grain merchant is planning for the harvest in August and it does not appear until September, there can be difficulties in comparing actual monthly figures with the original budget.
- **The budget should be prefaced by a review of the long-term plan:** If long-term plans are intended to be taken seriously, then they need to be linked into the annual budgets. Often, the original long-term plan needs some modification as a consequence of budgetary deliberations. But if the strategic milestones are not reviewed before the budget guidelines are issued, then the strategy is likely to be superseded by the short-term budget. Strategy should drive budgets, rather than vice versa. Key performance indicators (KPIs) derived from the strategy may also have a role to play.
- **The limiting factor to growth must be clearly identified:** Most well-run businesses are constrained by the amount of potential profitable sales that they are likely to generate in a given year. Accordingly, sales forecasting is the proper starting point for budgeting for most businesses. However, this need not be so in all cases. For an agricultural co-operative committed to buying milk from farmers, it may start with the available milk supply. For a nursing home with a waiting list, the starting point may be potential bed nights which can be charged. For a busy professional firm, the limitation could be available man days. For a utility company, the first consideration might be the revenue and price allowed by the regulator.

- **The master budget must be accurately consolidated before the year end:** Crunching the numbers accurately was once a problem with older manual systems. This is no longer the case with most modern computerised systems, which may need minimal manual intervention. Nevertheless, having the exercise completed needs all budgetary submissions returned by the due date to enable the financial controller to present the figures for final approval before the year end. The use of spreadsheets has enormously diminished the drudgery entailed in completing lengthy forms by hand and has allowed the focus to move from mathematical accuracy to the judgements and assumptions underpinning the figures.
- **The entire organisation must be committed to budgeting:** If any part of the organisation fails to complete the budgeting exercise in a diligent manner, then the overall budget will reflect this weakness. Those businesses that have a rigorous budgeting system tend to have a CEO deeply committed to the process.

## The principles of effective budgeting

If cost reductions are to be achieved in addition to having the budgeting system properly organised, the budgetary process should comply with best practice. For the process to work successfully, certain principles need to be observed:

- **Senior management need to set clear objectives and reasonable targets:** If targets are set that budget holders know to be impossible, either these targets will be resisted, or no commitment will be given to the final budget. Either way, the business will suffer. There may be all sorts of pressure to raise performance, but if impossible targets are imposed, this will normally be counter-productive.
- **The process must be two-way:** Budgeting cannot be simply top down or bottom up. If budgets are imposed from the top, there will be no buy-in. If, on the other hand, there is no guidance, meeting stretch targets is an unlikely outcome. Normally, those responsible for controlling costs have the closest understanding and need to be involved in the detailed preparation of the budget.
- **Difficulties need to be properly communicated and realistically negotiated:** If an industry is facing a downturn, it may be impossible to

achieve growth. For example, with an increase in smoking-related health scares, the consumption of tobacco may fall. With stricter drink driving regulation, the sale of alcohol in pubs may decline. With increased supermarket buying power, food manufacturers may be unable to maintain margins. In a recession, many businesses may discover that the assumption of growth each year needs to be re-examined. Realism is the key in all such negotiations.

- **Monitoring must be timely and regular:** Monitoring performance is usually conducted on a monthly basis. Significant technological advances have been made in recent years to speed up this process. The most advanced companies have practically moved to real-time performance analysis and aim to have accounts available in less than a week. Some systems also permit budget holders to drill down through several levels to investigate performance variances from budget on a continuous basis, enabling corrective action to be taken before the monthly accounts are available.
- **Performance variances from budget must be used properly for decision-making:** Variances may arise for reasons within or beyond the control of the budget holder, because of timing changes or simply because of bad budgeting. If the reasons for the variances are not understood and no appropriate action is taken, the whole budgetary system may fall into disrepute.
- **Where shocks arise, flexibility will be required:** Most companies are reluctant to reset budgets in response to a sudden shock. Nevertheless, it would have been futile to expect the income of travel companies to remain unchanged after the events of 11 September 2001 or, more recently, volcanic eruptions from Iceland. Similarly, banks could not ignore the sub-prime crisis in the mortgage markets. Many companies have moved to rolling budgets to deal with such eventualities. For example, in each quarter of a 15-month rolling budget, the first quarter is deleted and an extra quarter is added to the end, which permits changes to be assessed quarterly, rather than annually. Others track variances from the original budget and a revised budget.
- **Budgetary performance needs to be linked effectively to the rewards system:** The final and vital requirement of effective budgeting is that good budgetary performance is rewarded, and under-performance penalised. If promotions, pay increases or bonuses take no account of budgetary performance, then it is unreasonable to expect managers to

give their budgets much attention. All too frequently the system rewards the wrong behaviour. For example, a salesperson who obtains a commission purely based on the total sales he or she achieves may be tempted to discount the sales price or sell to customers who are unlikely to pay. If, however, a salesperson's bonus is based on sales for which cash has been received and the gross margin achieved, different behaviour can be expected.

## The usual budgetary problems

### Predicting sales

The top line or sales figure is often the most difficult to predict. To obtain a realistic target, it is vital to understand clearly the sector in which the business operates, the market environment, consumer demand and the strategy of competitors. Most businesses start with the previous year's expected outcome. The figure is then adjusted for changes in volumes from existing customers and customers gained or lost. Where there are large customers, they may be consulted individually and, in some cases, industry data will be available. This will vary in its usefulness, however, depending on its reliability and whether it is sufficiently disaggregated for the business concerned.

Some businesses are more predictable than others. For example, the supermarket business grows relatively slowly and steadily, but there will still be issues around market share and new competition. Other businesses, like the airline industry, are notoriously cyclical, with the turning points often unpredictable. The most difficult businesses to predict are those such as civil engineering, where business may either come in large contracts or not at all. In such cases, flexibility is crucial, and decisions on costs may need to be taken on an ad hoc basis.

### Unpredictable key costs

Another budgetary problem relates to key costs where the price is highly uncertain. For instance, one recurring issue is oil and oil-related costs, which are difficult to predict and expensive to hedge. Clearly, these costs are affected by geopolitical considerations far beyond the control of any business. For many businesses, the choice of exchange rates can present a serious problem, though this can be addressed by using the rates on the forward currency market. Some years ago, the key unpredictable cost for many was insurance, while at the start of the century, it was the availability and cost of computer personnel.

## Human behaviour and motivation

Finally, human behaviour may pose problems. If budgets are to be effective, they have to be linked to the rewards system. For example, a salesperson who has achieved the monthly budget may be tempted not to complete other sales until the next period. Inevitably, managers will seek budgets that they consider to be easily achievable and, therefore, tend to understate revenue and overstate costs. If there is a sufficient cushion in the costs, reductions can be achieved during the year as required without undue stress. CEOs and boards need to be satisfied that the budgetary process achieves an appropriate balance of individual motivation, teamwork and realism. If the culture of the organisation overemphasises individual budgetary performance, conflict between the budget managers and the financial controllers can become the norm rather than the exception.

# Prioritisation of costs for reduction

If the budgetary system is well-organised and operates on an equitable basis, and the problem areas are identified, the organisation will be in a position to locate excess costs, prioritise them and take actions to reduce them. Nevertheless, it can be strange how some chief executives select areas for cost reduction. For example, just months before one of the biggest corporate bankruptcies in history, Bernie Ebbers, the CEO of WorldCom, proposed secretly re-filling mineral water containers with tap water and monitoring the consumption of coffee filters to prevent the theft of coffee bags.[2]

If the target is to reduce costs by, for example, 10%, managers should focus on areas that will make a significant impact. While every economy can have a psychological impact on the organisation, there is not much point in devoting energy to targeting the elimination of biscuits accompanying the morning coffee if the effect is immaterial to the bottom line. There will probably be areas where the costs are significant, but which cannot be reduced and, therefore, should not be the focus of undue attention. The office rent may be large, but if there is no spare space, it will prove difficult to reduce this in the short-term. The aim is to find significant costs that can be reduced or achieve the best value for money.

A sensible approach is to set out all costs in a matrix such as that in **Figure 2.1** below. The potential for cost reduction is assessed on the horizontal axis, while the absolute costs are set out on the vertical axis.

The parameters of both the perceived reduction potential and cost significance need to be set according to the level of cost reduction needed and the scale of the business. If 10% is needed, any cost that could be reduced by over 10% could be classified as high, 2% to 10% could be medium, and less than 2% could be classified as low. What is defined as a high amount and a low amount depends on the scale of the business or department. For example, overtime might have considerable potential for reduction and, therefore, fall into the High–High category of the matrix, while rent, though a high absolute cost, might have little potential for reduction and so fall into the High–Low category.

Once all the costs have been distributed around the matrix, a start can be made on the High–High box, followed by the High–Medium combinations. There is unlikely to be much benefit from targeting any of the low boxes, unless some cost is of enormous significance, where even a 1% reduction would materially affect the bottom line. For example, 1% reduction in material costs could be very substantial, where material costs amount to 75% of total costs.

*Figure 2.1* **Matrix for Prioritising Cost Reduction Projects**

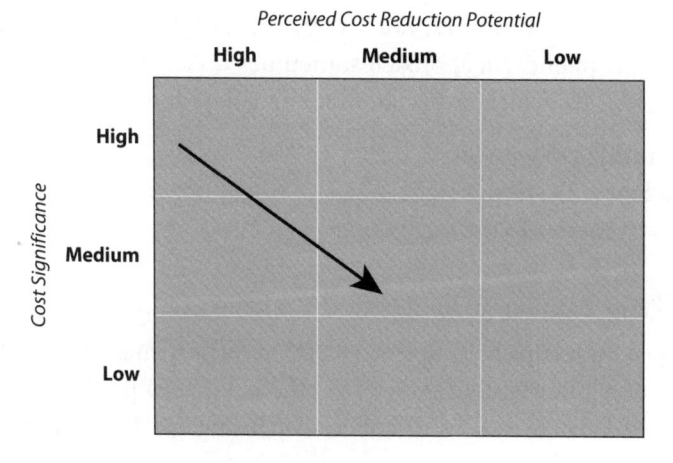

> ### Government spending cuts
>
> In the summer of 2008 the Irish Government announced that to balance the national budget with falling tax revenues it was necessary to make major cuts in expenditure. The target was set at €440 million in 2008 and €1 billion in 2009. A number of Government agencies were to be merged, but without any loss of jobs. Administration costs were also to be cut back and press reports[3] stated that the following suggestions had been put forward:
>
> - Using black-and-white rather than colour printing
> - Publishing annual reports on-line rather than in hard copy
> - Booking the cheapest air fares for official travel
> - Using civil servants rather than outside consultants
> - Providing staff with filtered rather than bottled water
> - Sending office notices using e-mail
> - Deferring capital expenditure projects
> - Reducing payroll costs by 3%
> - Switching off lights
>
> Into which of the nine boxes of the matrix would you place each of these proposals?

## Reducing individual costs through the '3 Es'

The public sector has sought, not always successfully, to provide 'value for money' to the public. An approach sometimes used is to address the cost in terms of the '3 Es', which are 'economy', 'efficiency' and 'effectiveness':

- **Economy:** Do with less
- **Efficiency:** Do things right
- **Effectiveness:** Do the right things

*Economy*

Economy is a relatively simple concept: it means managing with fewer resources or a lower level of service. In offices, for example, this might mean that the tea lady gives way to coffee dispensing machines. Farmers with declining EU subsidies understand the concept well. The labour force must be cut and inputs reduced. That means less expenditure on fertilisers and sprays, together with less reliance on vets.

There is waste and duplication in all organisations, and it is the challenge of good housekeeping to minimise waste. In the public sector, cost reduction may be enforced by setting cash limits for departments. Once the limit is reached, no further resources are available. It may, in extreme cases, be backed up by arbitrary rules of thumb: a ban on recruitment, a ban on new equipment, no overtime or restrictions on travel, etc. Such rules, however, tend to be short-term in effect, often doing longer-term damage.

Cutting resources may balance the books, but it may not necessarily lead to customer satisfaction. Restrictions in the health service may lead to long waiting lists and leaving patients on trolleys. When the roads budget is spent for a local authority, completion of a road may have to wait a year until further funds are available. Such outcomes may be unacceptable in the private sector, where customers may vote with their feet.

## Efficiency

Efficiency is trying to 'do things right', which means producing more output from a given level of input or providing the same level of output from a reduced level of input.

In essence, efficiency involves the simple idea of productivity. Metrics are usually applied to monitor efficiency, such as output per head, invoices processed per hour, etc. Care needs to be taken that the metrics are comparable. For example, the cost per mile of motorway is likely to be higher in the city than in the countryside, and the number of patients processed in a hospital per hour will vary with the complexity and seriousness of individual ailments. Pure efficiency metrics may overlook the quality dimension.

## Effectiveness

Effectiveness is the most difficult of the '3 Es' both to understand and to achieve in practice. In simple terms, it is 'doing the right things'. It seeks to find better ways of meeting the overall objective. Could many in-patients be better treated as outpatients to provide better healthcare? Could road deaths be reduced by safer roads, reduced driver alcohol levels or tighter speeding regulation? On a wider plane, it might consider whether an organisation's overall goals could be best achieved by a public–private sector partnership.

In assessing effectiveness, the overall objective needs to be clear. There are numerous tales in some centrally-planned economies of how efficiency targets were achieved in manufacturing plants by producing only left shoes or shoes of only one size. This may achieve efficiency narrowly in terms of volumes produced, but certainly does not provide effectiveness in terms of providing suitable footwear for the population. The ultimate goal should be consumer satisfaction, rather than a mere output target.

---

### Cost reduction in the hotel industry

Examples from the hotel industry illustrate how overall costs can be reduced using the '3 Es'. Many savings have been achieved without the loss of customer goodwill. Self-service at breakfast in the dining room, mini-bars, kettles and shoe shine in bedrooms all reduce labour costs, while careful portion control reduces food costs. Computerisation of keys and accounts can enhance efficiency, while such keys can also reduce energy costs. Group purchasing also can lower the cost of fixed assets through increased buying power, while substantial labour saving is possible through multi-skilling and flexible working arrangements. Finally, the whole selling process can be made more effective with good website and Internet booking options for customers.

Naturally, the '3 Es' should not be used indiscriminately. For example, if a hotel were to reduce cleaning or reception manning, savings should ensue. However, these savings may be outweighed by the damage done to the hotel's brand. Possible side effects on the quality of the service or potential revenue loss should not be ignored. Similarly, care must be taken to ensure that no regulatory requirements are overlooked.

---

Consumers will instinctively employ the '3 Es' when faced with a reduced household budget. Economy could dictate reduced consumption of luxuries; efficiency might lead to shopping at cheaper supermarkets; effectiveness might cause a household to relocate to a neighbourhood with a lower cost of living. The '3 Es' can provide a good starting point for managers to identify ways to reduce costs of dealing with their customers. For example, take the cost of having sales personnel on the road. Economy would lower the level of service, such as visiting customers once a month rather than once a week. Efficiency improvements might focus on the cost *per diem* or the routing of visits in order to lower travel costs. Improvements in effectiveness might focus on replacing the visit with electronic ordering, telephone or video linking.

The same approach could be applied at a higher level. Economy could be achieved through closing sales offices; efficiency might be improved by changing the basis of the sales personnel's remuneration between salary and bonus; and effectiveness might be enhanced by moving from sales personnel to e-commerce, particularly where customer decisions are primarily made on price.

Financial controllers often target travel and entertainment as a priority for cost reduction. It is frequently a cost which can be both large in amount and has considerable potential for reduction. Once it is curtailed, word will quickly spread around the organisation that cost reduction is being taken seriously. Questioning in terms of the '3 Es' provides a practical approach to identifying cost reduction targets.

The FÁS Science Challenger programme (also discussed in the next chapter) attracted much adverse criticism with suggestions that the high costs of trips to Florida constituted junketing and were a poor use of public funds. The costs could be challenged as follows:

- **Economy:** Were there too many trips?
- **Efficiency:** Was the use of business or first class air travel for officials and their wives, together with the meals and accommodation, value for money?
- **Effectiveness:** Could the objectives of the Science Challenger programme have been met by video conferencing, or other means rather than overseas trips?

## Conclusions

- The attitude of top management is critical to the effectiveness of budgetary control. The organisation of the budget should not present major difficulties for a competent financial controller, provided a proper costing system is in place and top management is supportive.
- The key to the operation of the budget in practice is a sense of fairness and realism, the absence of which will lead to apathy and cynicism.
- The attention given by managers to budgeting will be strongly influenced by its link to the rewards system. Ill-considered rewards can lead to antisocial behaviour.

- The use of the '3 Es' (economy, efficiency and effectiveness) provides a mechanism for managers to reduce their departmental costs.

The recession and the credit crunch have forced many organisations to review the effectiveness of their budgeting systems in the pursuit of cost reduction.[4] The question remains: Is the reliance on individual departmental managers to obtain economies the best approach, or will a silo mentality result in the overall welfare of the organisation being overlooked?

Before tackling this topic, organisations may wish to review how and where costs are reduced in the different functional areas, and this is discussed in the next chapter.

## Management checklist

1. Is your budgeting system organised in such a way that it will achieve material cost reduction?
2. Do you review the long-term plan prior to the commencement of the budgeting process?
3. Is the process sufficiently robust and equitable to provide a framework for significant cost reduction?
4. If cost reduction is a guideline, how do managers prioritise targets for reduction?
5. Can managers use a '3 E' framework to reduce targeted costs?

Chapter 3

# The role of the functions in traditional cost reduction

"Money is the most important thing in the world. It represents health, strength, honour, generosity and beauty, as conspicuously as the want of it represents illness, weakness, disgrace, meanness and ugliness."

*"Major Barbara", George Bernard Shaw*

If Shaw's desired abundance of money is to be achieved, costs need to be managed and controlled in a thrifty manner. Before embarking on a major cost-reduction programme, it is worth reflecting on who is currently responsible for cost reduction in the organisation, how it takes place and when.[1] When businesses need to save money, the problem is often approached through departmental heads.

To some extent, every manager who has a budget has a responsibility for cost management and, therefore, cost reduction, when required. *Cost control,* coordinated by the financial controller, should be the mechanism by which the budget is implemented, but *cost management* remains the task of every manager up to the CEO and, therefore, is also a matter of concern for the Board. However, some functional parties tend to be more involved than others.

Naturally, every business is different but, in this chapter, we discuss the role of the standard key functions which apply to most businesses, progressing to a treatment of management by objectives, and the overall approach a business should adopt for cost reduction. These are dealt with under the following headings:

- Financial control
- Operations
- Procurement or purchasing
- Engineering
- Human resources (HR)
- Information technology (IT)

- Logistics
- Sales and marketing
- Internal audit/organisation and methods
- Management by objectives (MBO)
- The most likely areas for cost reduction
- A holistic or piecemeal approach?

## Financial control[2]

The time is long since past when the cost accountant merely acted as a scorekeeper, analysing costs into various cost centres and presenting the results to management for action. Management accountants now have a key role in controlling business performance. As the budget coordinator, the accountant will inevitably have a role in cost containment. Typically, there will be a focus on ensuring that gross margins are achieved and overheads contained with the aim of keeping them fixed or, better still, having them reduced. If management accounts are produced on a monthly basis, it is the job of the financial controller to investigate adverse variances and to report accordingly. The financial controller will also check that all payments are duly authorised, which should prevent wayward cost escalation.

In addition to the everyday role of controlling costs, accountants may periodically undertake studies to make more lasting savings. Frequently, accountants will analyse a business's sales by product type or geographical territory. If the returns on investment are inadequate, an accountant may recommend that products or customer groups be discontinued and the associated costs thus saved. Historically, accountants have intervened in the 'make or buy' decision, which was usually regarded in purely financial terms. If the cost of a component from the market was less than the cost of manufacture, being the direct cost and the associated overhead, it should be purchased and not made. Finally, financial controllers are likely to be involved in investment proposals, vetting the forecasts and setting out required rates of return. In particular, their involvement may prove vital to the evaluation of mergers and acquisitions.

It has been suggested that the 2008 financial crisis has thrust chief financial officers (CFOs), as the true guardians of corporate health, more centre stage.[3] According to the CFO of the Dutch conglomerate Philips, often considered to be a role model in the budgetary process, the CFO has ceased to be a referee and become more of a player. This necessitates greater involvement of CFOs in cost reduction and even more emphasis on cash control to ensure the survival of the business.

## Operations

In manufacturing, if gross margins are to be maintained, costs must be carefully managed. This is the task of the operations function. The three key elements in manufacturing are the cost of materials, direct labour and factory overhead. If a standard costing system is in place, it will break down the materials cost into price and efficiency, as it will with direct labour. Production managers must manage these two elements continuously, together with the factory overhead. Accordingly, efforts should be made to reduce material waste, particularly scrap and rework. The purchasing department must negotiate favourable prices with suppliers. The labour force must be managed to minimise absenteeism, increase productivity and contain rates of pay. To maximise efficiency, downtime of machines should be minimised by careful scheduling and proper maintenance. Overheads, especially indirect labour, need to be minimised in a manner consistent with reducing other direct costs.

Service industries are much more straightforward: the determinants of success are buying well and maximising the productivity of the labour force.

There is one challenge common to manufacturing and trading companies: the management of stocks. In the case of manufacturing, these are raw materials, work in progress and finished goods while, for trading companies, only finished goods need to be managed. The costs of holding stocks can be considerable, although not readily visible in financial accounts. There can be the costs of storage space, light and heating, damage, handling costs, insurance, 'shrinkage' or theft and the cost of capital tied up in the investment in stock. It is in the overall management of stocks that some of the most significant cost reductions have been achieved in recent years.

In former times, productivity of production labour was measured by time and motion experts, the bane of trade unionists' lives. This, in turn, transformed into work study, which sometimes changed into the study of 'organisation and methods'. This has brought a whole new emphasis on processes, systems, activities and quality. If the production of goods and services is not set up in the most efficient way, higher costs will be the result. This, of course, should not be a once-off exercise, but a matter of continuous improvement in a lean manufacturing environment.

## Procurement or purchasing

The greater the percentage of the final product comprising bought-in materials or services, the more important is the role of procurement. In much of manufacturing, therefore, good buying is critical, since the cost of raw materials can be a high proportion of the cost of the finished product. In a world of increased competition and tight margins, many businesses place greater reliance on their purchasing departments to reduce their cost of goods sold. Buyers have access to much more information in a world of volatile commodity prices through the Internet and are usually empowered to continually reduce costs.

In retailing, skilful purchasing is even more vital. In some sectors, such as fashion or antiques, the buyer's ability to match customer tastes is the key to the success of the business, and price may play a less significant role. In other sectors where customer tastes are more stable, cost is the key. Where the company is in a position to place large orders, it is in a strong position to obtain the best possible price for goods. For example, supermarket chains have enormous buying power and can drive down supplier costs dramatically, as Tesco in the UK, Wal-Mart in the US or Dunnes Stores in Ireland can testify. However, this can lead to the supplier's margins driven down to a level where the survival of the business is put at risk. Supermarkets can also extract favourable credit terms, such as Tesco's increase from 30 to 60 days for its non-food suppliers, which it announced in 2008.[4]

The organisation of purchasing can have an important influence on prices paid. As supermarkets show, a business's negotiating power increases with the scale of its purchases. Many businesses have found that centralising purchasing in a group enables them to increase their purchasing/negotiating power and ensure that all parts of the group obtain the keenest price. Likewise, small businesses may form buying groups to achieve a similar end. However, the greatest potential for savings by centralised purchasing must be in the public sector, where, if well managed, the gains could be enormous. The Health Service Executive (HSE) in Ireland, facing massive budgetary cuts for 2011, was reported to be seeking cuts from suppliers of up to 30% in its €2.4 billion procurement budget and expected to save €200 million in 2012.[5]

Bought-in services can also be the target for cost reduction, although the purchasing decisions may only partly be made on the basis of price. Many businesses have found that they can significantly reduce their costs by looking for multiple quotations for services, such as energy or telecommunications.

Similarly, if the costs of insurance, audit or even banking are to be addressed, the simplest way is to put them out to tender periodically, although this may be difficult in the current banking climate. Where the supplier of such services is to change, a carefully drawn up service level agreement may be critical to assure that quality levels are not reduced. If the outcome of the service is more difficult to define, as in the case of management training or advertising, price is likely to be secondary to meeting the overall objective.

Skilful negotiation can enormously assist cost reduction. Good negotiators clearly understand their goals, anticipate problems and plan meticulously. This necessitates a thorough knowledge of the relevant standards which need to be met and the needs or interests of the other party. Frequently, good negotiators can find solutions which are mutually beneficial and safer. Negotiating skills fall outside the scope of this book, but are well documented.[6]

While most businesses wish to negotiate directly with their main suppliers, they may choose to use brokers for certain specialist areas, such as insurance or travel. This can result in considerable savings with regard to secondary costs, such as packaging, telephony, property facilities and bank charges. Some consultants specialise in these areas and can advise on a gain sharing basis to mid-sized or larger companies, thereby avoiding any consultancy fees.

In recent years, many businesses have reduced their supplier base, having only one or two providers of certain goods. This enables them to achieve favourable prices, which may be the subject of regular re-negotiation. However, good supplier management involves more than just price cutting.

Since the loss of a key supplier may cause irreparable damage to a business, many organisations try to approach supplier management in a more strategic manner. Some businesses choose to protect their global supply chain in a recession. It is sensible to assess how important your business is to your supplier and, conversely, how important their business is to you. This can be gauged in terms of the overall scale of the revenue or profit, but it will also be affected by how critical the business is overall to the success of the organisation and whether or not there are substitutes. Diagrammatically, supplier management can be shown as in **Figure 3.1**.[7]

The approach to supplier management is governed by the respective importance of the transactions to both supplier and buyer. Where the business is not important to either party, the relationship should be easy to manage. Efficiency may be achieved through the '3 Es', possibly through e-procurement or e-tendering, which can reduce the labour cost. Where your business is unimportant to the supplier, but important to you, it is usually necessary to have available alternatives. Where the business is important to the supplier, but not to you, it should be possible to obtain very beneficial terms and push inventory costs back to the supplier. It may very well be possible to exploit this relationship by methods such as conducting an auction by e-tendering to the point where the supplier's continued trading is put in real jeopardy, but company values and longer term self-interest may constrain unfair exploitation by a powerful buyer. The interdependent relationship needs careful management and may involve partnership with suppliers, collaborating closely to find mutually beneficial solutions.

*Figure 3.1*  **Supplier Management**

|  | Importance to Supplier | |
|---|---|---|
|  | **High** | **Low** |
| **Importance to Buyer — High** | Interdependent<br><br>Win-Win | Supplier Leverage<br><br>Find Substitutes |
| **Importance to Buyer — Low** | Buyer Leverage<br><br>Exploit Fairly | Free market<br><br>Manage Efficiently |

## Engineering

Engineering may have a major role to play in designing capital investment projects. Often, a substantial part of future product costs is determined by the initial investment in plant and machinery. If a production line is poorly configured, the products will be hampered by higher costs, which may be impossible or very expensive to remove by re-engineering.

Furthermore, the design of the product and its packaging will greatly impact on its cost of manufacture. Sometimes, the customer may design a complex product, as in the case of Dell computers. In general, the greater the complexity of a product, the more the components will number and the more physical movements needed in the process, the higher the cost of the finished product. Frequently, products are over-engineered, containing features or functions that are not valued by the consumer, as happened with many of the early personal computers. The same principle applies in the service industry, where businesses may decide to eliminate frills not appreciated by consumers. The case of low fare airlines and the value chain illustrates this point in **Chapter 9**.

Value analysis seeks to identify the elements of the product or service which are important to the customer. While packaging may be an important component of value with consumer goods, it may play a less significant role in industrial goods. Fewer parts, simpler packaging and more standardisation will reduce stocks and, therefore, costs. Sometimes, cheaper materials can be used, but this can be at the expense of quality. In times of volatile exchange rates, alternative materials at competitive prices can emerge unexpectedly. Value engineering involves the continuous search for the right balance between quality and cost.

Engineering in the guise of research and development can also devise ways to reduce energy consumption or incorporate desirable 'green' features, which indirectly reduce costs by avoiding legal claims from affected parties against the business. In an era of rising energy costs and socially responsible investment, it is natural to seek out opportunities in these fields. In some cases, it may be possible to avail of government grants or fiscal incentives, thereby enabling a business to undertake projects which might not otherwise be justified.[8]

## Human resources (HR)

The human resource function is tasked with providing an organisation with the tools to manage and maximise the contribution of its workforce. Typically, payroll costs feature in the top three expenses faced by an organisation, so it is a critical element that must be actively managed, just as much in periods of cost reduction as in times of growth. Part of HR's role is to provide credible information to managers on rates of pay, performance metrics and staff efficiencies. In addition, HR can provide the organisation with details on associated staff costs, such as pensions, healthcare, incentive planning, etc. The HR function should also create robust processes to manage staff-related expenditure, e.g. recruitment, training, travel, etc.

These inputs can be best realised if the human resource function provides an integrated service to the organisation. This begins with the selection and induction of staff supported through on-going training and development, directed by the management of performance, efficiency and attendance. The integration of these HR activities facilitates early and grounded decision-making regarding costs on an informed basis. For example, how can you objectively identify the best performers in any given team without a mechanism for managing and reporting performance? Absence of such basics makes the management of costs more difficult.

Since they engage with staff on a continuous basis, there is much that the HR department can do to improve the *productivity* of labour. Multi-skilling is often important and, for this to be achieved, training may be required. Staff rotation, enlargement of the job and empowering employees too can play their part in improving productivity. The presence of trade unions can be a complicating factor in this process. Where changes in work practices need to be negotiated and paid for, change will tend to be slower and more expensive to implement. In a crisis, particularly skilful HR management is vital to ensure rapid and smooth change.

Another major factor is the *price* of labour. The rewards system will have a major impact on morale and productivity. The cost of recruiting skilled employees may be high and short-term economies may be counterproductive if they lead to greater employee turnover. Pension schemes have traditionally comprised a significant element in the rewards package and have provided a strong loyalty incentive. Nevertheless, many businesses have recently found that they have been obliged to close defined benefit pension schemes because of their enormous cost. Flexible benefits packages examine the total costs of remuneration, permitting individual employees to choose their own particular mix of salary and benefits. For example, one employee may opt for a company car, while another might prefer an increase in salary. Ways of reducing the cost of labour are examined in **Chapter 16**.

Frequently, efforts to reduce labour costs attack both the productivity and price of labour by a process of de-layering. The removal of a supervisory level, for example, can obviously reduce costs, but may also reduce control. Too often, key workers that have been made redundant have had to be re-hired as consultants at considerable cost. The banking industry has seen the extensive use of lower paid workers in the branch network, which may have impacted adversely on the level of customer service. If labour savings impact negatively on operational effectiveness, it needs to be approached cautiously.

The management of human resources is bound to impact the cost of labour. The management of pay and absenteeism have an obvious immediate effect on labour costs. But the skilful management of recruitment, promotion and work organisation also affect costs, whether in the short or long term. HR implications are usually central to any cost reduction proposals.

## Information technology (IT)

Economists advise that capital can be substituted for labour as a factor of production. In view of rising labour costs, it is to be expected that increased mechanisation and automation of production lines through the use of machinery and computer-based technology will continue to be used to reduce labour costs. This trend has enabled many businesses to substantially reduce their manufacturing workforces, not only reducing direct costs, but also often increasing quality and reliability, since computers are unable to take industrial action. Ultimately, this can lead to the creation of robotic factories with minimal human input and robotic warehouses, where picking and handling are automated.

Investment in IT has also lowered the cost of communication. The widespread use of the Internet has enabled managers to obtain valuable information instantaneously and frequently at no cost. It has also revolutionised stock and credit control. While it is difficult to measure the benefits of this service, it clearly has been substantial. Likewise, the cost of internal communication has greatly benefited from the use of intranets. Above all, the universal use of e-mail has massively reduced postal costs.

It is natural to expect that the IT department will play a central role in cost reduction. In some cases, IT may be outsourced but, whether or not an IT department exists as a separate entity, the function can be expected to influence radical cost reduction by adopting labour saving technology. While this can be the case, all too often the reverse occurs. Frequently, computer investment proposals are approved on the basis of labour costs saved. Yet, this is rarely the case in practice. Few projects come in on time and on budget, while the labour saving is often elusive in the short term. The benefits of better information for decision makers are difficult to quantify, but the cost overruns are much more apparent. However, the skilful use of available technologies is fundamental to achieving massive savings in a successful business process re-engineering project, discussed in more detail in **Chapter 13**.

One interesting trend that has enabled businesses to reduce the cost of their IT investment is the increase in software rental, particularly since the advent of cloud computing. 'Software-as-a-service' is now available over the Internet, and this can help businesses to improve the efficiency of areas such as sales force management through an annual fee, rather than a large capital commitment with an uncertain outcome. 'Infrastructure-as-a-service' and 'platform-as-a-service' are available also, enabling businesses to replace traditional capital invesments with an annual service cost.

High-technology businesses have often had an ambivalent attitude to cost management. In the dot-com boom, engineers too often developed their products with little regard to cost. When the funds were exhausted, they returned to venture capitalists for further cash, which they assumed would be available. There were some notable exceptions where IT businesses adopted a thrifty approach to costs: one surviving company selling relatively small specialist systems to the global market insisted on prospective customers paying travel costs in advance of the sales presentation. More normally, this cost was considered secondary in IT departments and treated in a somewhat profligate manner.

## Logistics

Transport has always been an important cost for many businesses, particularly for those with heavy or bulky goods. One key decision was whether or not to own your own fleet or use an external supplier. Distribution and warehousing can also add up to large costs in some industries. Importing and exporting add further complications and costs.

Logistics, a discipline which manages the supply of goods from the point of origin to the ultimate destination is an old military tradition, dating back to the Greek and Roman eras. Armies then needed to obtain supplies from great distances in an efficient manner and locate lodgings for quartering personnel. Today, global businesses, also operating over vast distances, often have problems integrating their transport, inventory, warehousing, materials handling and packaging processes. The discipline of logistics evolved in the 1950s as a business concept, involving the flow of goods, information and other resources from point of origin to point of consumption, leading to the entire management of the supply chain.

The integrated study of inward and outward logistics has provided new possibilities for cost reduction. Those organisations that have a logistics function have discovered economies from integrating activities which were traditionally independently managed. Businesses with sophisticated supply chain management systems have for years endeavoured to rationalise their supplier base and achieve dramatic reduction in costs. This can involve the use of lean techniques to reduce waste, as outlined in **Chapters 11, 12 and 13**.[9]

Some global supply chains were severely tested in 2011 following the loss of energy supply and transport problems in the aftermath of the earthquake and tsunami in Japan.[10] Many global businesses found themselves critically dependent on goods from Japanese suppliers who could not deliver due to forces of nature beyond their control. Some extra cost incurred by always having an alternative supplier may be justified to prevent the disruption of the supply chain, which can halt production. In future, supply chains may need to consider 'just-in-case' as well as 'just-in-time'.

## Sales and marketing

The sales and marketing department is rarely a place where cost reduction takes place of its own accord. Sales personnel may resist economies which, in their view, jeopardise the placing of an order or closing a sale. However, in view of the customary magnitude of the expenditure, it is potentially a source of considerable saving. Unsurprisingly, costs such as travel and entertainment can become a battlefield between growth-conscious salesmen and cost-conscious financial controllers. (A possible logical approach to containment of these costs has already been covered in **Chapter 2**, under the '3 Es'.)

Wider marketing expenditure on items such as advertising and sponsorship can also become a target for financial controllers. If nothing else, these costs are easy to cut by simply refusing or reducing the expenditure. The difficulty, of course, is measuring the impact of such culling on future sales and revenues over the long term. As Lord Leverhulme of Unilever is reputed to have remarked, 50% of advertising is a waste of money, but the question is which 50%? A wider review of the costs of different distribution channels, such as the cost of direct versus indirect channels, can reveal considerable savings, particularly since the advent of the Internet, which has made information about and access to alternatives much simpler.

## Internal audit/organisation and methods

Larger organisations sometimes have an 'organisation and methods' department or, more usually, an internal audit function which typically examines the various functional departments, such as finance, IT, purchasing, sales and HR, and may be able to identify duplication between departments and examine existing systems with an impartial eye. With access to the external auditors, an internal audit department may be in a position to discover best practice in the industry, and with direct access to the Board through the audit committee, the department is well-positioned to bring about change.

> ### Internal audit at FÁS
>
> It was the internal audit team in FÁS, the Irish training agency which, in 2008, brought to the attention of its Board serious irregularities in procurement procedures. After some months of investigative journalism, the *Sunday Independent*, having obtained details of internal audit reports and expenses paid under the Freedom of Information Act, published a damaging exposure of expenses paid to senior management in connection with travel and entertainment in Florida under the Science Challenger programme.[11] This led to the resignation of the Director-General and a public outcry about expenses paid to Government officials.

For most internal audit departments, however, their focus may be on detection of irregularities and compliance, so cost reduction, value for money or even risk evaluation may not be their priority. Nevertheless, there may be scope for a more proactive role to promote efficiency in the way that the Comptroller and Auditor General performs this function in the public sector.

## Management by objectives (MBO)

One traditional approach to finding cost reductions in each of the functional areas throughout an organisation is 'management by objectives' or MBO. This technique, originated by Peter Drucker, was popularised in the 1960s in the UK by John Humble[12] of Urwick Orr, a firm of management consultants. Applying it to cost reduction, both functional and line managers were asked to set their own goals and identify ways to achieve them. While it did have the merit of involving all managers in cost reduction, in practice, managers tended to pitch the target too low and, as a consequence, the technique is less widely used today. However, many contemporary performance management systems still maintain elements of management by objectives with a keen focus on budgeting.

## The most likely areas for cost reduction

The kind of cost reduction suggested thus far is neither radical nor strategic. It is simply the application of best practice to the continuing issue of controlling costs and usually fits in readily with existing structures. While most CEOs at least pay lip service to cost reduction, the extent of its application varies enormously. In an increasingly difficult economic environment, it is reasonable to expect a greater emphasis in the future on cost reduction.

It is difficult to identify the most likely areas for cost reduction since no two businesses are the same, but research in the US is informative. The Institute of Management and Administration in 2002 surveyed thousands of financial controllers in companies of all sizes.[13] The findings of the survey indicated that the areas where controllers had most success in controlling costs were (in order of significance):

1. Capital expenditure
2. Materials
3. Stocks
4. Insurance
5. Professional services
6. Production costs
7. Compensation
8. Travel and entertainment

The priorities may be different in other countries, with different legal systems now, a decade after the survey was conducted, but perhaps these items may at least provide food for thought to organisations seeking cost-reduction targets.

## A holistic or piecemeal approach?

One way forward is to approach the problem of cost reduction in a piecemeal way within the existing business framework. In this approach, the key functional areas are addressed in turn with a view to making the cost base competitive. For those who favour such an approach, there are books which provide lists of places to look and tips for solutions.[14] Alternatively, teams can be set up to find areas of waste where economies can be achieved in a more bottom-up manner.[15]

The issue with this approach, however, is whether or not it will cut the most appropriate costs. Any business can cut costs by reducing budgets in a haphazard or political manner, where personal relationships count for more than competitive considerations. The danger in a piecemeal approach is that cuts in some particular area will have repercussions elsewhere to the detriment of the business as a whole.

Rather than addressing the functional areas of a business separately as silos, which will typically defend their traditional interests, it may be better to approach the issue of cost reduction in a more strategic, cross-functional way. Many functional heads will need to be involved as part of a team if the requisite expertise is to be assembled. The team may be led by the chief executive and will usually include the chief financial officer, in view of the link to the annual budget.

## Conclusions

- All managers have responsibility for controlling the costs within their area of activity, although some may take this task more seriously than others.
- It is possible to make savings in most or all of the functional areas.
- Focusing solely on individual areas may lead to an individualistic, silo mentality with damaging effects elsewhere in the organisation.
- If any organisation is to reduce costs, some financial goal is desirable. Without financial targets, strenuous efforts to reduce costs may succeed, but be inadequate, leading to eventual failure.

Once the target for cost reduction has been established, the remainder of this book will address the more daunting task of making dramatic reductions in costs where traditional remedies have proven inadequate. Tinkering with existing systems can indeed reduce costs, but greater savings are usually made by fundamentally examining what lies behind the systems and seeking a better way of achieving the overall objective. This approach continuously questions the effectiveness of existing systems by placing them in a strategic framework.

## Management checklist

1. What are the main functional areas in your organisation where cost reduction is achieved?
2. How often is cost reduction tackled: at budget time or continuously?
3. Are substantial improvements required?
4. How does the business ensure that savings in one functional area do not have adverse consequences elsewhere, for example, on product quality or staff morale?
5. Is there a need for radical or strategic cost reduction outside existing organisational structures?

# Chapter 4

# Is there a problem with current performance?

"The greatest danger for most of us is not that our aim is too high and we miss it, but that it is too low and we reach it."

*Michelangelo*

Reducing costs is rarely a pleasant or easy task. Consequently, if there are neither rules for the process nor targets for the outcome, managers may choose to neglect cost reduction. Some organisations may have an obvious or legal obligation to reduce costs. If a not-for-profit organisation is also not-for-loss and precluded from incurring a deficit, it may have no alternative to cutting costs when revenue falls. Similarly, governments may have limits imposed on the scale of their deficits and may be forced to cut costs when taxation and other revenue are reduced.

For commercial enterprises, the appropriate level of costs may be less obvious. Managers of such businesses should know the level of profit that they must achieve if they are to survive and prosper. In practice, this is the return on investment expected by their owners. To answer the complex question of how large this return should be, it is necessary to see if there is a problem, what the overall objective should be and how progress toward the objective should be measured. This chapter will address these issues under the following headings:

- Health check
- Worrying symptoms
- The health objective: shareholder value
- Return on invested capital (ROIC)
- Benchmarking ROIC
- Setting a target ROIC
- The drivers of ROIC
- Setting a cost reduction target
- Limitations of ROIC
- Prognosis without intervention

## Health check

Most executives undergo personal health checks throughout their careers. Before attending the doctor, they will probably have an idea of how fit they are and what health problems they are experiencing. They may also have noticed certain symptoms that may or may not indicate a health problem.

The doctor will conduct an array of tests on different aspects of the patient's health, for which there are benchmarks for acceptable, normal parameters. When the results of the different tests are available, the doctor will diagnose the situation, provide a prognosis of what will happen if no action is taken and may prescribe some form of treatment. In the case of mild disorders, the prescription may simply be a matter of sensible diet and regular exercise. In more serious cases, minor procedures or even major surgery may be recommended, in which instance the alternatives will be outlined and the inherent risks set out.

Ultimately, it remains the responsibility of the patient to decide what action he or she is prepared to take. To some extent, the decision will depend on the patient's overall fitness goals. For some, average good health is quite acceptable. For others, say, members of the security forces, a higher level of fitness is essential, while for Olympic athletes, nothing short of the highest level is acceptable.

Assessing the fitness of a business is broadly analogous to a personal health check. Managers need to understand what factors make for corporate fitness. Some businesses are content to maintain their current level of fitness. If normal budgeting and periodic simple dieting suffice to keep the body corporate in good shape, then perhaps no further action is required. Others may decide that they need a superior level of fitness and prepare themselves for a major weight-loss programme and all the unpleasantness that such a regime may entail. Still others will ignore the medical advice and subsequently become seriously, perhaps even fatally, ill.

## Worrying symptoms

Organisational problems may surface in the marketplace in a myriad of different forms. If they are not recognised in time, remedial action may be too late. Here are a few worrying symptoms which managers should look out for:

- A gradual decline in profit margins
- Falling share price or demands from new investors, such as private equity
- Threats from head office to relocate the business
- Loss of a valued major customer over price
- Inability to recover increased material or energy prices from customers
- Adverse exchange rate movements weakening competitiveness
- The arrival of a new competitor with a lower cost base
- Increased borrowings and bank pressure
- Loss of turnover in a recession

Many companies that have experienced continuous growth over many years will not be unduly perturbed by having some of these symptoms. Yet, while growth should ideally be accompanied by efficiency, it can often hide a multitude of difficulties and management errors. For businesses weakened by recession, the policy of simply muddling through may not work. The more prudent managers may decide on a health check to ascertain if corrective treatment is needed.

## The health objective: shareholder value

Ask most business people what the overall objective for a business should be, and they will typically reply, "Make as much money as possible for the owners." Though this is not the only possible goal, with some preferring a wider stakeholder objective, it has become widely adopted as the underlying foundation of the capitalist system. Creating value for shareholders is more complicated than maximising short-term profits. Companies can destroy value by failing to invest in their future or by exposing the business to higher levels of risk. In general, the success of value creation should be reflected in the share price. For companies without a stock exchange listing, the task of assessing value creation is more difficult.

A business in its simplest form may fit with the model shown in **Figure 4.1** below:[1]

It can be seen from the diagram that the ultimate aim of a business is to make the best possible return for shareholders. The company will decide what dividend, if any, should be paid out, with the remainder re-invested in the business, which should result in a capital gain for the shareholders.

*Figure 4.1* **Shareholder Value**

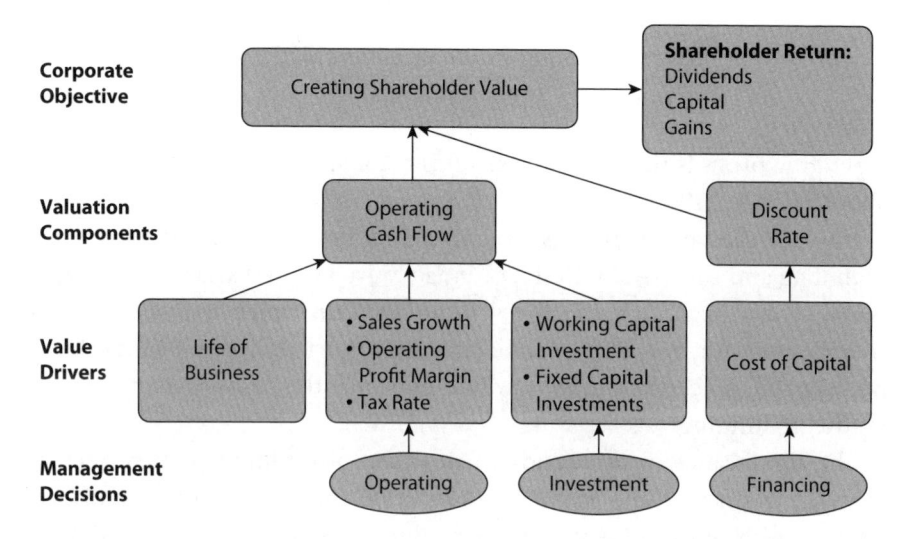

```
Corporate Objective:          Creating Shareholder Value  →  Shareholder Return:
                                                              Dividends
                                                              Capital Gains

Valuation Components:         Operating Cash Flow             Discount Rate

Value Drivers:  Life of Business | • Sales Growth       | • Working Capital Investment | Cost of Capital
                                 | • Operating Profit   | • Fixed Capital Investments  |
                                 |   Margin             |                               |
                                 | • Tax Rate           |                               |

Management Decisions:            Operating                   Investment                  Financing
```

The value of the business is seen as the sum of the future cashflows of the business over its life, discounted to a present value by the company's cost of capital. Management can influence the overall valuation by their decisions in three areas: operations, investment and finance.

The three operational levers to increase operating cashflow are increasing sales, increasing operating margins and reducing tax rates. If sales growth is limited by recession, the focus turns to operating margins.

Investment comprises periodic capital expenditure and the working capital needed to support the business on a day-to-day basis. The smaller the investment, the easier it will be to achieve a satisfactory return. The relentless drive to reduce stocks, a key element of working capital, has provided a challenge for many businesses.

The cost of finance is the average cost, after tax, of debt and equity. The cost of debt is simply the rate of interest on borrowings, reduced by the tax it saves. The cost of equity[2] is a complex topic. Suffice it to say, however, that the cost of equity is substantially higher than debt, since investors take greater risks and, so, can command higher returns. The result is that the average cost of capital, comprising both borrowings and equity, is much greater than the cost of bank borrowing. A business can only prosper if its returns considerably exceed the cost of borrowing.

## Return on invested capital (ROIC)

The key ratio to assessing whether a business is creating value for its shareholders is the return on invested capital, or ROIC. This comprises:

$$\frac{\text{Net Operating Profit after Tax (NOPAT)}}{\text{Invested Capital}}$$

Operating profit is the profit or earnings before interest and tax, sometimes abbreviated to PBIT or EBIT.

Invested capital comprises shareholders' funds + all financial borrowings, both long and short-term. ROIC is, in fact, just a slight variant on the traditional return on capital employed ratio (ROCE), which defines capital as shareholders' funds + long-term borrowings. Short-term borrowings should be included, since they may, however imprudently, be used as permanent hard-core funding.

The significance of this ratio is that it sets a minimum return required from the business. If the business has an ROIC that exceeds the cost of capital, it is creating value for shareholders. But if the ROIC is less than the cost of capital, then it is destroying value. Unfortunately, academic research, both in Europe and the US, seems to show that many businesses are actually destroying value. Accordingly, they can have difficulty attracting investors, unlike those that can show a positive return.

## Benchmarking ROIC

If a business is to set a target ROIC for itself, it is helpful to compare returns available in the relevant industry. Some companies may accept the industry norm, while others may strive to match or beat the best in their class. When managers know what the highest return is, they can start to analyse the gap with their own business and see whether fundamental differences exist in the cost bases of the two businesses.

It can be instructive to compare your business's ROIC with that of a leading competitor. If accounts of the requisite standard are available, the ratios can be readily calculated. While choice of accounting policies or date of the financial year-end can explain some differences, nevertheless, if a competitor has a significantly higher ROIC, it is important to understand the underlying reasons.

It is helpful to know the typical ROIC in any industry. Frequently, published industry data is available domestically or internationally. Information on listed companies may be available from stockbrokers and banks, derived from numerous statistical databases or from Internet websites. Sometimes, trade associations gather data that they make publicly available. Firms of accountants may also be able to advise what the financial norm is for different types of business. If ROIC is not calculated, then it may be possible to use the broadly similar return on capital employed (ROCE)[3] if the data on ROCE is available and calculated on a consistent basis.

## Setting a target ROIC[4]

Any company needs to set its target ROIC. Higher risk businesses will need a higher return than low risk businesses if they are to attract investors, so norms may vary significantly in different industries. Investors always have a range of potential propositions in which they might invest; it is logical to decline any investment if the return is inadequate for the inherent risk of the business. It is also logical for management to return capital to shareholders if they are unable to identify suitably profitable investments. Many investors with funds to invest in a recession have increased their required rate of return, as the perceived risks have increased.

For multinational companies, with businesses throughout the world, intra group benchmarking may be possible. With a uniform system of accounting, many of the problems experienced in external benchmarking disappear. Using a common base, it should be possible to draw up a global league table in terms of ROIC. If the group knows which subsidiaries generate the highest returns, after allowing for extra transport costs, it can be expected that they should attract the investment when the group seeks to expand. Accordingly, it is not surprising that many multinational groups in labour-intensive industries are relocating operations from the United States or Western Europe to lower wage economies in the Far East or Eastern Europe.

It is not important whether the benchmark return is initially calculated before or after tax, since the two calculations are simply related. If a business has a target rate of return of 14% and operates in Ireland, where corporate tax is 12.5%, then the pre-tax rate is 14%/.875 or 16%. For countries with higher corporate tax rates, the gap will be wider. It is, therefore, not surprising that Ireland, with 12.5% tax rate for business, has been able to attract a disproportionate amount of foreign direct investment.

## The drivers of ROIC

ROIC can be broken down into two constituent elements:

$$\frac{\text{Operating Profit}}{\text{Invested Capital}} = \frac{\text{Operating Profit}}{\text{Sales}} \times \frac{\text{Sales}}{\text{Invested Capital}}$$

or

$$\text{ROIC} = \text{Operating Margin} \times \text{Capital Turnover}$$

A company with an ambitious target ROIC of 16% could achieve its goal by either obtaining a 2% operating margin and a capital turnover of 8 or a 16% operating margin and a capital turnover of 1. Clearly, the greater the capital turnover, the less onerous the operating margin required.

When sales are static, it is usually difficult to increase significantly the capital turnover in the short-run. 'Invested capital' is invested either in capital expenditure or working capital. The capital expenditure is sunk and cannot be readily changed, unless there are surplus assets to sell. (The issue of working capital management is dealt with in **Chapter 5**.) Unfortunately, many businesses in industries such as manufacturing have a major requirement for investment in fixed assets and have heavy working capital needs, so that, typically, the capital turnover lies in the range of 1 to 2.

## Setting a cost reduction target

For many companies without surplus fixed assets it is difficult to substantially increase capital turnover. The main exception is where it is possible to reduce working capital by changing the terms of trade with customers or suppliers to the company's advantage. If this is not possible the company will then have to look for improvements in the operating margin, if it wishes to improve ROIC. Since the operating profit is the profit before interest and tax, this means that it must reduce the cost of sales or overheads.

It may also be possible to improve ROIC by increasing sales, while holding invested capital constant. Pricing and marketing strategies may be directed at different market segments to improve profitability. The challenge for many businesses has proved problematic in a recession, when customers become more price conscious. The scope of this book is limited to improving profitability through cost reduction.

If sales can be increased and gross margins are held constant as a percentage of sales, then the operating ratio should improve. This is provided that overheads are kept fixed, since the overheads can be recovered over a larger sales base. On the other hand, should sales decline, as can happen in a recession, even with gross margins maintained, the operating margin will deteriorate. The alternative is to reduce overheads in order to maintain operating margins.

It is easy to set a cost-reduction target if both ROIC and capital turnover are known. For illustrative purposes, if the ROIC is 16% before tax and the capital turnover cannot be improved above 1, then the operating margin needs to be 16% also. The action required to plug the gap will vary according to the size of the gap. Take the following three cases, which fall short of the target:

- **The current operating margin is 12%:** An improvement of 4% is required. This may be achievable through the budgetary system and traditional sources of cost reduction, as outlined in previous chapters.
- **The current operating margin is 8%:** An improvement of 8% is required. While it is possible that a similar solution to that above may be found, unless there is a lot of inefficiencies in the business, a more radical programme is required. Possible approaches which can be taken are discussed in **Parts II, III** and **IV** of this book.
- **The current operating margin is 2%:** An improvement of 14% is required. After financial charges, the company is losing money. If it has been in this position for any length of time, it may be hard to find its way out. Once the bank facilities are fully utilised, the company will be living from hand to mouth, worrying about how to pay the next wages bill. For those in such an unfortunate position, the issue of emergency cost reduction is tackled in the next chapter.

## Limitations of ROIC

ROIC is not, of course, the sole driver of shareholder value. Since the value of the business is theoretically the sum of the future cashflows, any action that has a bearing on the probable growth of the business will impact the share price. Frequently, the share price will drop after good results, if the shareholders believe that the long-term future has been damaged by inadequate investment. In particular, if shareholders believe that short-term profits have been obtained by taking on extra risk, this will adversely impact the share price. A good example of this has been the dramatic collapse of the value of many banks in 2008 (aspects of which are dealt with in greater length in **Chapters 15, 16** and **17**).

The pursuit of shareholder value in the longer term is the goal of most businesses. Nevertheless, this does not mean that short-term results are not important, since businesses can fail in the short term. Comparative price–earnings ratios still have an influence on share valuations, however much 'short-termism' is decried. In the absence of information to the contrary, the reported profits may be the best indication of corporate health. All too often, hopes for a future upturn are used as an excuse for avoiding unpleasant cost-cutting decisions. Businesses that fail to grow their profits or incur losses may not be around to experience the long-term future.

## Prognosis without intervention

Companies with inadequate ROIC, particularly those with heavy working capital needs, may experience a sharp decline in their corporate health if the problem is not treated. Growth needs to be profitable and controlled. Over-trading, one of the classic signs of business failure discussed in **Chapter 18**, can develop into an insidious disease, which can spread unnoticed when sales growth is strong. In many ways its development is similar to that of alcohol abuse.

Initial elation, accompanying the growth in sales, is soon replaced by worry over cash shortages. Liquidity problems usually lead to relationship problems with financiers, which can develop into acute depression, when extra borrowing is forbidden. Quite quickly, this leads to further operational inefficiencies, as higher costs arise from loss of supplier discounts and extra bank interest charges, developing into a vicious spiral.

In the later stages of overtrading, difficulties can be experienced with suppliers, customers and staff, any of whom may decide to leave, as well as with tax authorities. Companies may panic and focus on short-term management, not having sufficient time or resources to tackle the underlying problems. While companies may sometimes delude themselves and their stakeholders for a period by resorting to creative accounting, the untreated disease of overtrading is normally fatal.

If the overtrading is diagnosed in its early stages, a simple course of treatment can be prescribed. Addressing working capital, reducing operating costs and effective budgeting are essential. If this initial treatment is unsuccessful, more radical surgery in the form of strategic cost reduction may be necessary. While the disease does not spread as quickly in times of stagnant sales, the same outcome can be expected in due course. If sales decline and competitive pressures impair gross margins, it is imperative that overheads are reduced. We will address how to achieve this in subsequent chapters.

## Conclusions

- Businesses with failing financial health often exhibit their symptoms in the marketplace.
- If businesses are to maximise their value to shareholders, they should have a clear view of the return on invested capital (ROIC) expected of them by their owners.
- The pursuit of a higher ROIC in the short term does not mean that prudent businesses can ignore risk or the longer-term growth of the undertaking.
- ROIC can be improved by enhancing capital turnover or operating margins.
- In times of declining revenue and stable capital turnover, it is essential to reduce costs in order to maintain ROIC.
- If traditional budgeting and functional cost reduction do not produce the desired result, it may be necessary to consider a more strategic approach.

## Management checklist

1. Are symptoms of financial problems evident in your business?
2. What is your current ROIC?
3. What is your cost of capital?
4. What is the ROIC of your competitors?
5. If your ROIC is lower than your competitors, why is this so?
6. What are the requirements of the owners in terms of ROIC?
7. What level of cost reduction is required to meet the target ROIC?

# Chapter 5

# Emergency cost reduction in a cash crisis

"I operate on the shoe-box method. Everything else is manure. Accounting is not an exact science . . . It is a weird science . . . The cash scenario is what is relevant."[1]

*Richard Murphy, CEO Chartbusters, 1996*

Richard Murphy is entitled to his viewpoint. He founded Xtra-vision, an Irish video rental chain in 1982, which went public in 1989, with sales of over £4 million and 82 stores, raising £2 million on the stock market and a further £20 million the next year. Profits for 1989–1990 were over £4 million on sales of £17 million. However, these profits were subsequently converted to a loss, when the accounting policy for video tapes was changed. Following the practice employed by Blockbusters in the US, it was decided that tapes had a commercial life of only six months, rather than the three years previously employed, thus fundamentally changing the rate of depreciation. By 1993, the group's sales amounted to £22 million, borrowings were more than £12 million and shareholders' funds less than £1 million. The business went into examinership the following year, before being acquired by Blockbusters in 1996. This case shows that businesses do indeed fail because they run out of cash, not profits.

Occasions can arise where businesses have to make cost reductions at short notice. The problem may be as simple as how to pay the wages at the end of the month. In such instances, businesses may have little opportunity to examine the strategic implications of their actions and view the exercise simply as a cost of just staying in business. In these circumstances, cash truly is king.

In dealing with the issue of emergency cost reduction, this chapter will look at the following issues:

- The cashflow model of business
- Working capital management
- Short-term cash generation
- The credit crunch
- Initial reactions to the credit crunch

- Addressing the credit crunch
- Consequences of emergency cost reduction

## The cashflow model of business

Most trading businesses share certain characteristics. Broadly speaking, they can be regarded as systems to generate cash. The centre piece of the system is a type of cash water tank (or "shoe box"), which must not be allowed to run dry. Some inputs are purchased from suppliers, taken into stock, possibly changed by having some value added, and then sold on to customers. Suppliers of goods, services or labour need to be paid on an on-going basis, draining the tank of cash. Other overhead expenses and capital expenditure are further drains from the tank.

The tank is usually refilled by customers. Where sales are made for cash, this occurs at the time of the transaction. More usually, however, goods are sold on credit, so that the tank refills more slowly. If, of course, a customer fails to pay, there will be a leakage from the tank. Another source of cash is the occasional sale of fixed assets.

From its beginnings and as a business grows, there is normally a requirement for capital. This can be provided by the owners of the business, who may wish to be recompensed by dividends, or from financial institutions, which will require interest and repayment over a certain period of time.

The cashflow process is represented diagrammatically in **Figure 5.1**:

*Figure 5.1*  **Cashflow Model: Trading Company**

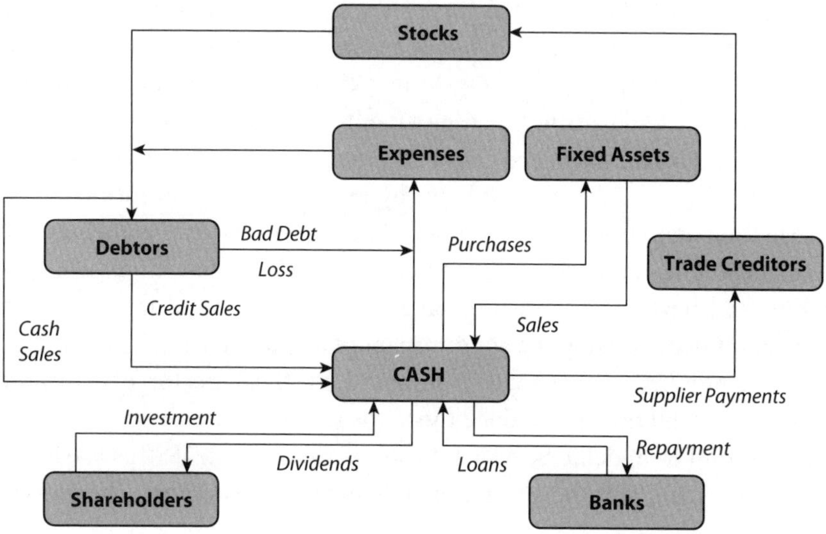

In the case of services, rather than goods, there will be no stocks, thereby simplifying the model. For manufacturing, the model is more complex, since the cost of manufacture will be included, which comprises materials, direct labour and factory overhead. Thus, stocks will be of even greater significance because, in addition to raw materials, there will be work-in-progress and finished goods.

## Working capital management

The key to the successful operation of this cycle is the speed with which the tank refills with cash. To this end, management have three important tools to regulate the flow: creditors, debtors and stocks. If debtors pay more slowly than creditors need to be paid, businesses are likely to experience increasing working capital needs as they grow, unless large gross margins are sufficient to compensate for the adverse timing.

The first tool managers can employ is the payment of creditors, which is governed by the terms of credit negotiated. Powerful suppliers may insist on the strict application of 30 days, either from the date of invoice or the end of the month, which equates to 45 days. For example, a publican may have to sign a direct debit for the supply of Guinness and would not wish to have the supply withdrawn. The other key creditor is wages and, whether they are paid weekly or monthly, the credit period is very short indeed.

In previous recessions in Ireland, some industries, such as the building-related industry, obtained credit illegally from the tax authorities: payroll and social security taxes or sales taxes were not paid over to the tax authorities on the due date. When this was eventually discovered, the defaulters attempted, sometimes successfully, to negotiate settlements on the substantial arrears to avoid causing unemployment. This led to unfair competition with tax compliant traders and could not, therefore, be tolerated by the State. The practice was made more difficult by legally obliging businesses to disclose in their annual accounts the amount of the various taxes in their audited accounts. The tax authorities have since tightened up their monitoring procedures and have been known to take severe measures against those who abuse the system, seeking the appointment of a liquidator if necessary. These actions, combined with penalties imposed by the Director of Corporate Enforcement, did much to reduce this antisocial practice.

The second tool, debtors, relates to sound credit control. This starts with prompt invoicing and the issuing of statements to customers. The terms of sale may include reservation of the title to the goods by the seller until payment is received, though this may offer limited protection in practice. Terms of credit and any cash discounts offered need to be enforced, while credit limits need to be set and observed. Aged debtor analysis reports are produced by most businesses and translated into action with follow-up letters and legal action, if appropriate.

Obviously, it is sensible to provide payment options to customers, enabling them to choose the most convenient way of settlement. On occasions, there can be a cost, such as the charge by credit card companies on the merchant. If, however, the credit card option is withdrawn, higher collection costs may follow from reminder letters and subsequent enforcement. In this context, it is surprising to discover that the automatic charging to credit cards of consumer payments which are notoriously difficult to collect, such as television licences, is no longer available in Ireland.

Excuses for late payment are plentiful. The invoice has been lost, the second cheque signatory is away, the cheque is in the post, etc. Naturally, there are many cases where payment is legitimately withheld, for example, due to poor quality of the goods or service supplied. Technicalities, such as the failure to quote order numbers, can also be invoked. There are numerous petty queries on invoices which unforthcoming debtors can employ to delay paying an invoice or bill. Ultimately, the choice may need to be made to discontinue trade with the customer and pursue payment through legal channels. The withdrawal of credit insurance during the recession has also increased the risk of unrecoverable losses for many businesses.

The third tool available to the manager to regulate working capital is stock control. In this area, more than any other, businesses have been transformed over the last few decades. The time when production managers could provide limitless buffer stocks, when buyers could issue massive orders to obtain the keenest terms, or sales managers build up finished goods to cater for the unexpected order, are long since gone. The mentality of the finance controller, who wants the minimum capital tied up in stocks, has won the day, courtesy in the main to Japanese management thinking, which developed the modern approaches to stock management.

In most businesses, the drive to increase the rate of stock turnover has continued relentlessly. Manufacturers have driven down their work-in-progress and sometimes enter into arrangements with suppliers for just-in-time delivery. For those in a strong enough position, the stock holding problem has been pushed back to the supplier through consignment stock

54  *Strategic Cost Reduction*

agreements and other arrangements to ensure on time delivery, without the manufacturer having to hold large volumes of raw materials.

From a working capital perspective, the ideal model is that of a supermarket. Customers pay in cash or by credit card, suppliers do not have to be paid for over a month, and the stock may be turned over on average in a week or so. Such businesses are cashflow positive, so that cash generation increases as sales grow, and their working capital needs are negative. However, the model is not restricted to supermarkets or the service sector. Manufacturers, such as Dell Computers, produce to order, receiving payment with the order and effecting delivery long before their suppliers require payment.

## Short-term cash generation

Where conventional management of working capital fails to generate sufficient cashflow and financiers are unwilling to inject further capital, businesses may be able to produce a plan based on the cashflow model as outlined above. The taps that release cash need to be turned off or tightened, and any tap that increases the flow turned on or loosened. Keeping cash in the tank is critical for survival.

The first obvious outflow for cash is capital expenditure. In times of economic downturn, it is unwise to increase capacity in most businesses. Machinery may be renovated, rather than replaced. Machinery leases may be renegotiated. Company cars and vehicles may be kept longer. Computer upgrades may be postponed.

The second obvious outflow is dividends to shareholders and bonuses or perks made to staff. These outflows are discretionary and, therefore, can be withheld, however much it may annoy the recipients. In the past, banks were reluctant to reduce dividends because of the expectations of their shareholders and the resultant impact on confidence. Ordinary shareholders may not be able to analyse bad debt provisions, but can certainly understand a cut in their dividends. Similarly, banks, afraid that they could lose key staff if large bonuses were not paid, sometimes actually guaranteed bonuses irrespective of overall performance. In times of financial crisis, recession and limited employment opportunities, bonuses of any size are hard to justify, particularly in banks which have destroyed much of their shareholders' wealth.

The final outflow of cash is the payment of other expenses. The payment of suppliers may need to be reviewed on an individual basis, so that the key suppliers are identified and a supplier payment plan can be drawn up.

In practice, non-key suppliers are likely to have their credit terms stretched, although small payments may still be paid promptly to avoid any unproductive diversion of scarce management time.

Any expenditure that is not absolutely necessary is likely to be sacrificed in an emergency. This puts under the spotlight all discretionary expenditure, such as marketing, product development, training and research, etc. While the cancellation of these expenses for any considerable length of time may do severe damage to a business, it may be possible to sacrifice them for a limited period if survival is at stake.

The remaining possibility is to generate cash inflow from the sale of surplus assets. The main consideration is how much cash the assets can raise, rather than whether the transactions show a profit or a loss. All non-core investments should be considered. Stock exchange listed securities may be the easiest to realise, but other investments should not be overlooked, even though they may take longer to sell. The main fixed assets to consider are land and buildings, which could be sold outright or, if there is no surplus space, be sold and leased back. Reductions in the fleet of vehicles or equipment may also be possible. Finally, surplus stocks can be the subject of a special sale. Retailers are familiar with such tactics, but manufacturers may also opt for a factory sale of their wares.

## The credit crunch

Before the banking crisis of 2008, successful businesses which were well-managed generally had no difficulty in receiving adequate banking finance. The standard constraint was the amount of gearing banks would permit. Thus, for small and medium-sized enterprises (SMEs) that had limited access to equity capital, banks traditionally might have set a limit of somewhere between 33% and 50% of the total funding by imposing a debt:equity limit of 1:2 or 1:1. The actual limit would be determined by factors such as the track record of the business, the cashflow projections and the interest cover. SMEs would complain about the banks' lack of support, while the banks would protest that they needed to protect depositors' funds, rather than take disproportionate business risk. Some level of friction between SMEs wishing to grow and banks was inevitable.

During the early 'noughties', in the era of low interest rates, continuous economic growth and increased competition between banks, lending standards were often relaxed. If there was adequate security and a reasonable loan-to-value ratio, banks worried less about repayment capacity. Overdrafts were usually renewed as a matter of course, and banks would attempt to sell a range of other products to their customers. Sound businesses could usually find alternative sources of funding if they were unhappy with their current arrangements. Where a business had limited inherent security, it was sometimes possible to avail of more expensive finance, such as invoice discounting, which could assist fast-growing companies with a strong debtors' ledger. Unfortunately such facilities, which are provided as a percentage of sales invoiced, may automatically contract sharply with a decline in sales.

The availability of finance changed radically with the global banking crisis of 2008, as banks ran into serious problems caused by their own mismanagement of risk. For some banks, this was caused by their involvement in US or other subprime lending (discussed in **Chapter 16**). For others, it was lemming-like behaviour in pursuit of short-term profits at the expense of prudence, when they dabbled in the arcane world of derivatives or reckless property lending. When the property bubble eventually burst, the large loans to developers, highly-geared mortgages and consumer credit inevitably resulted in losses for the banks. While some financial institutions held an optimistic view on property prices and initially failed to provide adequately for bad loans, inevitably, in a prolonged downturn, the losses had to be recognised.

With banks weakened by losses and short of capital, the banking crisis quickly turned into a credit crunch for the rest of the economy. Banks sought, whether voluntarily or otherwise, to reduce their own gearing and reduce their loan-to-deposit ratios. Many businesses found their borrowing facilities suddenly reduced or cancelled, and could no longer turn to alternative suppliers for funding. Additionally, few owner–managers were in a position to inject further funds, and many businesses found themselves without access to capital. In recent years, personal savings had diminished and personal borrowings had significantly increased, while the value of properties and stock exchange investments, which might have been sold, suddenly collapsed.

The credit crunch for many businesses has led to emergency cost reduction. The immediate goal is cash generation for short-term survival, rather than growth or longer-term development. To this end, the reduction of borrowings and an increase in savings have become the overriding objective for many organisations. The credit crunch has also increased the risk of bad debts or, what can be equally serious, the failure of key suppliers.

## Initial reactions to the credit crunch

The credit crunch has been a global phenomenon. In November 2008 it was reported in Ireland that 57% of companies could not obtain the finance they needed to keep their business going, a figure which trebled since August of the same year.[2] Due to the particular weakness of the Irish banks, it has been difficult to resolve the problem, a situation which the EU and IMF rescue package is designed to rectify. Because restrictions on credit have not disappeared, many businesses have been forced to close since the first edition of this book was published in 2009.

Many businesses reacted to reduced financial facilities by paying their suppliers more slowly. According to the Irish Small and Medium Enterprises Association (ISME), the average payment period grew quickly from 50 to 65 days, and companies with good credit histories became unable to obtain funding. Some businesses, on the other hand, have taken a more understanding approach to supplier difficulties. Aldi, the giant German supermarket chain, was reported to have intervened to help its transport suppliers, who were facing losses as a result of increased diesel prices.[3]

Businesses in the UK had similar experiences. The Chancellor of the Exchequer accused the UK banks of refusing to lend, even though they have been recapitalised.[4] The banks may deny it, but many small businesses continue to find credit in short supply. The *Financial Times* reported that companies face their worst funding problems in 30 years and that the Governor of the Bank of England viewed the restriction in corporate credit as the most worrying feature in the economy.[5]

Furthermore, some powerful businesses have altered their terms of trade. As mentioned in **Chapter 3**, Tesco announced in 2008 that they were extending credit terms from 30 to 60 days for non-food suppliers. Fortunately for suppliers, this has not been the reaction of all businesses. Some have preferred a policy of collaboration to tackle the problem, since they foresaw a danger in losing suppliers, which can disrupt their global supply chain. The motor industry has a 'distressed Suppliers Support Unit'. One UK defence group, VT, similarly suggested that cash-strapped suppliers should contact them, a course of action which might be more fruitful than contacting their banks, intimating that, in certain circumstances, they might extend credit or advance a temporary loan.[6] Yet, overall, most suppliers have been forced to accept arbitrary extensions of payment terms from their customers, as pressure on businesses to conserve cash continues to become acute.[7]

## Addressing the credit crunch

Where businesses face an emergency as a result of the credit crunch, they need to revisit their sources of short-term cash generation and consider their options as a matter of urgency.[8] Large, strong corporate groups often have an advantage over smaller businesses. They may be able to sell off unwanted businesses, issue corporate debt, cancel share buy-back schemes, renegotiate their facilities with their banks on a longer term basis and draw down on unutilised facilities, such as revolving credits.

Smaller businesses, however, often have fewer alternatives available to them. They need to see what can be squeezed out of working capital and what expenditure can be cut. The key to any plan is the existence of short-term cashflow forecasts, as a minimum covering three to four months, but preferably six months. Survival in the short term may be dependent on remaining within available bank facilities. There may be a need for a weekly or even daily cash outflow plan, since borrowings may not peak at the month end.

The impact of every decision on the projected cashflows must be fully understood. Obligatory short-time working, the reverse of overtime, may be necessary to reduce labour costs. Manufacturers Bausch & Lomb took this course of action when it announced a mandatory week's leave every month for its 1,400 employees in Ireland to last for a period of six months.[9] Redundancies may be inevitable for many other businesses, and these need to be factored into the company's financial forecasts. It is worth bearing in mind that, while in Ireland it is possible to recoup a proportion of statutory redundancy from the State, this payment may take three or four months to arrive.

The other imperative is for companies to keep in close contact with their banks, particularly in times when it is difficult to change banks. Some businesses are careful to nurture trade relationships, but are singularly ineffective at managing bank relationships. Multi-banking enormously increases the complexity of the task, particularly in the absence of formal syndicate arrangements between the banks. It may be possible to negotiate a moratorium on capital repayments on term loans or even a roll-up of interest payments.

Businesses with close bank relations may have been far-sighted enough to have agreed stand-by facilities in reserve. If these facilities are committed and cannot be withdrawn by the bank, then the business may well weather the credit crunch without undue pain. They may well not, however, be renewed after their expiry date.

Above all, banks dislike unpleasant surprises. Audited annual accounts, current management accounts, short-term budgets and cashflow forecasts can help to allay the fears of nervous bankers. Overdraft excesses are unlikely to be tolerated and, if a temporary facility is needed, supporting cashflow projections are essential. Where such information is not currently sought, it should be helpful if it can be provided at short notice.

## Consequences of emergency cost reduction

When businesses experience a cashflow crisis, they have few options other than to cut all available costs. If they do not, they may have to cease trading and face winding-up. Legal advice may be required to ascertain whether continued trading could be considered to be 'reckless trading'.

In serious situations, it may be necessary to seek protection from creditors through the courts, either by entering into 'examinership' in Ireland or 'administration' in the UK.[10] This may enable the business to prepare a longer term plan to attract additional funds and negotiate with its creditors. Insolvent businesses in such situations may ultimately end up in receivership or liquidation, so they must rely heavily on legal advice as to the wisest course of action.

The downsides of emergency cost reduction are clear. It may irreparably damage the business in the medium or longer term. Excessive cost-cutting may lead to corporate anorexia, which can prove fatal. Discretionary expenditure on marketing, training or research is necessary for growth. Wherever possible, businesses should take a more strategic view of the business than is entailed in emergency cost reduction.

The remainder of this book will address **Strategic Cost Reduction**, looking at the longer term implications of cost reduction. It focuses on strategic objectives and seeks ways to achieve these ends more effectively. The approach is usually made on a cross-functional basis, which may not readily fit with traditional organisational structures.

## Conclusions

- In an emergency, the focus must be on cashflow, rather than profits.
- Prudent working capital management is essential, particularly in an emergency.

- Short-term cashflow can be generated by cutting capital expenditure, dividends, bonuses and all unnecessary expenditure, while realising any surplus assets.
- The credit crunch has forced many businesses into emergency cost reduction.
- Emergency cost reduction may be necessary for short-term survival, but can threaten the longer term future of a business.

## Management checklist

1. Are adequate short-term cashflow forecasts available?
2. Is there scope for improvement of working capital management?
3. What assets could be sold in an emergency?
4. Have you adequate financing in the present credit crunch?
5. Can you afford to take a more strategic approach to cost reduction?

# Part II

# Approaching cost reduction strategically to fit the cost reduction programme into the wider framework and values

# Chapter 6

# Preliminary strategic considerations

*"He who wishes to be rich in a day will be hanged in a year."*
*Leonardo da Vinci*

One major problem with cost reduction through the traditional budgetary system is that actions to save costs in one area may have adverse consequences elsewhere in the organisation. Another difficulty is that opportunities which cross several areas may be missed. Instant cuts may not lead to sustainable savings, and an excessively short-term approach may ultimately be a recipe for disaster. A strategic approach attempts to address these issues in a holistic, top-down way. The starting point is to understand the different strategies that are available to the board. This is followed by a discussion of values and the alternatives facing the CEO under the following headings:

- Cost reduction failures
- The strategic framework
- Memo from the chairman
- Issues for the board
- Overall cost leadership and the alternatives
- Core values
- Key issues for the CEO: style and participation
- Use of external resources: consultants and mentors

## Cost reduction failures

There exist many accounts of successful cost cutting in companies. More difficult to find are documented cases of failure in attempts to reduce the cost base, even though failures may be more common than triumphs. Success is, of course, a relative term and not many chief executives wish to talk about their mistakes. It can be tempting to proclaim the exercise a success, even if the cost reduction is only of a temporary nature. All too often, strategic considerations are ignored in favour of short-term cost cutting results, and ultimate failure is inevitable from the outset.

Sometimes, the process appears to have been conducted in a haphazard fashion or with strong political overtones, favouring one's friends and sacrificing one's enemies. On other occasions, there may have been a perfectly rational approach, but the execution has been poor, neglecting the fundamentals of project and change management.

Perhaps the most common cause of complaint is the damage done to future growth. The easiest costs to target in the short term are the discretionary costs, such as research and development, training and marketing. The immediate effect of cancelling or drastically reducing these budgets will be beneficial, with profits suitably improved. However, if the goal of the business is to create shareholder value, the consequence of any such sustained action can be disastrous. Innovation may be stunted, skills reduced and customers lost, leading to a fall in the value of the shareholders' investment.

The consequences of ill-considered cost cutting are obvious. There is much hard work for very little return. As well as stunting growth, inherent inefficiencies often remain in place. The business may experience undesirable side-effects, particularly in quality and customer service. Morale can also suffer. As crises arise, some of the reductions may be reversed and, slowly, costs can bounce back.

At its most Machiavellian, a vicious circle can be created, whereby savings will eventually disappear. It is established that costs are too high. Therefore, the business must be downsized or, more euphemistically, 'right-sized', but self-interest may outweigh business logic in the process. "You are not adding value and must be fired." "I must be rewarded with a share of the costs saved." After a period, preferably not too long, "I need an assistant to deal with the backlog." Costs start to rise ... "Naturally, as a highly skilled manager, it would never be appropriate to demotivate me by reducing my salary or cancelling my bonus," as no doubt many investment bankers can testify in the aftermath of the sub-prime banking crisis. Most managers will not vote to cut their own pay any more than turkeys would vote for Christmas.

## The strategic framework

All businesses operate within some form of wider strategic framework. The management react to stimuli from their stakeholders, which may trigger the need for radical cost reduction. It may be that customers in an era of globalisation demand lower prices. A new competitor may have entered the market. These direct stimuli from stakeholders could be reactions to changes in the wider environment. They could be *political*, such as the enlargement of the European Union, which led to competition from Eastern Europe. They may also be *economic*, such as the introduction of the Euro, bringing greater transparency to prices affecting tourism in particular. They may be *social*, such as the wish for greater flexibility in working hours. Finally, they may be *technological*, such as the rapidly increasing use of the Internet for purchasing and price comparison.

The public sector operates within the same changing environment as the private sector, but it has no single objective metric such as shareholder value with which to measure success. It must try to satisfy multiple objectives and the demands from competing interests, while operating within the economic framework of the time. However, if the Irish public sector funding deficit is to be reduced to 3% of GDP by 2013, enormous reductions in costs are required.

## Memo from the chairman

In the private sector, the stimulus to seek cost reduction may come from the board or from senior management. In either case, the CEO will need the continuous backing of the board to implement the programme successfully. In the course of cost reduction, it is vital that the management responsible for the outcome do not lose sight of the wider strategy and values of the business. In order to illustrate a strategic approach, we have used an imaginary memorandum from a chairman to his not very well-informed CEO and his subsequent memorandum to his management colleagues (see **Chapter 7**).

### Memorandum: Strictly Confidential

| | |
|---|---|
| **To:** | The CEO and Members of the Board |
| **From:** | The Chairman |
| **Date:** | 3 January |
| **Re:** | Cost Reduction |

You will have noticed an item on the Board agenda, yet again, about cost reduction. The item is there at my request, and I wish to explain the background to this request.

### Share Price

I do not need to remind Board members of the catastrophic fall in our share price over the last six months. At a recent meeting with a leading firm of stockbrokers, it was explained to me that the share had been classified as a 'Sell', since the market doubted our ability to trade out of the present, difficult climate.

The analyst drew my attention to our declining market share, falling gross margins and high level of overheads. The comparison of our financial ratios with those of our peers was unflattering to say the least. With increasing price competition coming from the Far East and Eastern Europe, the analyst saw little likelihood of this changing in the near future, as the recession in our industry is expected to deepen. She was somewhat scathing about the cost reductions we made last year, considering them to be of only short-term benefit. Our capital investment plans also failed to excite.

### Past Efforts at Cost Reduction

Our chief executive has reported his efforts to reduce costs wherever possible. Sadly, these efforts have been insufficient to stem the tide, as evidenced by our share price.

I believe that we need to take out a further 15% of operating costs as a minimum (preferably 20%) on a permanent basis, if we are to survive the current downturn.

### Strategy

I believe that our overall strategy remains sound. I also believe that we must remain faithful to our values as set out in our mission statement. Nevertheless, major costs must be removed in a way that is consistent with this strategy. To this end, I would ask you to re-read the strategy document approved by the Board last October. This will remain the framework within which cost reduction will take place.

### The Project

I have asked the CEO to take overall responsibility for the project. He should be free to co-opt whomsoever he chooses on to the team. I have asked him to report at our next meeting on how the project will be managed. This will include details of:

- The resources required
- Whether outside consultants should be retained

- The steps involved
- When the report will be available

I have stressed that this is to be conducted as rigorously as any other capital investment proposal. There can be no sacred cows, and all options must be examined.

I welcome your views and hope that I can rely on your support. In the meantime, I would ask you to treat this memo with the utmost confidentiality in view of the sensitivities involved.

## Issues for the board

For an organisation to achieve an effective and sustainable reduction in costs, it is advisable to ascertain how cost reduction fits into its broader strategic framework. The approach by Michael Porter to strategy classifies any strategy into one of three types:[1]

### Figure 6.1    Generic Strategies

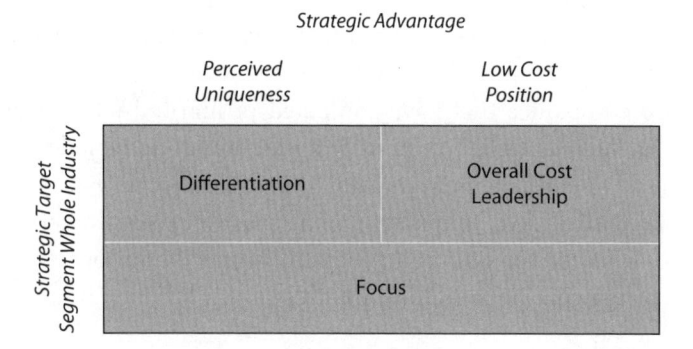

*Strategic Advantage*

|  | Perceived Uniqueness | Low Cost Position |
|---|---|---|
| Strategic Target: Whole Industry | Differentiation | Overall Cost Leadership |
| Segment | Focus | |

## Overall cost leadership and the alternatives

Strategic advantage can derive from having a low-cost position, so that the business has *overall cost leadership* in the industry. From this position, it can quote lower prices than the competition and achieve a dominant position. However, for many businesses the strategic advantage arises from a perceived uniqueness or *differentiation* that is valued by customers, which enables them to charge higher prices. Other businesses may choose not to compete across the industry, but to *focus* on some segment in which they may successfully compete, whether by differentiation or cost leadership.

Most SMEs do not have sufficient scale to be cost leaders. Therefore, they must be able to differentiate themselves in the eyes of their customers and establish a niche. This does not mean that costs can be ignored. A customer will pay a premium for a differentiated product, but there is a limit to the size of that premium. Full-service airlines can charge more for their tickets than low fares airlines but, when the price gap becomes too large, their customer base will be eroded. Similarly, skilled craftsmen producing hand-cut glass crystal cannot ignore competition from mass-produced imitators.

However, the leading company in an industry is not always the lowest cost provider.[2] Businesses can and do compete in different ways. It is important to understand how a business competes in practice to avoid cutting costs that are essential to its future development. For some companies, like Apple or Intel, product leadership is fundamental. They strive to be first to market and penetrate new market segments. Their internal focus is on innovation and research. Others, such as IBM and leading investment banks, succeed by providing a complete customer solution. The emphasis is more on the number of products and on customer retention. It would be dangerous to cut costs which keep them close to their customers. Yet others,[3] such as Microsoft or Gillette, lock in their customers through making it expensive to switch. Cutting costs in such a way as to allow competitors to gain access to your market would be foolish.

For those companies that have competed primarily by being the lowest cost supplier, such as Dell, Toyota or Ryanair, the fundamental requirement has been good operations management. The product or service must be produced to the desired level of quality and be available to customers as readily as possible, whether the business competes primarily on low cost or value. Any cost cutting that impairs the smooth running of operations is likely to be self-defeating.

If the cost-reduction exercise is to succeed, the starting point should be the overall strategy of the entity. This should highlight the areas where damage could be fatal to the business, and the cost-cutting team should always bear these areas in mind. For example, if a business needs to dispose of surplus assets and is considering selling a brand, it needs to consider whether or not this intangible asset is crucial for the survival of the enterprise in the longer term. It may be that there is some fat in such key spots and that it is possible to slim them down, but it is vital not to perform surgery in a way that risks the patient's life.

## Core values

Every business is run according to certain basic values, which are fundamental to its business behaviour and the way it implements its strategy. These values, therefore, cannot be ignored in a cost-reduction project. They include the way a business deals with its stakeholders, particularly customers, suppliers and employees (this is discussed in the next chapter). In addition to these values, many organisations have social values. Sometimes they are set out formally in a mission statement. In other cases, they are implicit in the behaviour of the management. These social or ethical values generally entail some cost. For example:

1. Does the organisation feel it has obligations to the local community?
2. Does it provide funds to selected charities?
3. Are its buildings aesthetically pleasing and maintained to a high standard?
4. Is it constrained by voluntary environmental standards in a 'green' agenda and matters such as global warming?
5. Is it acceptable to pay bribes to mitigate bureaucratic charges or bend rules under any circumstances?

Different businesses answer these issues in different ways. The lowest cost solution in a given situation may be obvious, but other social or environmental factors may outweigh mere costs. There is no one absolute standard as to how premises should be maintained. For example, the Japanese, who completely refurbish their homes every 15 or 20 years, may find Western standards too low.

Sometimes, the underlying values of an organisation need, at the very least, to be questioned. Western head offices can range from Spartan to luxurious in the same industry for no obvious reason. Traditionally, many banks have magnificent banking halls, which may once have conveyed the strength of the institution to the public. It is doubtful if the splendour and luxury of the offices contribute to the operational efficiency of the business. The public may not be impressed by the image any more than they are by a property developer's Rolls Royce or helicopter. The answer for most Western businesses may be a balance between cost and generally accepted practice. Governments may set health and safety standards, but many leading companies elect to adopt far higher standards. Such a position is, of course, compatible with the goal of maximising shareholder value. If a company wishes to attract and retain the best employees, they may need to adopt high social standards. Whether the pressure comes from employees, shareholders, customers or from espoused values makes no difference, the financial cost to the organisation will be the same.

More and more lobby groups are forcing wider social issues onto boardroom tables. Consider, for example, the supermarket industry, which has a major focus on cost reduction. While the industry leaders may be financially successful, they are more and more subject to criticism.[4] Some detractors concentrate on low pay and benefits of the employees or the net loss of employment as competitors are forced out of business. Others attack the way they deal with suppliers, such as levies or 'Hello money', the extended credit that they exact or unilateral changes to terms of trade that they impose. Still others focus on the damaging side effects on the community, such as the drabness of their buildings, their land hoarding, controversial planning permissions or their impact on global warming.

However strong the supermarket chains may be, few of them choose to ignore such criticisms and some have responded by publicising their social policies and their perceived obligations to society at large. These include measures to support Fair Trade, local sourcing, community support, reduction of the carbon footprint, promotion of green and healthy product alternatives, charitable giving, etc.

The public sector faces similar issues. Hospitals will want to maintain the highest standards of hygiene to prevent the spread of disease, and certain levels of patient service must be observed. Medical behaviour should conform to the Hippocratic Oath, and so forth. Often, a charter enshrines the core values of an institution or organisation which must be upheld.

What then are an organisation's social policies?

## Key issues for the CEO: style and participation

There are two key issues which a CEO must consider when tackling cost reduction:

- What style of leadership is appropriate?
- Who should be involved in the process?

It is hard to see how any truly strategic programme of cost reduction could be successful without the involvement of the chief executive. If he or she is not part of the team, it is likely that the chief executive will monitor the work closely to ensure that whatever proposals are eventually put to the board are achievable. Few boards would tolerate a CEO excusing a failed strategic cost reduction project by stating that he or she had delegated the entire exercise to colleagues. In any event, the chief executive will almost certainly wish to influence the way the exercise is approached and, in particular, how directive it should be.

Most successful CEOs will know instinctively how to approach change in their organisation. But the approach and style chosen will vary significantly across different organisation types. A leading management writer, Charles Handy, classifies organisations into four cultural categories, each one typified by an ancient Greek god.[5]

The club culture (Zeus), commonly found in SMEs, occurs where a strong leader can introduce change quickly. Systems tend to be informal and change is effected through a network of club contacts.

The role culture (Apollo) is typical of larger organisations in manufacturing and other industries, whether organised by function or division. Systems tend to be bureaucratic and authority is derived from position, with business conducted according to a strict set of rules and procedures. Change is slower and usually involves committees.

Task assignments (Athena) are structured around problem solving, such as is found in consultancies and professional firms. They encourage creativity and often entail teamwork in assembling the appropriate expertise to deal with a particular situation. To survive and grow, a task culture may morph into a role culture over time.

Existential cultures (Dionysius) are found where minimal control is accepted, such as barristers' chambers or even universities. Typically, however, these organisations remain small, perhaps organised in a loose partnership with a collegiate culture, where decisions have to be made democratically if change is to be accepted.

The CEO is free to choose his leadership approach and style. At one extreme is the traditional collegiate, *academic* approach, favoured by Dionysius. The management team is convened and provided with as much relevant cost information as possible. Managers are then asked to discuss the issue and formulate proposals to reduce costs. The projects selected will be decided by a vote. This type of democratic approach may well minimise the amount of conflict, but all too rarely produces proposals beyond token gestures, which require minimal change in a manner reminiscent of the BBC sitcom *Yes Minister*.

At the other end of the spectrum is the *military* style, favoured by Zeus. The changes are ordered from on high with both managers and the workforce coerced into acceptance.

In between the two extremes, however, there are several different ways of approaching cost reduction. The *economic* model relies on individual motivation through rewards and sanctions. Managers are encouraged to submit proposals with the incentive of gain-sharing from the savings. The *engineering* model first changes the structure of the organisation, then gives managers in the new positions the brief and authority to effect change. Lastly, there is the *political* way. The chief executive attempts to influence those parties, such as trade unions, who influence the behaviour of others, and the process becomes one of negotiation, trading benefits for acceptance of change.

The choice of style is not mutually exclusive. Nor is one style suitable for all situations. What works in a highly-unionised auto industry, for example, is unlikely to work in a professional partnership. The chief executive who knows at the outset where the excess costs are and how they can be reduced will manage the exercise in a wholly different fashion from the chief executive who understands the problem, but does not have a ready-made solution. The blend of styles may well be influenced by the seriousness of the situation, the time available and the degree of cooperation forthcoming from the labour force.

Typically, however, projects are undertaken by teams, whose composition will reflect the nature of the organisation, selecting either the style of Apollo or Athena. To some extent, the nature of the problem and the cost areas targeted for reduction will determine which discipline is central to the cost reduction plan. Practitioners addressing IMI cost reduction conferences approached the challenge from varied viewpoints. In a brewery seeking reductions in the workforce, the process was driven by the human resources department. A dotcom seeking to contract after the year 2000 was mainly sales driven, reducing the number of sales outlets. A world-class manufacturer had a strong operations focus. A traditional manufacturer seeking to outsource its manufacturing was finance and industrial relations focused. A construction business facing the property downturn had a strong human resources and industrial emphasis. But what all had in common was a cross-functional dimension.[6]

## Use of external resources: consultants and mentors

The initial decision for the board in approaching cost reduction is whether or not to use external resources and, if so, in what capacity. Many major organisations undertake cost-reduction projects without any external input or only in a very limited way. There is always the danger that consultants have a specific toolkit, which will be used irrespective of the nature of the problem. Tools, such as business process re-engineering, have their uses, but can do damage when used indiscriminately.

On the other hand, many companies do not have the experience of major radical restructuring and may wish to use consultants to fill the gap. If, for example, a company was considering a major outsourcing programme overseas, expensive mistakes may be avoided through the use of consultants with the relevant expertise. Where redundancies are involved, some companies may not have the necessary legal knowledge in-house. If consultants are retained, tight terms of reference and fee arrangements need to be agreed at the outset to ensure that the scope of the assignment does not creep ever wider and costs escalate out of control.

Consultants may have experience which they can bring to bear on a particular situation. They may also be considered to be objective, and a sceptical workforce, suspicious of bias in their own management, may more easily accept the recommendations of external consultants.

On the other hand, employees may treat consultants with suspicion, believing them to be nothing more than the vehicle for unpalatable changes already decided upon by management. Whatever the case, consultants are unlikely to understand a business better than its management and, of course, they may be expensive to hire. Thus, many businesses that have the necessary expertise in-house prefer to come up with their own solutions for routine cost-reduction projects.

An alternative to retaining the services of consultants is to use a less-intensive and cheaper external resource, such as a mentor. Mentors can help set the agenda for organisations, suggest alternative tools or approaches, generally act as a sounding board for a project team and provide a constant challenge to ideas. The business retains full ownership of the project and only avails of the mentor's service as circumstances demand. Since the use of the resource is restricted and controlled, the costs should be much lower than would typically be charged by consultants.

## Conclusions

- Being the lowest cost producer or provider is only one of several types of strategy available to a business.

- If cuts are to take place in the right areas, it is imperative to understand the overall strategy and how cost reduction fits in.
- The business will have certain values, either explicitly or implicitly embedded in its culture. Cost reduction needs to take place within the value framework.
- The choice of leadership style is fundamental to the success of the project: who will be involved, who will be consulted and how will the project be run?

## Management checklist

1. What is the company strategy, and in what way does cost reduction fit in?
2. What corporate values need to be borne in mind?
3. Who will lead the project and who will be involved?
4. What management style will be adopted to obtain participation, commitment and support of the various parties?
5. Is any use of external resources, such as consultants or mentors, deemed appropriate?

# Chapter 7

# Critical functional considerations

"There are two times in a man's life when he should not speculate: when he can't afford to and when he can."

*"Pudd'nhead Wilson", Mark Twain*

Once the strategic and values frameworks of the organisation are ascertained, consideration should be given to the various functional requirements that feed into the overall strategy. Every functional activity has its own set of values, which are sometimes not well understood elsewhere in the organisation. Usually, these values are jealously guarded by the specific functional heads, who act as their gatekeepers when they are under attack. These are addressed here through a fictitious memorandum from a struggling chief executive to his management team. Throughout the cost-reduction exercise, it is important to bear in mind that these critical issues are impacted and to consider what steps can be taken to mitigate the risks. The requirements of each function are considered in turn in this chapter as follows:

- Memo from the CEO
- Issues for the sales and marketing director
- Issues for the finance director
- Issues for the operations director
- Issues for the human resources director
- Issues for other disciplines
- Reconciling functional imperatives

### Memo from the CEO

**Memorandum: Strictly Confidential**

| | |
|---|---|
| **To:** | The Directors of Sales and Marketing, Finance, Operations, Human Resources |
| **CC:** | The Chairman |
| **From:** | The Chief Executive Officer |

**Date:**   10 January

**Re:**   Cost Reduction

---

At the last Board meeting, it was decided that further drastic action needs to be taken to improve our performance in view of our declining profitability and the dismal market outlook.

I have been given the responsibility for the project, which has a target of reducing operating costs by 20% over the next year. I am enlisting your help to form a steering group with a view to producing a firm plan within three months. At this stage, I do not envisage retaining consultants, but may do so once our overall plan starts to take shape. We will need to co-opt others, who can contribute to productivity improvement, such as the heads of purchasing, IT and engineering when appropriate.

The Board does not believe that a new strategy is needed. Accordingly, our mission statement and strategy document adopted last autumn remain in place. We simply have to find a more effective way of implementing the strategy. To this end, I would ask you to consider what aspects of your department are fundamental to the existing strategy. Matters such as customer needs, quality and values relating to employees are relevant here. We do not want to 'throw out the baby with the bathwater' or take unnecessary risks in this project.

At the outset, I believe that we will need to consider:

1. What activities we should outsource to a cheaper location
2. How to improve the efficiency of the remaining activities
3. Whether we need to reduce and restructure our labour force

At the Board meeting, I was asked a couple of questions by Mary Blunt, our new non-executive director. First, she asked whether we had adopted world class manufacturing. I replied that of course we had. A substantial part of our sales are exports, and if we were not world-class, we could not compete. The decline in our exports is purely due to the historic strength of the Euro.

Mary's second question related to our costing system. She wanted to know if it would provide the necessary information to help us reduce costs. I explained that we had a perfectly satisfactory product costing system for over 20 years, factory overheads being recovered on the basis of direct labour hours. Management accounts separate out fixed and variable costs. Last year, we rejected the introduction of the 'ERP' system, proposed by the SAP salesman, on the grounds of cost, and we will certainly not be in a position to change our system in our present straitened circumstances.

While accepting that we cannot invest in a new ERP system at present, Ms Blunt doubted whether the present system would provide much help in the task ahead. She also doubted whether we really are world-class manufacturers. The matter was put back to the next Board meeting. I would be grateful for your views on this in the interim.

This project is to be treated with the utmost urgency and, obviously, is confidential. If we do not succeed, I doubt that any of us will be here in two years' time. So, let us make cost reduction our New Year's Resolution. Please have your views ready for our next management meeting in 10 days' time, where it will be the priority item on the agenda.

---

This chapter will now address the issues raised by the CEO for each of the functional heads. Most competent managers will appreciate matters that are essential for the business, if their own function is to be conducted in a professional way. Accordingly, they may become the gatekeepers for these particular values, endeavouring to ensure that they are not lost in a cost-reduction programme.

## Issues for the sales and marketing director

In any cost-reduction programme, it will be important not to damage the product or service that you provide. In some businesses, there may be product managers who will defend their products and their key features. If damage is to be avoided, it is important to have a clear view of the attributes of your product or service which are valued by customers. This forms the basis of the differentiation and, therefore, the product or service strategy. A simple way of understanding this idea is to set down all the possible features of your product or service and decide which ones are in line with the industry norm, which ones are above average, and which ones are below average.

Take an example from the motor industry. Not everyone wants to drive the cheapest Lada. A potential car buyer might be influenced by a whole range of factors and features: power and speed, safety, space, styling, reliability, fuel economy, durability, comfort, high technology, ozone layer impact and, naturally, price. One manufacturer of mid-sized cars might target older, family drivers. Market research in this context might show that the key requirements are safety, comfort, space, reliability and fuel economy. The car could be designed to be above average for these features, average on price

78  Strategic Cost Reduction

and below average for the remaining features. Another manufacturer, targeting the younger executive market, might emphasise power, styling, high technology and environmental friendliness with an above average price, but below average for the remaining features.

These different product strategies could be depicted as shown in **Figure 7.1**:[1]

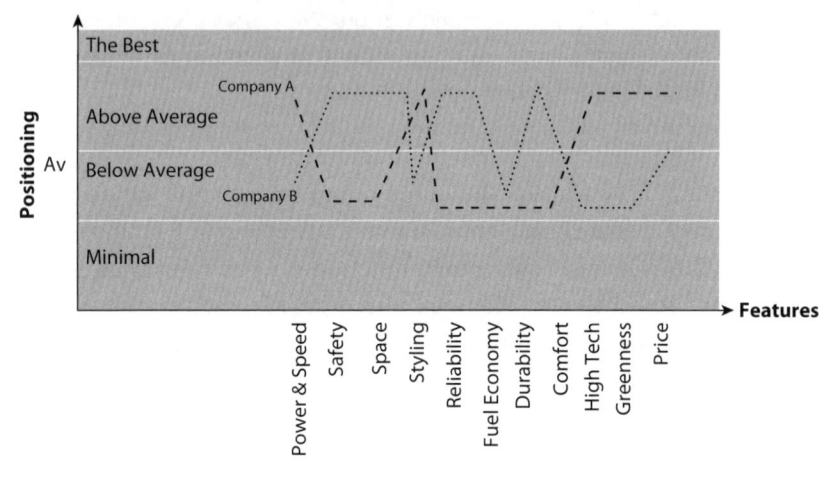

*Figure 7.1*  **Comparison of Product Policy of Two Motor Manufacturers**

[Chart showing Positioning (The Best, Above Average, Av, Below Average, Minimal) against Features (Power & Speed, Safety, Space, Styling, Reliability, Fuel Economy, Durability, Comfort, High Tech, Greenness, Price) with lines for Company A and Company B]

In a cost-reduction programme, it can be too easy to remove product or service features that are critical for sales. It is the job of the marketing director to make sure that this does not happen. It could be that the business is prepared to reduce or even eliminate some of the traditional features. However, this should be a conscious marketing decision and not an accidental by-product of a cost-reduction programme. If a cost-reduction programme adversely affects the quality of the product or service, as perceived by customers, organisations will need to seriously consider whether the savings outweigh the customers' loss of value.

## Issues for the finance director

There are at least two key questions that finance directors should bear in mind during cost reduction:

- What impact will the changes have on the risks and controls of the business?
- Will the accounting system help in finding costs to be reduced?

Most finance directors accept that there is more to financial management than profitability if the business is to prosper. The control of risk, in particular, is a key feature of prudent management. It may make excellent sense to hedge not only against adverse movements in currency or interest rates, but also in key input costs, such as energy. Insurance, of course, bears a cost, but the prudent finance director would no more consider eliminating a modest cost for this protection than he or she would wish to forego employee, third party or product insurance.

## Financing constraints

Similarly, prudent funding is basic to the survival of the business, as some banks have recently found out to their detriment. Constraints on businesses may be imposed by bank covenants or as a matter of policy, such as limiting the amount of financial gearing or setting minimum liquidity levels. A prudent finance director with a thorough knowledge of the business may well set more restrictive covenants than the banks. A modest commitment fee for a contingent line of credit may be a price worth paying. It is foolish to rely excessively on short-term funding purely because it is cheaper than longer-term facilities. Cost is only one element of effective financing.

## Risk management constraints

As part of risk management, certain controls need to be maintained for the orderly running of the business. Included in these controls are internal controls and the separation of functions to protect against fraud or reckless behaviour. Auditors are likely to have a problem if cost savings lead to a reduction in the level of control. If, for example, there is a cost in separating the back office from trading, it should be a price worth paying (as perhaps Barings Bank could testify).

## Financial and management reporting constraints

Management accounting systems serve many purposes.[2] Usually, the primary function of management accounts is to control performance. In practice, many finance directors have their origins in financial accounting, which sometimes results in monthly figures assuming a format similar to the annual figures. The management accounts may also attempt to break up costs by sales divided into various geographic areas or product types. While such information may assist in withdrawing from certain markets or pruning the product line, all too rarely does it provide assistance in finding ways to reduce costs in a strategic manner. Line managers frequently complain that the management accounts are not very useful for identifying targets for cost reduction.

## Cost models: fixed or variable; direct or indirect

Costs are basically cut two ways: fixed or variable, and direct or indirect. The division between fixed and variable costs has its uses, particularly in establishing break-even volumes. However, in practice, many costs turn out to be semi-variable, which leads to problems in using this model. Another difficulty with this model is the fact that most costs can be made more variable in the long-term while, in the short term, many so-called variable costs are hard to reduce with declining volumes. Rents may be fixed in the short term but, in the longer term, it may be possible to negotiate rent reductions or move premises. Production labour may, theoretically, be variable as far as the management is concerned, but trade unions, intent on maintaining employment, may beg to differ when volumes fall. The restrictions of the model to a single product or constant product mix may also limit its usefulness. Finally, treating volume as the sole driver of costs may be a serious oversimplification in an increasingly complex world.

Whatever the limitations of the fixed and variable cost split, the problems with the traditional direct and indirect cost split are even greater. In manufacturing, where costing systems were first developed, it was normal to identify the direct cost of material and direct labour on a product basis. Overheads were a relatively modest part of total costs, but needed to be included in the total costs when selling prices were determined. This was typically done by apportioning them to products on the basis of direct labour or machine hours. While such calculations may seem crude, they may have been sufficient in an era of full capacity, when it was possible to increase prices at will.

In the modern era, with the rise of service industries, increased automation and general complexity of many businesses, the scale of central overheads has risen drastically for most organisations. With rapidly increasing overhead rates, the crudity of such calculations has been exposed, and many businesses have found themselves unable to recover their overheads by simply increasing their prices. In such circumstances, many businesses have begun to question not only the accuracy of their costing systems, but also their usefulness when it comes to cost reduction.

Essential to the efficiency of operations is the improvement of processes, increasing throughput, balancing capacities and reducing stocks. Unfortunately, conventional accounting systems rarely help managers in this task. The key accounting question for the finance director is how successful can the costing system be at identifying those costs that managers can reduce.

## Activity-based costing (ABC) and activity-based management (ABM)

Modern operational techniques focus on improvements in processes or activities. These techniques try to eliminate, simplify or combine to increase efficiency. As discussed in **Part III** of this book, this entails examination of the various business or operational processes. Management may seek to eliminate activities that add no value, simplify others, possibly combine them or, in some other way, reduce their costs. If the accounting system can support such changes it will serve a much more useful function. The experience of many companies that adopt activity-based costing is that, by linking costs to activities, they can obtain a much better understanding of their costs. In particular, if it is possible to benchmark the cost of an activity, then inefficiencies should be brought to the surface.

Out of the need for businesses to allocate their burgeoning overheads on a rational basis, activity-based costing (ABC) was developed. If it is activity that gives rise to cost, then it is logical to identify these activities and apportion costs on the basis of the drivers of these activities. For manufacturing, there is no simple allocation of overheads based on machine hours, direct labour hours or headcount. But it should be possible to identify the various activities that give rise to costs. For example, machinery set-up costs can be very significant for short production runs. Once the cost of a set-up is established, different products can be charged with the appropriate number of set-ups.

Similarly, a customer service department could break up its activities into solving customer problems, processing returns and testing returns. The driver of the customer solution cost might be the number of customer calls; the driver for the processing returns cost might be the number of returns; and the driver for testing costs might be the number of test hours. The cost of these activities would then be allocated to products accordingly. ABC does not result in total and undisputed precision, but it provides a better basis than traditional methods, which often claimed spurious accuracy and a misleading allocation of costs.

ABC was adopted by a considerable number of large businesses in the 1990s, particularly in the United States, most of which found it increased their control of product and customer costs. Adoption was by no means confined to manufacturing, but included service businesses, such as banks and hospitals. While ABC was originally a management accounting costing tool, its influence has spread. 'Activity-based budgeting' and 'activity-based management' are now standard business terms, but they cannot work without the appropriate costing system to support them. Unfortunately, many companies baulk at the cost and time involved in introducing and maintaining such an accounting system. As a result, they are at a disadvantage when it comes to implementing strategic cost reduction. The use of activity-based budgeting in cost reduction is illustrated by the case of Irving Oil in **Chapter 11**.

Whether or not a business has adopted ABC, it should review the extent to which the costing system helps managers with the task of cost management. They may provide adequate assistance for budgetary control or analysis of product or customer profitability, but fail when it comes to identifying a route to cost reduction. If continuous improvement is to be an important element in strategic implementation, then it is at least worth reviewing whether the costing system is effective in supporting this goal.

## Issues for the operations director

Since operations directors in many organisations have responsibility for the largest part of the budget, they can be expected to play a major role in cost reduction. They will inevitably also attach importance to the values which impinge on their workplace.

### *World-class operations*

Many businesses have adopted in varying degrees the principles of 'world-class operations'. While the techniques primarily have their origins in manufacturing, they have been satisfactorily adapted for use in the services sector. Fundamental to this mode of thinking is the concept of 'lean' operations, where cost reduction is a way of life, subject to continuous improvement. (Details of the various tools and techniques of world class and lean manufacturing are set out in **Chapters 11** and **12**.) While many businesses pay lip-service to the philosophy of world-class manufacturing, the extent to which it is actually implemented in practice varies enormously. Naturally, those who have adopted this philosophy, with its emphasis on continuous improvement, start cost reduction with an in-built advantage.

Successful practitioners of lean manufacturing will be well aware of the benefits to be gained in terms of reduction of waste, elimination of defects, etc. Almost certainly, employees will have been empowered to make improvements themselves. In such an environment, thought needs to be given to whether there is scope for a cost-reduction programme and how it will fit in with existing structures and practices. It is perhaps not coincidental that the concept of lean manufacturing originated in Japan, where lifelong employment was the norm. If compulsory redundancy is foisted on a reluctant workforce, future cooperation for continuous improvement may be difficult to obtain. If the company does not currently subscribe to such lean thinking, the obvious question is: should it be introduced as part of the cost-reduction plan or in parallel with it? Thus, one key question for the operations director is: to what extent has the company adopted the general principles of world-class operations and lean manufacturing?

## Identifying bottlenecks and constraints

Operations managers who pursue a lean agenda have the ultimate goal of making as much money for the shareholders as possible. Their intermediate goals are to maximise throughput, reduce work-in-progress and manage total operating costs.[3] This entails the need to identify any bottlenecks or constraints in the system. Once the bottleneck is identified, effort can be focussed on its removal to improve the overall flow.

Yet, most accounting systems give operations managers little assistance with these key tasks. They examine processes which can be improved. Activity-based costing systems described above have considerable benefits in this regard and can fit much better with the needs of 'lean' operations managers. More traditional systems can give misleading signals and hinder efforts to reduce work-in-progress.

## Health and safety

Another important consideration for any operations director is the health and safety of employees. There may well be industry standards which need to be followed, but many organisations may choose to abide by stricter standards. Office buildings in Tokyo were built to withstand powerful tremors, which must have added significantly to the cost, but stood them in good stead when the devastating earthquake hit Japan in 2011. Unfortunately, the country's nuclear reactors were not built to deal with the loss of power experienced in the aftermath of the resulting tsunami. This has since caused many countries to review their own safety standards and the costs of nuclear energy. No employer wants to experience serious injuries or even deaths in their workforce. Such concerns are particularly prominent in certain heavy engineering, construction and chemical industries, where workers have experienced asbestosis or, in the case of the Union Carbide India Limited pesticide plant, the tragic loss of life at Bhopal caused by a gas leak in 1984.

Health and safety issues are not limited to the interests of employees. For many industries, the safety of customers is also of paramount importance. Airlines worry about having a crash, toymakers fear selling dangerous toys and supermarkets hope that the food they are selling is fit for consumption and not poisonous. All these industries may need to have costly procedures in place to avert calamities. Third parties can also be affected by health and safety issues as the 2010 drilling disaster by BP in the Gulf of Mexico has shown. One consequence of this has been a massive law suit and the creation of a $20 billion compensation fund, while another is the possibility of criminal prosecutions. If allegations of compromises on safety are substantiated, untold damage can be suffered by the company and its brand, however well established.

## Issues for the human resources director

Most organisations believe in certain values when it comes to the treatment of employees. Some of these values, such as respect for individuals, may be proclaimed in mission statements, but others may be assumed from the custom and practice in which problems are approached. The practice may be extended to indirect employees or subcontractors. For example, should a builder work with a subcontractor who flouts safety regulations or pays less than the statutory minimum wage?

### Basic human values

More generally, consider a situation where the workforce needs to be reduced by 10% to remain competitive. Will the organisation:

1. Rely on natural wastage to solve the issue?
2. Create conditions so that many or selected employees will leave?

3. Introduce an attractive early retirement or voluntary redundancy scheme?
4. Selectively target individuals for redundancy?
5. Introduce a mandatory redundancy scheme based on some objective standard, such as 'last in-first out'?
6. Provide redundancy on a generous or purely statutory basis?
7. Consult staff on how the problem should be addressed?
8. Provide outplacement services?

The choice of strategy may be constrained by the severity of the crisis, relevant legislation, the role of trade unions or staff associations, the culture of the country or simply ethical practices that the organisation espouses. Some approaches, such as the second above, might constitute constructive dismissal and, therefore, be illegal. Others, which might be perfectly normal in the United States, may not be applicable in Europe.

## Issues in headcount reduction

In a situation where an organisation has to reduce its headcount by, for example, 10%, the human resource function will normally take a lead role. In such situations, notwithstanding legal considerations, most employers will try to ensure that all affected staff are treated in a dignified manner and with respect.

When faced with the need to reduce head count, the human resource function will likely have preferences as to the best approach. Natural wastage is the most palliative approach, followed by voluntary redundancy or early retirement schemes. Only when these remedies fail will it be necessary to resort to less agreeable methods, such as temporary short-time working, pay cuts or even compulsory redundancy.

Many organisations will also try and support exiting staff by providing a range of supports that usually include outplacement and tax advice. The ideal result is an absence of acrimony, as illustrated in an interview aired on TV at a factory gate with a worker who had just received notice that the plant was closing. When asked by the reporter for their reaction, the worker replied, "It was a great place to work."

## Fundamental values or optional extras?

There are also, of course, many human resource values other than those relating to termination of employment. Naturally, human resource directors, like operations directors, will consider health and safety considerations to be vitally important. The difficulty is defining the limits where precautions turn into featherbedding of employees. Appropriate workloads are not easy to determine, as can be seen in the manning policies of different airlines.

Other factors include training, work conditions and space, workload, accepted perks, holidays, etc.

A further consideration is the establishment of minimal qualifications for any job, which may restrict the supply of available talent. Teachers, for example, may need certain academic qualifications, but may still not be able to teach well, even though this may be their primary responsibility. Trade unions have similar rules for manning levels. When useful minimal standards become restrictive practices is a matter of judgement, where there is room for considerable disagreement. These standards can vary over time and in different countries. The introduction of lowly-qualified 'barefoot doctors' might work in China, but fail disastrously in more litigious societies. Restrictive practices may not only increase costs, but also fail in the goals of improving quality and providing value for money.

Increasingly, organisations are forced to re-examine the values that have traditionally governed their behaviour, separating those that are fundamental and absolute from those which are merely nice to have. For example, many companies traditionally have considered that they have a duty to provide adequate pensions for employees when they retire. However, the burgeoning cost of defined benefit schemes due to increased longevity and falling stock markets have forced them to reconsider this value. On a lesser note: is the traditional Christmas party an important benefit, vital for the maintenance of staff morale, or a luxury which can readily be cancelled in times of economic hardship?

Careless cost-reduction programmes that breach established values may do permanent damage to employee morale and adversely affect the ability of the organisation to attract talent when recovery looms. The key question for the HR director is: what are the company's employee values that should be protected in a cost-reduction programme?

## Issues for other disciplines

The key issues here have been confined to sales and marketing, financial control, operations and human resources. But the values of other disciplines may also be relevant. The engineering function may need to foster creativity. The purchasing function may wish to avoid excessive dependence on a single supplier. The IT function may be concerned with data integrity, security, back-up and disaster recovery. Accordingly, it may be appropriate to consult these and other interests, where cost reductions impinge on them. Unwanted collateral damage is not confined to the military.

## Reconciling functional imperatives

In the memorandum at the start of this chapter, the CEO has requested functional managers to outline the issues that are important to them. This is wise, and it should not be surprising when they conflict, since gatekeepers will tend their own patch and pursue their own values. A degree of constructive friction is quite usual and needs to be resolved carefully, bearing in mind the organisation's overall strategy. If cost reduction is designed to produce real sustainable savings, rather than obvious but superficial savings, it is appropriate to question all costs which may be reduced and to listen to any defences of same which may be put forward. It is foolish to draw up a cost reduction plan that exposes the organisation to risks which have been overlooked, with potentially serious, if not fatal, consequences.

## Conclusions

- The product or service strategy of a business identifies the key features that are valued by customers. If they are damaged, sales may be lost.
- Financial controls form the foundation of risk management. If they are removed or weakened, the business may be imperilled.
- Most cost systems, other than activity-based systems, provide management with limited help in improving processes to reduce costs.
- Companies that have adopted world class manufacturing principles start cost reduction with a significant advantage over others.
- The choice of employees to leave and their departure terms are critical. Any perceived unfairness may leave an enduring legacy.
- An element of friction between functions is quite usual.

## Management checklist

1. What product or service features need to be protected in cost reduction?
2. What risks and controls need to be considered?
3. Is cost information available in a format that is helpful to the project?
4. What modern operational tools are already in use, and to what extent does the company espouse a world class operations and lean manufacturing approach?
5. What human resource values need to be borne in mind?
6. What other functional issues are important?
7. Have the relevant concerns of all the functional gatekeepers been carefully considered?

# Chapter 8

# Discovering the strategic drivers of cost[1]

"It is not the strongest of the species that survives, nor the most intelligent, but the most responsive to change."

*Charles Darwin*

For businesses to thrive, it is critical that they understand what gives rise to their costs and whether they need to be restructured. If any business compares its overall costs with those of a close competitor, it can be astonishing how widely they diverge. The reasons may not be in the efficiency with which each management team conducts its business, but rather in some deep-rooted causes more related to strategic decisions, some of which may have been made many years previously. An understanding of these broad strategic drivers will highlight how a business should respond to change by identifying the targets where the focus of the cost reduction should be aimed.

The topic is approached by examining the different drivers and illustrating them by two examples, as follows:

- Size and growth cost drivers
- Situational cost drivers
- Relationship cost drivers
- Discretionary cost drivers
- An example from the printing industry
- Service industry applications

Michael Porter identifies 10 major strategic cost drivers, which, for convenience, we will group into four broad categories as outlined in **Figure 8.1**.

## Size and growth cost drivers

The first set of drivers, which influence the running costs, relate to the absolute size of the business and how long it has been trading.

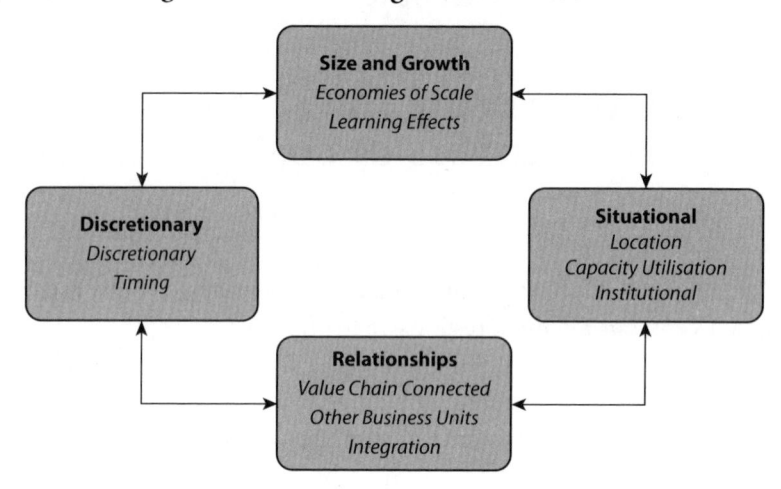

## Figure 8.1  Categorisation of Strategic Cost Drivers

**Size and Growth**
*Economies of Scale*
*Learning Effects*

**Discretionary**
*Discretionary*
*Timing*

**Situational**
*Location*
*Capacity Utilisation*
*Institutional*

**Relationships**
*Value Chain Connected*
*Other Business Units*
*Integration*

### Economies of scale

Large organisations can benefit from specialisation and, therefore, should be able to lower unit costs. Where labour is divided into smaller tasks, workers can increase output by specialising in a small number of activities in which they become experts. The classical explanation of economics of scale was set out by Adam Smith, one of the founder figures of modern economics, using a pin factory to illustrate the concept. The division of labour permitted savings by increasing mechanisation of the manufacturing process, reduction of movement around the factory and increased dexterity of individual workers. In this way, large volumes of pins could be produced at a much cheaper cost per unit than small volumes.

Businesses can also suffer from diseconomies of scale. For a variety of reasons, inefficiencies can be expected to increase once a business grows beyond a certain size. The whole issue of economies and diseconomies of scale will be addressed in greater detail in **Chapter 10**.

### Learning effects

The more often a particular activity is performed, the more efficient the process should become. In manufacturing, learning effects can come from better layout, improved scheduling, reduction of waste and increases in labour efficiency.

Typically, savings should arise from increased volumes, longer time in operation and overall plant investment. Learning effects can equally arise in the services sector. Skilled craftsmen, from lawyers to garage mechanics, who have repeated a particular transaction or operation on many occasions, should be able to reduce the time involved over a period of months or years by knowing what they should be watching for.

Businesses can help learning in various ways. Appropriate recruitment and training should accelerate learning. Policies that lead to low staff turnover, while remaining open to new ideas, may prevent the loss of 'know-how', while still encouraging innovation. The dissemination of ideas and improvements, together with the encouragement of useful external networking, to bring in new ideas should speed up enhancements.

Many organisations pride themselves on being 'learning organisations'[2] and endeavour to systematise improvements from experience. While small organisations often rely on informal dissemination, larger organisations may choose more elaborate systems to capture learning. It does not matter if this involves simply informal word-of-mouth exchanges, regular meetings or complex databases. If the 'know-how' is somehow captured by the organisation, rather than being contained within individuals who may choose to leave, learning should occur. Knowledge-based industries are particularly vulnerable to the loss of key employees, since expertise is the basis of their ability to compete, a view often expressed by investment banks.

Learning should not be limited to the experiences of one's own organisation. Many successful organisations seek the best ideas from their own industry or the 'best in class' organisations outside their industry, where new standards have been adopted. Successful organisations are constantly seeking new ways of learning from a wide variety of sources, giving real meaning to the mantra: 'work smarter, not harder'.

Factors that may assist organisational learning include:

- Policies encouraging and rewarding suggestions
- In-house newsletters
- Celebration of successes
- Attendance at relevant conferences
- Encouragement of professional qualifications
- Degree of employee mobility and rotation
- Culture of openness and trust

## Situational cost drivers

Costs are strongly influenced by historic decisions, such as where a business is located, the size of a plant, and resulting arrangements with institutions, such as government and trade unions.

### Location

Location impacts on organisations in two ways. Proximity to customers, suppliers and sources of energy will affect transportation costs. Location will also frequently give rise to extra costs or savings in terms of labour, taxes and material costs. For many service industries, transport costs are less significant than the availability of a skilled workforce, accustomed to lower wage rates, with a supportive government. In an era of globalisation, the possibility of realising substantial savings by relocating to low-cost economies has opened up exciting new possibilities for many businesses.

The current location of many businesses may derive from historical accident. Traditionally, higher costs, resulting from an uneconomic location, were accepted as a fact of life. For a truly multinational business, this is no longer the case. The current location of the business is now seen as a strategic choice.

However, if the location of a business gives rise to high operational costs, the capital costs of moving may outweigh the benefits of a lower cost operational base. Choice of location becomes another capital investment decision, and a key element may be the overall management of the business and the willingness of key employees to move.

### Capacity utilisation

Industries that experience high fixed costs need to concentrate on capacity utilisation. For example, to minimise unit costs in a cement plant or a packaging business, it may be necessary to operate 365-days-a-year, 24-hours-a-day. Aircraft similarly need to operate at high load factors with minimal empty seats to exceed break-even. Hotels that cannot fill their rooms out of peak season may struggle to be profitable. Professional firms, selling the skills of their employees, need to optimise their number of chargeable days.

Historically, many businesses could assume relatively full capacity, particularly where the products were in high demand. In an increasingly competitive world, where consumers have a greater degree of sophistication, knowledge and choice, full capacity may be the exception, rather than the rule. Flexibility to add or reduce capacity in an economic manner may be a key element of overall costs. Such factors need to be considered when capital decisions are made because, all too often, many costs are unavoidable after the investment has been made. (The operational tools that can assist in making the best use of capacity are described in **Part III** of this book.)

*Institutional factors*

Governments and regulators frequently make rules that impact on costs in a significant way. Unfavourable rules may take the form of tariffs and levies, employment laws, etc. Favourable rules may include capital grants, subsidies, tax holidays, low rates of corporate tax, etc. Ireland introduced its 12.5% rate of corporation tax as a carrot to attract and retain foreign direct investment to the country. The determination of successive governments to maintain this institutional advantage in the face of constant EU pressure for tax harmonisation underlines its overall significance.

Another source of institutional cost can be agreements reached with trade unions or staff associations over remuneration and work practices. In particular, restrictive practices relating to manning levels, permitted absenteeism and overtime arrangements can add enormously to costs, especially in a labour-intensive industry.

In highly-mobile industries, especially those that can take advantage of modern telecommunications (such as parts of the financial service sector), certain institutional factors can be critical in determining location. The absence of unnecessarily onerous regulations and a favourable tax regime, together with a good supply of skilled labour, can act as a powerful draw to companies, as the International Financial Service Centre (IFSC) in Dublin has demonstrated. For authorities imposing regulatory costs, the difficulty may be drawing the line between unnecessary bureaucracy and effective 'light touch' regulation to ensure the orderly operation of the system.

## Relationship cost drivers

Costs can be seriously affected by the way the organisation can benefit from certain linkages, either internally or externally.

## Linkages connected to the Value Chain

The Value Chain (as discussed in **Chapter 9**), sets out the separate elements of both the five primary and four support activities. In practice, many of these activities depend on the smooth connection between the different elements. In manufacturing, there are obvious connections between machining and maintenance, quality assurance and customer service or purchases and operations. Good stock management involves the linking of operations, purchasing and sales. If these linkages do not operate smoothly, extra costs will be incurred.

Important linkages also exist with customers and suppliers. Some supermarkets obtain merchandising savings from suppliers, who are required to place the stock on their shelves. Pharmaceutical wholesalers may improve their selling by placing terminals with the pharmacists who are their customers, enabling them to order automatically when stocks fall below a predetermined level. On a wider front, the presence of major industrial players in any given location may attract suppliers to locate nearby, thus providing better service and lower costs. The clustering of global information technology companies in Ireland, and pharmaceutical businesses in the Munster region, provide illustrations of how important these savings are for multinationals selecting locations for their business.

To enhance the benefits of linkages within the value chain, some businesses have operated supplier partnerships, where they obtain very detailed costing data from their suppliers and help them to run their operations more efficiently. While some Western companies, such as Marks & Spencer in clothing manufacture, have adopted such a policy, many businesses are reluctant to divulge sensitive competitive information. So, such close supplier relationships are much rarer outside of the more trusting culture found in Japan.

## Interrelationships with other business units

In the case of large corporate groups, there may be the possibility of sharing certain costs between different business units. As already noted, many groups wish to capture and share learning. They may also choose to share some activities, such as purchasing or distribution. Increasingly, groups are looking to centralise activities which have traditionally been managed independently, such as HR, IT and invoicing.

Any activity that is performed in the same manner in different locations can be considered a candidate for centralisation. Centralisation is more difficult when different locations require different treatment. If different legal systems exist, or ways of handling customers diverge due to cultural factors, the gains from centralising a service are diminished.

Treasury is one service which is commonly shared. A specialised treasury unit, handling all of a group's cash and borrowing requirements should have more negotiating power than smaller autonomous units. In the management of currency exposures, it may be possible to identify opposite positions in different parts of the group and, so, save duplication and unnecessary transaction costs. Most importantly, the Board may also want to see the group's aggregate exposure to risks such as currency and interest rate movements.

## Integration factors

Some industries have traditionally been vertically integrated. Oil companies, for example, may undertake exploration, operate their refineries and own their retail outlets. Utilities often provide complementary services, such as the generation of electricity and its transmission to customers. Vertical integration can provide greater control and generate savings, particularly by eliminating the margin of the middleman.

In recent years, the trend of most industries has militated against vertical integration. With the increasing tendency to outsource functions where no competitive advantage exists, all parts of vertically integrated groups have come under increasing scrutiny, since captive markets can generate cost inefficiencies, which would not survive in a more competitive marketplace. In the case of utilities, regulators have sometimes intervened to ensure greater competition. Yet, today, many businesses may reconsider their strategy in the light of highly volatile material costs and uncertainty of supply.

Assessing the benefits and costs of integration is often a complex problem. Where one business unit purchases from another member of the group, the transaction may or may not be at the market price. If the price is based on cost plus a margin, parts of the group may be subsidising or penalising other parts. In some cases, the benefits of integration can be outweighed by the inefficiencies involved. Profits 'may' become distorted and performance hard to measure.

## Discretionary cost drivers

The last set of cost drivers exist because businesses have deliberately incurred them as a matter of policy.

### *Discretionary policies*

All organisations spend money deliberately in ways that could, in strict terms, be avoided. It is not necessary to spend money on discretionary areas, such as research & development, marketing and training. The easy, though not necessarily the wisest, way to reduce costs is to eliminate or drastically reduce these activities. Many businesses elect to do so in times of economic adversity in order to maintain a required level of profit.

While such economies are easy to effect in the short term, they may result in serious long-term damage to the business. Over a period, if there are no new products or services, customers may leave. If there is no advertising, the brand may be affected, and prices may be hard to maintain. If there is no training, staff may become disaffected, and morale often suffers as a consequence.

The choice of the appropriate level of spend on these discretionary items is grounded in the overall strategy of a business. A true low-cost producer of goods or services will take a harder look at discretionary expenditure than a company whose strategy is based on some form of differentiation. Other costs arise as a consequence of the company's espoused set of values, such as their treatment of employees.

Nevertheless, many companies with a differentiation strategy can easily find that the levels of discretionary spend can grow without necessarily providing a competitive advantage. Some costs may be required by regulatory considerations but, for other costs, the real test is whether or not they add value to the consumer. All too often, where organisations budget on an incremental basis, such questioning of costs does not occur.

Most discretionary costs provide some benefit and may grow rapidly if they are not challenged. Organisations should question their range of policies as follows:

- Which add value to the customer?
- Which are core values?
- Which might reasonably be reduced:
    - The range and options of products or services?
    - Customer service policy?

- Marketing and advertising spend?
- Pay and conditions of employment?
- Recruitment and training costs?
- Plant maintenance?

*Timing decisions*

Many costs are the result of decisions regarding the timing of entering the market. The timing of a product or service launch can have a fundamental influence on the cost base. It can result in either of two ways: the business can be the 'first mover' or a 'follower'. If the first mover is successful, it may be difficult for followers to achieve a sufficient scale to compete effectively. The product can become synonymous with the brand. For example, it is hard for late entrants to effectively challenge Guinness in the stout market or, more recently, Baileys in the cream liqueur market.

On the other hand, the first mover may have incurred enormous start-up costs, which can be avoided by a follower. MS-DOS, the precursor of Windows, was not invented by Microsoft. Many Apple enthusiasts claim that the company invented icons, yet Microsoft had the ability and resources to exploit the opportunity at a lower cost. Sometimes, followers have the ability to learn from the mistakes of inventors and, consequently, can employ a technology with a much lower cost base. If patents permit, copying may be cheaper than original research.

## An example from the printing industry

The Adare group, in 1993, was a small Irish printing company listed on the Dublin stock exchange, led by Nelson Loane, a CEO with long experience in the industry. In an industry noted for intense competition and low margins, Adare's profitability was a considerable achievement. It set about a strategy of acquiring similar businesses in the UK midlands, which was accessible by cheap air travel. The targets were under-performing businesses with a strong customer base.

The strategic cost drivers in the business were economies of scale and full utilisation of capacity. The key to managing the balance sheet was tight control over capital expenditure and working capital. To grow the business profitably, it was necessary that costs of sales and overheads were minimised. The key ratios were material cost, which was kept to a maximum of 50% of sales and direct labour, which should not exceed 25% of sales. Accordingly, material purchasing was centralised and head count monitored by head office to ensure rising sales per employee.

Between 1993 and 2000, the group acquired 14 companies. By 2000, the group was generating an operating profit of UK£15.2 million on sales of £160 million, and a return on invested capital of 33%. At this point, a management buyout was undertaken and the business was taken private for a consideration of £108 million.

## Service industry applications

The main cost in service industries is payroll. An understanding of cost drivers is essential if cost reduction is to be approached in a rational manner. The reduction of costs in the public sector is fundamentally different from that of professional firms.[3]

### Public sector

The basic driver of costs in the public sector is institutional. Public sector unions are a feature of the civil service everywhere and, often, they have agreed work practices with the government, which are severely constrained by onerous restrictive practices. Secondary cost drivers are connected to relationships – in particular, interrelationships between departments and integration factors.

The Irish Government, facing a major fiscal crisis in 2010, decided to embark on a policy of cost reduction. Benchmarking indicated that civil servants were paid around 20% more than their counterparts in the private sector and significantly more than nearly all of their European peers, excluding their generous pension benefits, generous leave, numerous allowances and security of employment. After an initial pay cut, further savings were to be achieved by reform of the public sector.

In 2010, the Croke Park Agreement[4] was reached with labour leaders and, subsequently, with a majority of their members that, subject to no further budget deterioration, there would be no further pay cuts or compulsory redundancies for a four-year period. In return, there would be a reduction in the number of civil servants, a moratorium on recruitment and a voluntary redundancy scheme. Additionally, it was agreed that:

- The terms and conditions of employment would be standardised and redeployment over sectors allowed.

- Selective external recruitment would be permitted, and promotion would be based on merit.
- Systems would be reconfigured to increase productivity and services integrated, permitting a sharing of services, together with greater centralisation.
- Duplication and waste would be reduced and advantage taken of improved technology and on-line services.

The Croke Park Agreement should be understood in the context and the experiences of other countries where fundamental, strategic change in the management of public sectors has been undertaken. Throughout the OECD countries from the 1980s onwards, the reform agenda was driven by a body of doctrines, known as 'New Public Management'. There was a shift in emphasis from policy-making to management skills, from a process focus to an output focus, from orderly hierarchies to competition in service provision, from fixed pay to variable pay, and from a uniform structure to contracted services. This was a world characterised by privatisation and market pricing of services; decentralisation was favoured over centralisation; and results were judged on output measure, quality and intensity of implementation.[5]

Not all countries adopted New Public Management with equal enthusiasm. Australia, Canada, New Zealand, Sweden and the UK led the way, while Ireland, whose public sector was originally modelled on the UK, moved more slowly. Perhaps Ireland's lack of enthusiasm could be attributed to the fast economic growth of the 'Celtic Tiger', the reluctance of coalition governments to tackle the issue or, possibly, it could be explained by the strength of vested interests. Under a benchmarking exercise with the private sector in 2000, generous pay increases were granted to public servants for increased productivity, which failed to materialise. In any event, rates of pay and benefits in the public sector for both public servants and politicians grew rapidly under the agreements negotiated under a programme of 'Social Partnership' with serious consequences once recession hit.

These public sector issues are by no means unique to Ireland. A recent review[6] by *The Economist* indicated that the same problems exist in the US, UK and elsewhere in Europe. Public sectors tend to be heavily unionised and have been able to extract deals from weak governments, so that most of their members are better off than their private sector equivalents. In the US, public sector pay and benefits have grown twice as fast as in the private sector. Powerful unions have negotiated generous pensions and light workloads, while providing maximum job security and limited accountability. In Greece, the country's railways generated revenues of only €174 million in 2009, but spent €246 million on wages, while posting an overall loss of €937 million. Yet, the unions sought assurances over job protection and services as part of the privatisation package.[7]

The burgeoning cost of the public sector and government fiscal problems have led to increasing pressures to rationalise the public sector in many countries. The heart of reform is the tackling of benefits, in particular pensions, and improving productivity through changed work practices.

A further study[8] by *The Economist* reported that the state almost everywhere is "big, inefficient and broke". It predicted that "how to slim the state" would become the great political issue of our times. The cutbacks of the Thatcher/Reagan era had been reversed, with government spending typically representing 50% of GDP and the debt burden of OECD countries averaging over 100%. Few countries, other possibly than Sweden and Canada, have successfully addressed the matter. Productivity could be improved by greater use of technology, while greater selectivity in social transfers is vital to reduce the size of the public sector.

It is one thing to identify the drivers of cost and target areas for reduction in the public sector, but it is another matter to overcome resistance and implement the changes. In Ireland, enormous waste has been exposed by a prominent independent politician,[9] but that does not mean that the problems can be readily rectified. Without a crisis, it is usually difficult to generate sufficient energy to bring about reform, but a serious crisis, although it may be necessary, is not always sufficient to bring about radical change.

Many commentators consider the progress made in the year following the Croke Park Agreement in Ireland in April 2010 to be disappointing or even negligible. The new Irish Government in 2011 committed to creating a better, smaller and cheaper public sector. This was to be achieved through radical reform and the elimination of waste, which requires skilful management. But where the drivers of cost are restrictive practices, interrelationships and integration factors, solutions may be difficult to achieve. Most of the issues around implementation of change and leadership of the process, discussed in **Chapter 19**, are fundamental to the success of public sector cost reduction.

## Professional service firms

Virtually every professional service firm faced a reduction in business and pressure on fees charged as a result of the economic downturn. Those connected to the building industry, such as architects, surveyors and structural engineers, were hardest hit, as were recruitment agencies. Others, such as advertising agencies, accountancy and legal practices faced the same problems in varying degrees.

The main cost driver in professional firms is capacity. Employees are paid salaries, which are largely fixed and are recovered through fees charged to clients. To the extent that time cannot be fully recovered, profits suffer. The financial model has been described as follows:[10]

To maximise profits per partner, there are essentially three levers:

$$\frac{\text{Profits}}{\text{Partner}} = \frac{\text{Profits}}{\text{Fees}} \times \frac{\text{Fees}}{\text{Staff}} \times \frac{\text{Staff}}{\text{Partners}}$$

In a recession, with pressure on professional fees, there is little scope for increasing the first element of fees per partner. Similarly, there is minimal scope for increasing the third element of staff per partner. Consequently, the middle element of fees per staff member must bear the brunt of the adjustment.

Professional firms have little choice but to reduce their staff payroll in an economic downturn. Initial moves include reducing or ceasing recruitment, encouraging sabbaticals and offering early retirement. If these measures to accelerate natural wastage are insufficient, there is little alternative to cutting staff pay and benefits through foregoing bonuses, cuts in rates of pay, short-time working or redundancies. Alternative ways to reduce labour costs are considered in greater detail in **Chapter 16**.

Thus, the approach to cost reduction fundamentally differs in the public sector from that in professional firms. Yet the difference is not based on the fact that one sector is public and the other is private. Traditional cost-cutting in the car industry, which is also heavily unionised, very much resembles the public sector model with its focus on improving work practices.[11] The key distinction between the two sectors is the differing drivers of cost. Any organisation approaching cost reduction in a strategic manner is well advised to start by understanding these drivers, as applied to its own activities.

## Conclusions

- There are 10 basic cost drivers, relating to size, the historic situation, relationships and discretionary choices.

- In any given business, it should not be difficult to work out what the significant cost drivers are.
- A benchmarking exercise may provide some measure of the relative significance of cost drivers.
- Those drivers that damage competitiveness should be the first targets of a cost-reduction exercise.

## Management checklist

1. Do you know how your costs compare with your leading competitor?
2. Which three strategic cost drivers most impair your competitiveness?
3. What measures are available to you to tackle the strategic disadvantages caused by these cost drivers?

# Chapter 9

# Exploiting the value chain

> "We are operating on the multiplex cinema model – they make most of their money from the sale of popcorn, drinks and sweets, not cinema tickets. It is our ultimate ambition to get to a stage when the fare is free."
>
> Michael O'Leary, CEO Ryanair

Where goals to reduce costs are ambitious, traditional costing systems may fail to provide appropriate guidance. As already noted in **Chapter 7**, divisions of costs between 'fixed' and 'variable' or 'direct' and 'indirect' are of limited use when seeking ways to reduce costs in a strategic manner. Likewise, activity-based costing may be too detailed as a starting point to assess costs. Managers need to focus on the wider systems and the ways in which activities or processes can be improved.

One generic way of examining costs from a strategic perspective is through the 'value chain' and is explored through the example of the low fares airline industry, and in particular Ryanair, in this chapter under the following headings:

- The value chain
- Ryanair
- Ryanair and the value chain

## The value chain

The value chain[1] model breaks down businesses into five 'primary' and four 'support' activities, as shown in **Figure 9.1** below.

The primary activities (inbound logistics, operations, outbound logistics, marketing and sales, and service) follow a sequential order. In manufacturing, for example, the inbound logistics ensure that the raw materials are delivered. Operations transform the raw materials into finished goods. Outward logistics despatches the goods to the customer, either directly or through an intermediary. Marketing and sales arrange customer transactions. Servicing provides back-up to generate customer satisfaction, which should set a platform for further sales.

*Figure 9.1* **The Value Chain**

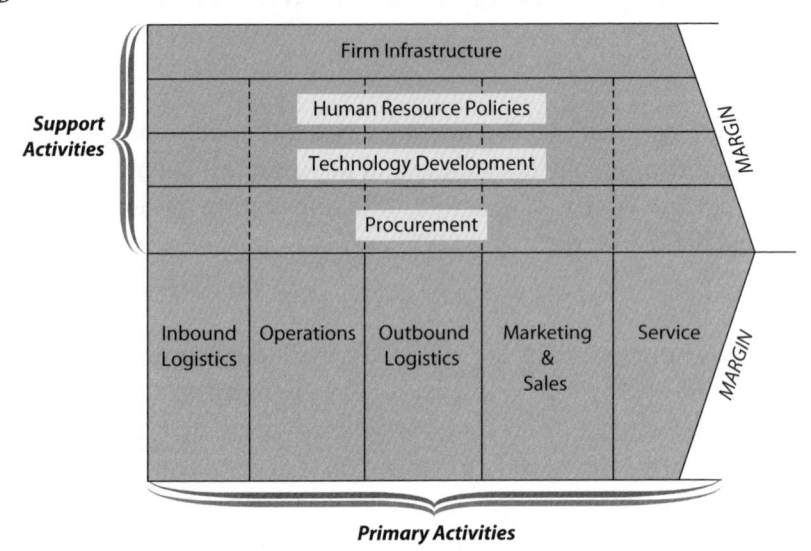

|  | Firm Infrastructure |  |  |  |  |
|---|---|---|---|---|---|
| **Support Activities** | Human Resource Policies |  |  |  |  |
|  | Technology Development |  |  |  |  |
|  | Procurement |  |  |  |  |
|  | Inbound Logistics | Operations | Outbound Logistics | Marketing & Sales | Service |

MARGIN

**Primary Activities**

The primary activities could not exist without the support activities: procurement, technology, HR and infrastructure. Procurement deals with the purchase of capital and revenue items. Information technology coordinates the different elements of the system. Human resources policies are needed to manage the labour force. The firm's infrastructure will also include its head office and finance functions.

To illustrate the use of the value chain model to guide cost reduction, consider a grain farmer trying to reduce his costs. Initially, he might decide to cut back on certain luxuries on the farm, such as 'The ponies have to go,' but this is rarely sufficient. He orders his seed, which he probably collects himself from the supplier ('inbound logistics'). He sows, sprays and harvests using the minimum amount of inputs, both materials and labour, possibly outsourcing some activities ('operations'). The grain merchant collects the finished product, though some crops may be sold on the basis that the customer cuts the product ('outbound logistics'). The sale price is agreed in advance, based on tonnage, quality and moisture content, after checking prices with different merchants ('sales and marketing'). Servicing does not apply.

Both operating inputs and capital expenditure will be kept to low levels, with purchases negotiated with the cheapest provider ('procurement'). The Internet may be employed to obtain information on prices, products, etc.

('technology'). The labour policy will be to maintain the smallest full-time employment, consistent with the size and complexity of the farm ('human resources'). The business may be run from an office or maybe the farm's kitchen with family labour, though the accounts function may be outsourced to a Chartered Accountant, who prepares the tax return ('infrastructure').

The value chain model can also be applied to service industries with minor modifications. A service is offered to customers; it is then performed, sold and usually accompanied by some form of back-up. The support activities also follow a similar pattern. It may be instructive to see how the model can be applied to a larger-scale business than a family farm. We have selected an industry familiar to most readers, where low cost is the essence of competition, namely the low fares airline business.

Two of the best known low fares airlines are Southwest Airlines in the US and Ryanair in Europe. Though Ryanair was originally modelled on Southwest, there are some differences in their modes of operation. While both are focused on low cost, Southwest[2] is renowned for its excellent staff and customer relations. It welcomes unions and works in partnership with suppliers, such as airports, security providers, air traffic controllers and aircraft manufacturers. Ryanair does not welcome unions and is generally more confrontational with suppliers. Southwest too only outsources off-line maintenance and fuelling, while Ryanair outsources more widely. We shall focus here on Ryanair.

## Ryanair

Ryanair is a relatively new airline. It was launched in 1985 by Tony Ryan, an Irishman who had earlier set up what was to become a leading aircraft leasing company, GPA. The first plane was an old 15-seat turboprop Bandeirante, for which GPA obtained permission to operate from Waterford in the Republic of Ireland with routes to Dublin and London. In 1986, it opened a route from Dublin to Luton at a competitive fare of £99. Luton was not an ideal destination for many Irish passengers and a significant break came in 1989, when the company succeeded in ousting Aer Lingus from Stansted.

At this juncture, Tony Ryan contracted his personal assistant, Michael O'Leary, to stem the considerable losses that the company was suffering. Faced with possible closure, Tony Ryan urged O'Leary to examine the model of Southwest Airlines in the US. In 1992, O'Leary visited Southwest, which was run by Herb Kelleher, a charismatic lawyer of Irish-American extraction. O'Leary resolved to apply the low fares model to Ryanair. Shortly afterwards, the GPA flotation failed and O'Leary was appointed CEO of Ryanair. Ryanair floated in 1997 and made a bold expansion in 2001 after the 9/11 attack on the Twin Towers in the US. Since then, it has developed into a major competitor in Europe in the short-haul business.

Ryanair is now a well-known airline, not only for its low fares, but also, at least until 2008, for its high profitability and considerable stock market capitalisation, which outstripped BA and Lufthansa, both long-established national carriers. In 2008, however, the company became a hostage to rising oil prices, which it had not initially hedged, reversing its historic growth pattern significantly. Operating profits declined dramatically from €537 million in 2007/08 to €92 million in 2008/09, but trebled the following year, since when strong growth has continued.[3]

While its low-cost model is based on that of Southwest Airlines, Ryanair has not copied the excellent staff and passenger relations for which Southwest is renowned. O'Leary comes across as a colourful and confrontational CEO, who features in the media on a regular basis, often dealing with staff and customer disputes.

Although Ryanair's low cost model owes little to consultants or formal models, it may, nevertheless, be instructive to see how low cost has been achieved both in its service offering and in each element of the value chain.

## Service offering

Obviously, the main feature of Ryanair's service is low fares. However, there are a small number of other features that the company emphasises. In its in-flight magazine, the airline is described as "the most punctual airline with the lowest cancellations and lost bags". This service offering, mainly based on the Southwest Airlines model, stresses:

- low cost
- punctuality
- most completed trips
- minimum lost baggage, and (naturally)
- safety

Ryanair does not offer many of the service elements that a lot of full service airlines consider to be important. Where other services are required, they may be provided at a much lower level than would be available from a full services airline. On board, for example, there are no frills or 'freebies', no pre-seating, no business class, minimal comfort, minimal assistance for the disabled and often minimal information or even courtesy. Its ticketing policy is also basic, since it is a point-to-point airline, offering no interlining with other airlines. There is little ticket flexibility and rebates are difficult or expensive to claim. The service, in short, resembles basic train travel, rather than traditional airline travel.

Ryanair's service policy, compared to full service airlines, could be depicted roughly as shown in **Figure 9.2**.

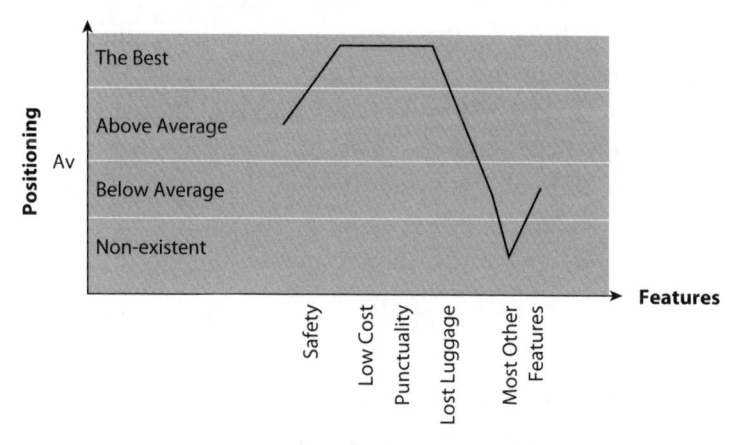

*Figure 9.2* **Ryanair's Service Policy**

Unsurprisingly, Ryanair's service does not appeal to everybody. Some passengers swear that they will never use the service again, particularly if they have been unexpectedly stranded and had to pay for their own way home. In 2006, Trip Advisor polled 4,000 travellers around the world[4] on their flying experiences. Low cost airlines fared badly in the study; Ryanair was voted the world's least popular airline, with Easy Jet not far behind. Complaints centred on unfriendly staff, followed by delays and poor leg room. Ryanair responded[5] with the fact that 42 million people in 2006 chose Ryanair for the lowest fares and best punctuality. A further survey in 2011 showed that 97% of Ryanair's passengers planned to fly with them again, citing cost as the main reason, followed by the airport location.[6]

To compete effectively in the low fares industry, Ryanair must have a lower cost base than its competitors, and it strives to achieve this by reducing costs in all elements of the value chain.

## Ryanair and the value chain[7]

### Inbound logistics

The first part of the value chain is the customer ordering process. Traditionally, this service was provided by travel agents, who charged their commission and also for the use of the central airline computer booking system. From its early stages, Ryanair decided to pay no commission to travel agents, preferring to sell, in the main, through telephone booking. This service had its drawbacks. Customers could be kept waiting on the phone only to discover that no cheap seats were available on their preferred flights.

A breakthrough came when two students were commissioned for a small fee to produce a website for the company. Customers could now do their own booking and print their own tickets. The Ryanair website has been upgraded several times since and is now localised in many languages. It generates not only ticket sales, but also considerable advertising revenue. By 2007, 99% of all bookings came through the website. In a 2008 cost-reduction drive, the company's telesales operation in Dublin was closed, leaving telesales only in Germany and Romania.[8]

### Operations

The first element in operational cost reduction for Ryanair is the choice of routes and, in particular, airports. Following the Southwest Airlines maxim, an airline only makes money when its planes are in the air. This means a maximum number of flights per day and rapid turnaround on the ground, typically within 25 minutes. Such performance is not possible in large congested airports, so Ryanair chooses small and sometimes remote airfields, often former military bases. Competitors may challenge the names given to the airports, due to their distance from the related cities. For example:

- Beauvais to Paris: 80 km
- Reus to Barcelona: 80 km
- Torp to Oslo: 110 km
- Hahn to Frankfurt: 124 km

The local authorities may be anxious to attract business and employment, so landing charges may be negotiated down to a tiny fraction of the norm at major hubs and generous marketing support also provided.

The second element creating cost savings in the running costs is the streamlining of all operational systems. Ticketing, baggage handling, check-in and docking are reduced to the basics. Passengers without hold luggage can check in online and, if they miss the flight, need not expect rebates. Neither airbridges nor buses are used to facilitate passenger movement. Handling and fuel costs are reduced by discouraging hold luggage.

Governments and airport authorities are vehemently opposed when landing charges are increased or new charges introduced to cover additional security costs or carbon emissions.

Finally, Ryanair contains labour costs by insisting on flexibility. There is no demarcation and everyone is expected to help out when required. As O'Leary explains, he will do everything except fly the planes.[9] Unions are resisted and, where they exist, as with the airline's pilots, they have been confronted in the courts.

## Outbound logistics

Given the nature of service industries, these costs do not exist, as in manufacturing. Once the service has been delivered through the flight, the contract with the passenger is fulfilled.

## Sales and marketing

While offering low fares, maximisation of revenue is a critical component of the Ryanair business model. The pricing policy is the reverse of the traditional charter companies, which offered bargains at the last minute to fill their planes. With Ryanair, early bookers normally receive cheap tickets, but late bookers can pay considerably more. When extra demand is anticipated (for example, on the day of a major sporting event), fares may increase dramatically. In effect, the price of any ticket is fixed according to the customers' willingness and ability to pay, rather than the costs incurred. Skilful yield management through varying ticket prices and achieving high load factors are at the heart of Ryanair's low fares airline model, as well as its unrelenting attacks on all costs.

A further source of revenue is from what are euphemistically termed 'ancillary services'. To change a ticket costs money, as does checking in at the airport, placing luggage in the hold or receiving priority boarding. If a passenger has paid tax, but does not fly, there is no automatic refund, nor is the tax paid to the State. While it has not introduced a fuel surcharge to cover rising oil prices, there are other charges. When the airline was obliged to provide wheelchairs, which it considered to be the duty of the airport authority, it introduced a general wheelchair levy on all its passengers. Passengers are obliged to pay by credit card for which a credit card levy is imposed.

There is also revenue from ancillary on-flight sales and website sales. Cabin crew are encouraged to sell anything from drinks and sandwiches to watches and scratch cards. On the website, there is a casino and sales of anything from skiing holidays to financial services. Where a service does not prosper, it is withdrawn.

Possibly the biggest source of revenue other than ticket sales comes from partnership arrangements, where Ryanair receives a commission on sales of other services to passengers. Substantial revenue is generated from rail fares, car hire, hotels and insurance, while revenue from mobile phone usage is being introduced.

Advertising is a major form of income and occurs on the website, on seatbacks, luggage lockers or even on the fuselage, though the latter usually consists of messages aimed at competitors. O'Leary has likened the model to that of a multiplex cinema:[10] give away some seats for free and make a profit from selling other products or services to the passengers. Since ancillary revenue totalled over €800 million in 2010/11 and substantially exceeded total operating profit, this claim seems reasonable.

Promotion of the Ryanair brand is often achieved for little or no advertising cost with regular coverage in the media. There are numerous publicity stunts by Michael O'Leary, where he is photographed pulling faces, driving a private taxi to beat the Dublin traffic or poking fun at competitors. Offending people is not a problem. When Ryanair was taken to court for failing to provide the millionth passenger with the promised free travel, the judge was highly critical of O'Leary. The publicity was bad, but bookings soared by 30%.[11]

The airline's aggressive advertising policy can lead to problems. In 2008, the UK Advertising Standards Authority found against Ryanair on a number of fronts and referred it to the consumer watchdog.[12] The findings were that:

- Ryanair made exaggerated claims about the extent of availability of flights at advertised prices.
- Advertised prices did not include taxes and charges.
- The company did not clearly state restrictions that would exclude customers from taking advantage of an offer.
- It made misleading and derogatory comparisons with rivals.
- It did not provide evidence to prove the claims it was making.

Finally, the brand is exploited. The Ryanair name is widely recognised and has become synonymous with low cost. Companies offering other unrelated products, such as credit cards, are willing to pay for the use of the name. If the product is withdrawn, such as with Ryanair Telecom, this does not harm the company.

## Service

When Ryanair was originally launched, good service was a key feature. This is no longer the case. There can be minimal assistance for children, the aged, disabled or stranded customers. Complaints are not easily made, and are often ineffective. If rebates are granted, the processing charge may exceed the value of the rebate. Celebrities can be refused boarding like anyone else, if they do not have the required documents. Even the Irish Minister for Tourism was refused permission to board, because he did not have picture ID.[13] Undoubtedly, after a bad experience, some passengers will refuse to use the airline again. However, overall, passenger numbers have been growing at a spectacular rate over recent years.

## Procurement

Procurement for an airline can include general products or services required for everyday operations and also capital goods, of which the most important are aircraft. The most significant running cost is fuel. Kerosene is an international commodity, with the result that no airline is at an advantage when it comes to price. Efficiency may be influenced by the age of the aircraft, flying speeds and weight. However, these factors are much less significant than fuel prices, which can be affected by hedging policies. While some airlines bought fuel forward in 2008/09, Ryanair failed to do so, with the result that its profits were significantly reduced for the year due to rising oil prices. Its control over other running costs, however, is now legendary.

Ryanair outsources all activities where it has no competitive advantage. Maintenance is a case in point. With overcapacity in this global industry, the company can negotiate good contracts for the maintenance of its substantial fleet. The provision of cabin crew may be outsourced. The company may or may not need full-time check-in staff at any location, depending on the volume of business. Pilots, on the other hand, are a core competence and are company employees, some of whom are members of trade unions.

Every effort is made to reduce the cost of purchased goods or services. In some cases, the cost is avoided. For example, the purchase of highlighter pens is banned. Employees of all levels clean their own offices. Employees provide their own coffee and have been asked not to charge personal mobile phones using company electricity. There can also be elements of 'free sourcing'. Employees are urged to take free hotel stationery to save costs. 'Staff sourcing' also reduces cost. Employees may have to pay for their own training, their uniforms and even applications for job interviews.

With external suppliers, Ryanair's search for cheaper prices is unrelenting. No costs are beyond scrutiny, with battles fought over such issues as the price of ice. The company's volume of purchases is such that it can negotiate with suppliers as effectively as any supermarket chain. In March 2008[14] the company announced a €400 million cost-cutting exercise to counteract the rising price of fuel. Renegotiation of airport, handling and maintenance contracts was announced, as was an indefinite management pay freeze, designed to generate significant savings. It was intended to reduce costs in every single area of operations.

The purchase of aircraft is another major source of saving. The company has a single supplier, Boeing, which enables it to save on maintenance and spares. Aircraft are designed with a view to minimising running costs. There is only one class with the maximum number of seats, which do not recline. Headrests and blinds are eliminated. The traditional seat pocket is removed to save on cleaning. Cabin luggage space is designed to hold genuine hand luggage up to the permitted size.

But it is the buying price of the aircraft where the greatest economies are to be found. Ryanair announced a major expansion of its fleet in the aftermath of the Twin Towers attack in 2001, when Boeing was struggling for survival. When it announced purchases worth in total €9 billion the price was never publicised, but it was widely rumoured that the discount exceeded 40% of the list price.[15]

## Technology development

As has already been noted, Ryanair uses information technology with great effect to locate customers through the Internet and also to enable them to book online. However, it also uses technology to support low costs, reduce labour and assist operations. It is used to control sales and, in particular, to manage third party products, where commission is payable. It is also used to assist flying through crew allocation and control over flight paths. This enhances flexibility, since pilots on new routes will find familiar systems.

The skilful use of technology helps minimise manning levels. However, any investment needs to be justified in terms of savings generated. The latest technology will not be adopted just because it can save labour. For example, while Ryanair does offer online check-in, it does not provide the equipment to permit customers to check themselves in at the airport in the way provided by other carriers.

*Human resource policies*

High productivity is fundamental to Ryanair's low cost base. To achieve this end, restrictive practices are strongly discouraged and multi-skilling encouraged. Cabin crew are not only expected to sell a wide variety of products, but also assist with cleaning and luggage if required. When the company took over Buzz, the low fares subsidiary of KLM, it was made clear to the staff that they would need to fly the same number of hours and sectors as Ryanair staff if they wished to retain their jobs.[16]

Employees are given responsibility to negotiate new purchase contracts, but they are also accountable for the outcomes. Various sanctions and incentives are available to achieve results. If pilots fail to complete the requisite number of flights per day, they suffer financially. Commissions are paid on in-flight sales to cabin crew. Since many staff members are also shareholders, they are owners as well as managers. However small the shareholding of any employee, he or she can thus, in some way, identify with the company's overall success or failure.

The culture in Ryanair is youthful, casual and irreverent, as illustrated by O'Leary's use of blunt and colourful language. It is supremely cost conscious and also confrontational. Cost reduction is a central policy, and no effort is spared to achieve that goal. Litigation with opponents is widespread, be they governments, the European Union, airport authorities, other airlines, unions, regulatory authorities or passengers themselves.

*Firm infrastructure*

The company is run on as lean a basis as possible and could never be accused of being over-manned. Staff perks, common in various legacy airlines, find no place in Ryanair. Consultants are rarely employed. There is no large head office. The former Dublin city centre office has long since been closed. Instead, the company operates from modest, largely open plan premises at Dublin airport.

## The overall strategy

Ryanair has grown spectacularly since its creation in 1985, particularly since Michael O'Leary was appointed CEO. The number of routes and destinations throughout Europe has increased rapidly over the years. Where routes fail to live up to expectations, they are unceremoniously axed. Consideration was given to extending the model to long-haul on the Atlantic routes, where the model might be more difficult to operate, but in due course this idea was shelved. Ryanair has retained its dominant low cost position with short-term price wars if appropriate, as the airline GO found to its cost. It has, on occasion, attempted predatory moves on other carriers such as Buzz and Aer Lingus. Mindful perhaps of Tony Ryan's former business, aircraft leasing company GPA, Ryanair has maintained a very strong liquidity position since its flotation.

Ryanair has, to date, managed to maintain a relatively low risk profile in a high-risk industry. O'Leary identifies the three major risks[17] as nuclear war in Europe, a major accident, and management failure. In 2010, he might have added a volcanic eruption. The airline's success is in no small measure due to the skilful management of each component of the value chain. The model is not rocket science, but implementation is taken to the extremes.

The value chain can provide a useful perspective on total costs. If it can be compared to that of a relevant competitor by some benchmarking process, as discussed in **Chapter 14**, then it can highlight costs needing attention. If there is no strategic reason for a higher cost, then the question arises as to why the organisation needs to continue with this activity. Why should it not be outsourced, as discussed in **Chapter 15?** In this way, any business should understand the basis of its competitive advantage and decide which activities could be better conducted by third parties. For a business providing a specialist product or service, it should be helpful to understand how it fits into the industry value chain, and whether it wishes to expand into other parts of the chain.

## Conclusions

- The value chain can provide a useful tool to examine the overall costs of any organisation.
- There are interesting features in the maximisation of revenue by Ryanair. These include:
    - The service offering
    - The product line

- Ryanair's approach to reduction of operating costs has some unusual features:
  - Differential customer pricing
  - Sources of income from customers
  - Income from partners
  - Exploitation of the brand
- Ryanair's approach to reduction of operating costs has some unusual features:
  - Staff flexibility and manning levels
  - Customer ordering and ticketing through the Internet
  - Systems for processing customers
  - The use of IT
  - Dealings with suppliers
  - Outsourcing
- Finally, there may be lessons from Ryanair's control of overheads:
  - The role and scale of the head office
  - Cheap sourcing
  - Publicity
  - Rewarding of staff
  - General elimination of costs
- Whether or not these ideas can be readily transferred to another business depends on the company's strategy and, in particular, its values.

## Management checklist

1. What is the value chain of the industry and how does your business fit in?
2. What are the key elements in your value chain and is it a useful way of examining your costs?
3. Would it be possible to use any elements of the Ryanair approach to its value chain in your business?
4. Which elements of 3. above would you decline because of a conflict with your strategy or values?
5. Would any ideas you could adopt lead to a sustainable cost advantage for your organisation?

# Chapter 10

# Deciding on size[1]

> "There are no great limits to growth because there are no limits of human intelligence, imagination and wonder."
>
> *Ronald Reagan*

The size of an organisation is likely to influence its costs in a very profound way. All too often smaller businesses believe it is impossible to compete effectively with much larger businesses, which can benefit from economies of scale (as mentioned in **Chapter 8**). Sometimes, however, large corporations are broken down into smaller business units to increase efficiency and reduce cost. In this chapter, a discussion of the drivers of economies and diseconomies of scale is followed by a review of some of the factors that may have caused the underlying determinants of economies of scale to have moved over time. This chapter is set out as follows:

- An optimal size?
- Economies of scale
- Diseconomies of scale
- Franchising
- Impact of globalisation
- Impact of technology
- The choice to remain small

## An optimal size?

What is the best size for your business? Most businesses are the size they are as a result of their particular history. Occasionally, owners such as Richard Branson of the Virgin Group will split businesses once they have reached a certain scale. An even more radical course of action has been adopted by Ricardo Semler, a Brazilian who divided his business, Semco, into highly autonomous factories run on democratic principles, involving the workforce in factory management. More normally, companies keep growing in size, provided the business is prospering, so that it is difficult to see what factors constitute the limits to growth. Key questions for any organisation to ask are: 'Would unit costs be lower if the business doubled its present size, or would they be lower if it were half the size?'

The question about size is frequently asked in the public sector as well as in the private sector. For example, what is the optimal size for a hospital? Larger hospitals can afford expensive equipment and a fuller range of consultants, which should assist in better diagnosis of patients' illnesses. But accusations are sometimes levelled at large hospitals for failing to follow up with proper procedures once problems have been detected. Are inefficiencies a likely or inevitable consequence of being large scale? Similarly, will a child obtain a better education from a secondary school of 200 pupils or one of 800 pupils with better facilities and a greater choice of courses?

This opens up the question of economies of scale, a topic which has been studied by economists for many years. The generally accepted economic theory of the firm is that, as a business grows, it should benefit from economies of scale up to a certain point. Beyond this point, diseconomies of scale arise, which results in higher unit costs to the firm. The costs are represented diagrammatically in **Figure 10.1.**

**Figure 10.1** illustrates that, under competitive conditions, firms are assumed to be price takers and face unlimited demand for their product at a given price, 'P'. As they grow initially, the marginal revenue from selling extra product declines, due to economies of scale. After a certain volume, diseconomies of scale arise, causing marginal costs to increase. Eventually, the marginal cost reaches the selling price at point 'S'. At this point, further

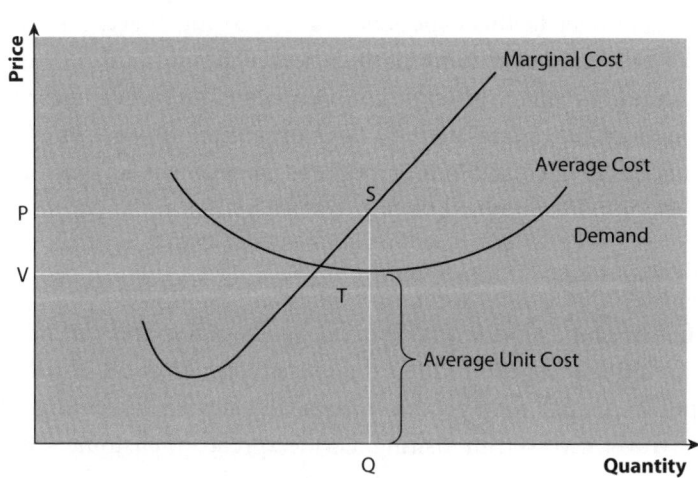

*Figure 10.1* 'Tracing the Typical Cost Curves of a Business'

expansion will diminish profits, so an optimal size is achieved. At the level of output at point 'Q', the average unit cost is significantly below the selling price, and total profit is maximised. The profits are represented by the rectangle 'PSTV'. So, what are these economies and diseconomies that limit the growth of the business and set a ceiling to profits of PSTV? We will examine these below.

## Economies of scale

Most people would expect that a large company should be able to produce goods more cheaply than a smaller company. But what are the underlying reasons for this advantage?

### Specialisation

The more specialised workers become, the better they should be able to perform a particular operation. Adam Smith's classic case of the pin factory, illustrating the savings, was described in **Chapter 8**. Other examples include shoe manufacturing or car production. In a service industry the same principle applies. If, for example, a large multinational business wished to retain an audit firm, it would be unlikely that a small practitioner would have the range of expertise required. Four large firms now dominate this business internationally and would expect to be able to produce experts on any complex audit problem.

As discussed in **Chapter 8**, the more times an operation is performed, the more efficient it should become and, therefore, the cheaper it should become. People loosely refer to this experience as a 'learning curve'. For example, it should not be necessary to reinvent the wheel each time a car is made. A large business should be able to generate core competencies that can be made available throughout the organisation. In large organisations, such as McDonald's restaurants or GEC, considerable trouble is taken to ensure that this knowledge is properly disseminated throughout the group.

### Economies of scope

Economies of scope arise when different goods or services can be provided more economically together rather than separately. Physical distribution is a case in point. A small food producer supplying supermarkets might find the time and travel involved in visiting a wide spread of customers to be very expensive. If the goods are distributed with another range of goods that the buyer needs, a lower cost might result. The use of a common brand with its associated image of quality can similarly provide economies of scope.

## Indivisible costs

Certain industries are subject to high fixed costs. For example, a toll road may be expensive to construct. The more people that use the road, the wider the cost can be spread, so that the fixed cost per traveller reduces as traffic increases. To research a drug sufficiently to obtain Food and Drug Administration approval in the US can take many years. A small company cannot afford the time and investment in research and development required to obtain approval.

## Economies of increased dimension

Transport and storage costs tend to relate to area, while capacity increases with volume. If the height of a tank is doubled, the capacity will double, but the cost of material will not proportionately increase, because no new base is required. Similarly, the cost of stocks or inventories should not increase proportionately to sales. Network costs behave in the same manner, which is an important consideration for the telecommunications industry. Metcalfe's Law, first propounded around 1980, states that the value of the network enterprise increases with the square of the number of participants. It is, thus, hard for a small network to compete with a large rival.

## Increased buying power

Large-scale organisations have the ability to negotiate favourable prices from suppliers, as any supplier to a supermarket chain knows too well. The supermarket can offer to take large volumes, which lessens the number of transactions and costs of the supplier. A telephone call to sell one screw costs the same as a call to sell a million screws. The same volume of business undertaken by one salesman to a supermarket may equate to five or more salesmen selling to smaller outlets. The large business may have a similar advantage in negotiating rates of interest with its bankers.

It can be seen that economies of scale impact most cost areas of a business. Larger companies should have the advantage in purchasing, manufacturing, storage, distribution, marketing, research and finance. But what stops businesses growing ever bigger until all industries are dominated by a small number of businesses? Are there factors which can lead to the extinction of the mammoths or at least inhibit their further growth? In practice, it seems that scale can generate diseconomies, as well as economies of scale.

## Diseconomies of scale

### Communication requirements

As networks grow, so too does the number of relationships, which leads to demands for extra management information. The small firm owner–manager will often make decisions by the 'seat of his pants'. As people meet less face-to-face, there is a need for more formal information systems. Good decisions need good information, which comes at a cost. Complex enterprise resource planning systems, such as SAP, used by large organisations, do not come cheaply.

### Management control

As the volume of information increases, so normally does the amount of control. The number of managers and the managerial levels increase. Control systems are introduced and decision-making slowed down. Bureaucracy increases and responsiveness to customers' needs suffers. As companies become more dominant, they may become subject to greater regulatory scrutiny, obliging them to introduce yet more controls. Often, duplication occurs and internal rivalries flourish. All these features can add significantly to cost and diminish flexibility.

### Loss of employee motivation

Specialisation should enhance skills but, if carried to excess, can lead to boredom, loss of motivation and inertia. Individuals often become isolated and less connected with the overall success of the business. This is not limited to the operator on a production line repeating the same monotonous task day after day. It can apply equally to a call centre employee in his or her cubicle, reading from some manual in response to customer problems. Disenchanted workers may join trade unions, introduce restrictive practices or resort to industrial action, all of which can add considerably to the cost base.

Diseconomies of scale have sufficiently worried businesses into considering their optimal size, particularly those that value high flexibility and speed of response to customers' needs. There have been surprising changes in the scale of some businesses where large scale was traditionally a prerequisite. Micro-breweries and mini-steel mills now exist. Even governments sometimes attempt to find ways to reduce their scale. In large-scale manufacturing there has been an increased tendency towards working in small teams, rather than on one giant assembly line, thereby enhancing communication and motivation, while not sacrificing control. In the field of communications, bloggers can reach thousands of readers with minimal investment, transforming the economics of that industry.[2] 'Small is beautiful' has emerged as a motto for organisations, where traditionally size and scale were seen as desirable.

While the economies of scale are based on a certain inherent logic, the same cannot be said for the diseconomies. Communications, control, motivation and industrial relations are issues for management to address. While these problems are commonly met with growth in scale, they can in many cases, when combined with good management, be at least mitigated There is no point in growth where economies must become diseconomies. Effective outsourcing, modern operations methods that emphasise 'lean' management philosophy and management of the labour force may provide assistance. But, before addressing these matters in subsequent chapters, it may be helpful to examine some factors that may cause businesses to reconsider their optimal size.

---

*Factors influencing the optimal size*

- It may be possible to organise a business to minimise the diseconomies, while benefiting from economies of scale.
- Globalisation may have shifted the goalposts.
- Changes in technology open up new possibilities.
- Some businesses may opt to remain small, irrespective of the disadvantages.

---

## Franchising[3]

Franchising has shown how businesses can grow by combining the advantages of scale with the entrepreneurship of the small-scale organisation. The word itself is derived from a French word for 'freedom from slavery'. It is a widely used concept, particularly in the service industry, from the motor trade to printing, but especially in the area of fast food. In retailing, the turnover of the leading symbol groups can challenge the scale of the large supermarket chains.

The franchisor can provide many of the benefits of a large organisation: the original research and development, the brand, equipment, training, accounting systems and bulk buying of materials. The franchisee, on the other hand, should be able to avoid the usual diseconomies, being motivated to maximise sales and avoid red tape, while employing a small workforce. The fees payable and the responsibilities of the two parties are set out in the franchise agreement.

In some cases, franchising can be set up to reduce the traditional adversarial relationship that can exist between customer and supplier, as they negotiate terms of trade. For example, some department stores have used their established brand name, customer base and location to benefit franchisees or 'concessionaires'. Instead of charging the market rent for the premises, a commission is charged as a percentage of the franchisee's sales.[4] The effect is to change a high fixed cost into a more manageable variable cost. Thus, in a recession, the franchisee may continue in business, while paying out a smaller fee and the property owner can avoid vacant space.

While franchising is normally associated with the service sector, it is not restricted to that area. Agriculture has adapted the model to mushroom production through a system of satellite growers who produce mushrooms independently. The franchisee or grower buys compost and supplies from the franchisor, who buys the product at predetermined prices once it has been harvested.

Franchising also operates in the hotel industry. In Britain, the Intercontinental group, which owns the Intercontinental, Holiday Inn and Crown Plaza brands, has sold most of its hotels and franchises the brand. The hotel owner may delegate the running of the hotel either to the brand owner or a totally different company. Another company may provide the staff, and an outside caterer may manage the restaurants, creating a 'virtual' hotel.[5] Thus, small businesses can run large hotels with famous brand names.

## Impact of globalisation

Some multinational companies may have seen themselves operating in a global market for many years, but the process has enormously accelerated in the last 20 years.[6] Just as many EU-based companies were wrestling with opportunities arising from the Single European Market and the enlargement of the EU, an even wider world vista was opening up. This not only opened new markets, but also offered new ways of working on a global platform. 'Think global, act local' became the new mantra.

Technological developments have, in many cases, revolutionised the costs of working across national boundaries. Technological changes can be spread with incredible speed. The advancement of the Internet and online communications such as e-mail provided a cheap means of communication throughout the world. Search engines, in particular Google, allowed users access to information almost instantaneously at negligible costs. Mobile phones too have improved the effectiveness of communications and greatly reduced costs.

These technological changes have affected companies in different ways. Larger global markets may lead to greater scale and provide scope for greater economies. Change has been aided by forms of collaboration that were previously inconceivable, and the world of 'Wikinomics'[7] was created. With information often free, it has become possible to research projects that would previously have been eliminated due to indivisible high fixed costs. In future it may be possible to dispense with some in-house specialist skills, and learning curves may be rapidly accelerated.

A by-product of globalisation and the relaxation of immigration controls have resulted in much greater transnational labour mobility. The availability of industrious immigrants, whether skilled or unskilled, has provided many businesses facing labour shortages with the possibility to reduce their labour costs. There may also be deeper benefits from the information these diverse diasporas bring with them.[8] Immigrants tend to maintain strong ethnic social networks, which enable them to import innovative cost-saving ideas and resources from their home countries which rely more heavily on skilful workforce management rather than intensive capital investment.

Nevertheless, the changes brought about by globalisation can be two-edged. They have not only enabled companies to look outward from their domestic base at lower cost, but have also permitted others outside their company to communicate inwards more cheaply. Small operators can now easily upload information. Common standards, open sourcing and software packages all assist the transfer of back-office functions from high-cost developed countries to lower-cost developing countries. Small businesses may be able to compete as part of a global business against elements of the large, traditional, well-established, integrated multinationals.

The above changes have provided a powerful impetus to outsourcing, discussed in **Chapter 15**. Outsourcing tended originally to be 'on-shore' sourcing. Now it can be equally 'off-shore' or 'near-shore' sourcing. The era of low oil prices and cheap energy also assisted the process, although now, with increased transport costs, some of these benefits may have been dissipated.

Nevertheless, very many businesses must now look at their costs on a much broader basis than before. Whether this is forced on them by new competition in their existing markets or by the exploitation of new opportunities globally does not matter. For all these reasons, it may be time to re-examine the traditional economies of scale.

## Impact of technology

Technological developments have caused managers to reconsider fundamentally their business models. It may be profitable to exploit the 'long tail'[9] of a normal statistical distribution, where a relatively small amount of the population is to be found. One such example on product range is the impact of electronic distribution at minimal cost through the downloading of products over the Internet by the customer. In the music industry, the focus was on the big hits. If a record could sell millions of copies it was worth the investment needed to distribute it as widely as possible. If, on the other hand, it was only likely to sell a few thousand copies, then it was unlikely to be heavily backed. The old rule of thumb, promulgated by the Italian economist Vilfredo Paretto, was that 20% of the products generated 80% of the profits, so it was that 20% where the focus of effort should be made.

With the arrival of electronic distribution of music, the goalposts moved. Investment in physical stocks was no longer necessary. It was easy to upload music and distribute it by download at minimal cost. It, therefore, became economic to cater for minority interests. Albums could be assembled to cater for individual tastes. In short, most or all of the remaining 80% could become profitable business. The tail, as measured in statistical terms, had lengthened. The traditional economies of scale no longer applied.

Emerging technologies may further transform economies of scale. It has been suggested that three-dimensional printing will change the world fundamentally.[10] It may be possible to produce individual items almost as cheaply as those that are currently mass produced based on parts standardisation, combining efficiency and flexibility. Manufacturing may no longer require factories, thus reducing barriers to entry to many industries. If three-dimensional printing were to become widely used/available, many businesses may choose not to be supplied by remote factories, which result in high transport costs. It has even been suggested that these technological changes will create a third industrial revolution, reversing the trend to offshoring and causing businesses to relocate nearer to their customers.[11]

Interestingly, technology businesses look at scale from a novel viewpoint, that of 'scalability'. A new product requires substantial research costs but, often, minimal cost of adding additional users. Thus, it has high fixed costs and low marginal costs. If the business can be expanded exponentially without significant extra cost, then large profits are possible. In this context developments of the social media, such as Facebook and Twitter, have enabled businesses to access new customers at very little expense. The business model and IT architecture need to be designed to achieve this scalability. Changing technology may provide yet another reason why the basic determinants of the economies and diseconomies of scale may have changed.

## The choice to remain small

It may well be that many businesses could lower their unit costs and increase their profits if they were to operate on a larger scale. Nevertheless, many owner–managers prefer to remain small, because profit maximisation is not their overriding objective. Owner–managers may resent the discipline and loss of freedom that inevitably accompany growth, so sometimes the less onerous reporting and regulatory requirements afforded to SMEs provide an incentive to remain small. Some restaurateurs or shopkeepers may wish to run multiple premises, but many more do not share this ambition. In most countries, the vast majority of businesses remain SMEs, though not necessarily representing most of the output and employment.

Staying small, of course, does not guarantee survival. Many family businesses, which have traded successfully for generations, may find it impossible to compete with the giants that invade their territory. Most independent shopkeepers suffer when supermarkets open in the same vicinity. In a recession, business failures increase and competition may intensify as large businesses seek new outlets for their products or services. For many small businesses without a very distinct market niche, staying small may not be an option. Without significant financial reserves, many are forced into a struggle for subsistence.

It would appear that globalisation and changes in technology offer the possibility for businesses to expand very significantly, if they so wish. If the diseconomies of scale can be avoided through good organisation, such as that provided by franchising, or simply better management, then the barriers to growth can be shifted, if not eliminated.

Diagrammatically the cost curves would change as shown in **Figure 10.2**:

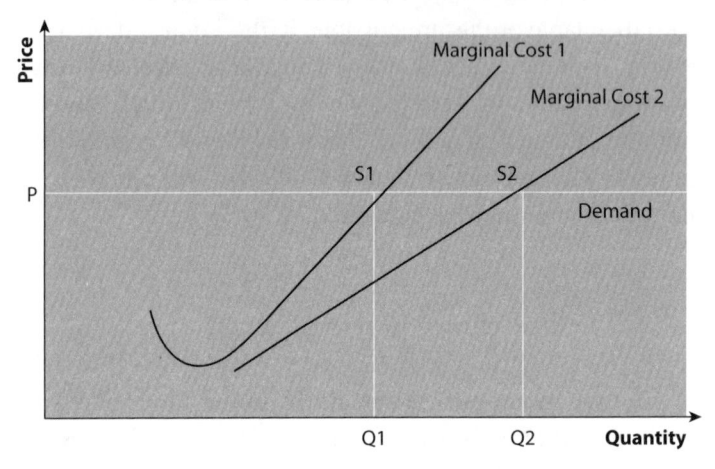

*Figure 10.2*  **Tracing the Cost Curves of a Business Successfully Managing Diseconomies of Scale**

The marginal cost curve of a business which can successfully manage diseconomies of scale would rise much more gradually, so the point where it intersects marginal revenue would occur at a significantly higher level of production. This in turn would lower average unit costs and increase average profit margins. Both the size of the profits and the optimal size of the firm are also much increased from that shown in **Figure 10.1** above.

There is no obvious optimal size for many businesses, but the balance seems to be moving in favour of larger organisations. Certainly big firms can be slow to respond to changing tastes or disruptive technologies. But the Southern Eurozone peripheral states, dominated by small firms, have experienced slow economic growth. A shortage of big firms has been linked to sluggish productivity and loss of competitiveness.[12] The skilful use of modern operational techniques, described in **Part III**, points to the way costs can be contained as the business grows.

## Conclusions

- Without doubt, economies of scale can be achieved by specialisation and other factors.
- Equally, some large organisations develop diseconomies due to their scale.

- Franchising has enabled some businesses to grow, while avoiding the diseconomies of scale.
- Changes in globalisation and technology have enabled businesses to increase their scale very substantially, while avoiding most of the diseconomies of scale.
- There is no obvious optimal size for a business. It is the challenge of management to grow the business, while minimising the diseconomies.

## Management checklist

1. Would your unit costs be:
   a) Lower if your business was twice the size?
   b) Lower if it were half the size?
2. Do you benefit as much as you can from economies of scale?
3. Do you suffer from diseconomies of scale?
4. To what extent could you curb diseconomies of scale by:
   a) Better use of technology?
   b) Outsourcing?
   c) Better use of modern operational tools, especially 'lean' techniques?
   d) Better human resource management?
5. Do, or will, the forces of globalisation affect your economies or diseconomies of scale and the optimal size of your business?
6. Do new means of distribution or emerging technology change your economies of scale?
7. What size business do you wish to be?

**Part II** of this book, covering strategic considerations, is now complete. In the next part we will look at the modern operational ways of analysing and managing costs. This will outline how leading companies can embrace growth, while simultaneously reducing their cost base. While many of these aids are drawn from the experience of large global companies, it will also be shown through examples how these techniques can be used by much smaller organisations.

# Part III

# Using modern operational aids to analyse and manage costs, providing a path to 'leanness' and continuous improvement

# Chapter 11

# World class and lean manufacturing

"A leader is best when people barely know he exists, not so good when people obey and acclaim him, worse when they despise him...But of a good leader who talks little when his work is done, his aim fulfilled, they will say, 'We did it ourselves'."

*Lao Tzu, Chinese Philosopher*

Advances in the field of operations have provided managers with new ways to examine and analyse their costs. In the 1980s Western businesses sought to improve their operations by becoming *quicker, better and cheaper*. Their aim was to achieve superior performance and become 'world class' by choosing best practice, wherever it was to be found. To assist themselves in these tasks, they inevitably focussed their attention on the country usually considered to provide the best role model, namely Japan.[1] While many of these advances originated in manufacturing, they have also been adopted within the service industry. We will start our treatment of these tools, which fall within the broad ambit of 'World Class Manufacturing (WCM)' and 'lean' manufacturing, under the following headings:

- Introduction
- WCM techniques
- Core principles of WCM
- WCM – getting started
- WCM roadmap
- Continuous improvement
- The 7 Steps sequence of problem-solving
- Aids to each of the steps
- 'Lean thinking'
- Service industry example – specialist legal practice
- Combining 'lean' with activity-based budgeting: a North American example

## Introduction

Strategic cost reduction involves a systemic approach to eliminating waste, enhancing quality and expanding throughput. The powerful techniques outlined in this chapter require a shift from a traditional approach to a 'lean' thinking approach, which is the pursuit of perfection using a rigorous approach to creating value and reducing cost.

The lean thinking technique inverts traditional hierarchical approaches, creating instead a team-based culture and a focus on the customer. Once the domain of large manufacturing companies, the approach (usually termed World Class Manufacturing or WCM) is now successfully applied in service companies, professional service organisations, government organisations and, increasingly, in small companies. Diagramatically,[2] it is summarised in **Figure 11.1** below.

The set of techniques within WCM is so comprehensive that it can actually serve to obscure the simplicity of the approach. Fundamentally, WCM and all its variants are pre-planned, customer-focussed, evidence-based, team-oriented, learning experiments. As will be shown later, if the philosophy is embraced, substantial benefits, including cost savings, can be gained almost immediately.

*Figure 11.1*  **World Class Manufacturing**

## WCM techniques

The array of WCM techniques includes:

- TQM (Total Quality Management – the philosophy of WCM)
- TPS (Toyota Production System – the original version of WCM)
- Just-in-time (JIT – delivering just what is needed, when needed)
- Lean operations (the elimination of all kinds of waste in resources)
- Six Sigma (the pursuit for zero defects through statistical control)
- TPM (Total Productive Maintenance) – practical application of TQM
- Kaizen (7 Steps – continuous improvement – problem-solving)
- Benchmarking (the search for best practice – see **Chapter 14**)
- Outsourcing (re-configuring the value chain – see **Chapter 15**)

The essence of WCM is the elimination of waste, such as lost time, overproduction, production of defective goods, unnecessary motion, re-work, bureaucracy, approvals and inspections. This strategically reduces costs to their inherent minimum. While elimination of waste is the goal, it can only be achieved by applying the techniques to the underlying processes and by consciously developing a learning culture in an organisation willing to confront reality and embrace change proactively.

WCM can be assimilated into an organisation by examining in turn:

- The core principles of WCM
- Continuous improvement
- Radical improvement
- Business process re-engineering
- Benchmarking
- Outsourcing

## Core principles of WCM

WCM is effective in reducing costs because it goes beyond traditional thinking. It rests on the belief that there are no limits to improvement, and that improvements can be systematically accessed through an unending series of planned changes ('experiments') undertaken in the workplace.[3] The tools and techniques are summarised in **Figure 11.2**.[4]

The WCM credo maintains that those closest to the work are best positioned to see the opportunities for improvement. These people, therefore,

134  Strategic Cost Reduction

*Figure 11.2*  **World Class Manufacturing – Tools and Techniques**

| Lowest Cost |||
|---|---|---|
| **Radical Improvement**<br>**Lean – Zero Waste**<br>Business Process<br>Re-engineering<br><br>***Just-in-Time***<br>Quick change-over<br>Flow: Pull, not Push<br>Simplicity<br>Total coordination<br>Outsource non-core | **People and Teamwork**<br>Ongoing Learning<br>Common Vision<br><br>**Disciplined Approach**<br><br>**Process Innovation**<br>Customer Orientation | ***Continuous Improvement***<br>***Six Sigma***<br>Zero defects<br>Total quality<br>Team Problem-solving<br>7 Steps<br>Autonomy<br>Empowerment<br>Pride in the work<br>TPM + 5 S |
| Deliberate Design of Operations |||
| Stable Standardised Processes as Baseline for Improvement |||
| Simplicity and Simplified Management |||
| Management Philosophy – TQM – Employee Engagement |||

*must* be 'empowered' to implement the resulting changes. While acceptance can seem like management *nirvana*, with the workforce implementing an endless series of planned changes, many managers are uncomfortable making the leap, as it implies a reduction in their own authority. Those who do accept are usually amply rewarded with lower costs and a reputation for progressive thinking, in addition to being seen to be capable of delegating and of unleashing workplace creativity. The management role becomes one of leading by example, of teaching rather than supervising, of developing processes rather than controlling people. As John F. Kennedy said: "Leadership and learning are indispensable to each other."

## WCM – getting started

While WCM can seem daunting, real benefits can readily be extracted, provided a *philosophy of learning and controlled experimentation* is adopted. The success of this approach rests on a *willingness to challenge, coach and confront staff in a systematic way.* **Figure 11.3** below illustrates its dimensions.[5]

The tools are important, but the main challenge is the adoption of the WCM philosophy, especially 'lean thinking'. As John Shook, Toyota's first

American manager in Japan, stated: "WCM is a manufacturing *philosophy*, which shortens the timeline between the customer order and the shipment by eliminating waste."

*Figure 11.3* **WCM – Philosophy of Learning and Improvement**

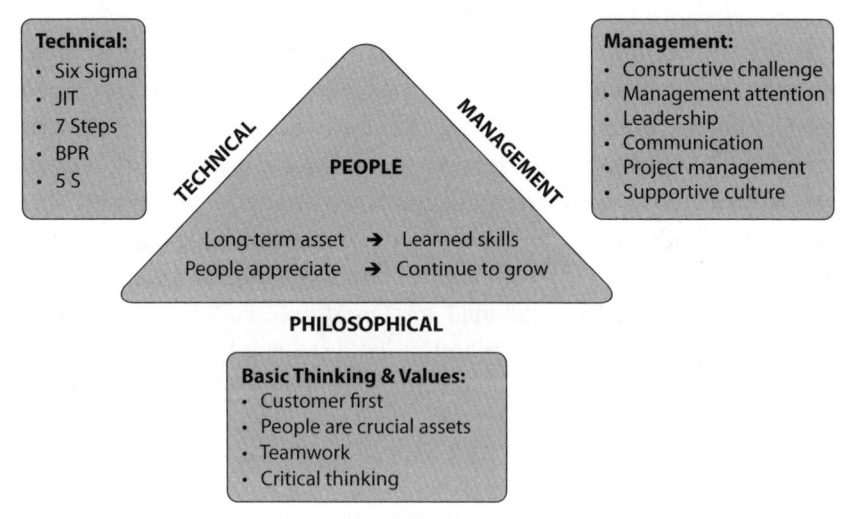

**Technical:**
- Six Sigma
- JIT
- 7 Steps
- BPR
- 5 S

**PEOPLE**

**TECHNICAL** / **MANAGEMENT**

Long-term asset → Learned skills
People appreciate → Continue to grow

**Management:**
- Constructive challenge
- Management attention
- Leadership
- Communication
- Project management
- Supportive culture

**PHILOSOPHICAL**

**Basic Thinking & Values:**
- Customer first
- People are crucial assets
- Teamwork
- Critical thinking

## WCM roadmap

There are many ways in which to embark on WCM, but perhaps the most practical is to convene a small team to address issues in a particular part of a troublesome process; to simply learn-by-doing. This provides the opportunity to develop understanding of the WCM philosophy, to generate team spirit and, indeed, to make cost savings immediately.

It also sets the tone and captures early benefits by soliciting, refining and applying ideas about selected work areas, and does this in an informal way, in the workplace itself, close to the operation concerned, involving those doing the work.

When the more obvious areas for cost reduction have been exhausted, the manager then moves to a more systematic approach, using group-based problem-solving techniques to foster continuous improvement (see the '*7 Steps*' panel at **Figure 11.4**).[6]

When this approach reaches its limits, managers should analyse an unsatisfactory process and see what can be done to streamline it. Then they should re-design the operation to make it leaner, cheaper and better able to deliver just what customers actually need.

While suggestion schemes and 'quality circles' have very low success rates due to their unstructured, serendipitous nature, the simple act of bringing together staff to address easily-rectifiable problems usually generates excellent responses. It can also enhance staff morale by providing a convivial forum for staff involvement and relieving some of the trivial, but burdensome, issues which bear down on most organisations.

The initial meeting, typically of less than an hour's duration, should be stage-managed to promote a suitable atmosphere which encourages problem identification and potential solutions. The key to success, in what is essentially a structured brainstorming exercise, is to limit the range of suggested improvements to those which can be implemented at no-or-low cost almost immediately. Under such conditions, there is little likelihood that people will feel their idea was unfairly rejected, a common cause of team collapse. If personalised criticisms are excluded, as they should be, and if management proceeds without delay, the momentum gathered can be considerable, with significant cost savings and/or productivity gains within the first few months.

## Continuous improvement

After the initial wave of fixes and solutions, which are often the correction of simple issues, such as repairing broken equipment, moving equipment, or communicating better, momentum tends to dry up. To obtain continuous improvement, there is a need to move to a more refined and systematic approach, using a defined routine, team-based form of problem-solving, following a sequence of defined steps, such as those shown in **Figure 11.4**.[7]

This system helps overcome the usual difficulties in problem-solving by specifying each step and by clarifying goals, roles and responsibilities. It discovers true root causes by repeatedly probing 'why' something is happening. It promotes good planning and checks that the solution actually works. Proven solutions are then standardised to become new best practice and the platform for the next round of changes.

The problems to be addressed, in this case, should not originate from staff, but should be proposed by management. Teams are recruited to join the initiative and to prepare solutions after examination of the facts. Actual implementation can often be understood by a different team if the solution involves, for example, a modification to an IT system, a new marketing campaign or another cross-functional project.

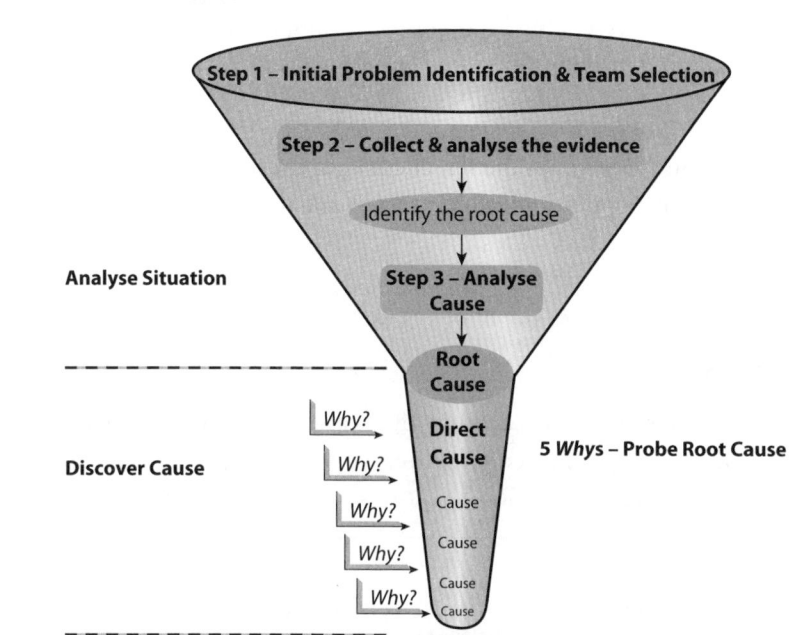

*Figure 11.4* **Continuous Improvement and the *7 Steps* Problem-Solving Method**

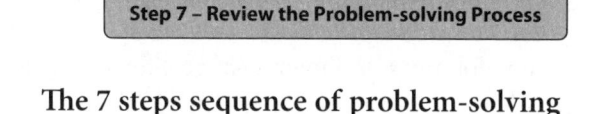

*The diagram shows a funnel with:*

- Step 1 – Initial Problem Identification & Team Selection
- Step 2 – Collect & analyse the evidence
- Identify the root cause
- Step 3 – Analyse Cause
- Root Cause
- 5 Whys – Probe Root Cause (Why? Why? Why? Why? Why? → Direct Cause, Cause, Cause, Cause, Cause)

*Left-side labels:* **Analyse Situation**, **Discover Cause**, **Plan and Implement Solution**

- Step 4 – Decide and Plan Countermeasures
- Step 5 – Evaluate if Solution is Effective
- Step 6 – Standardise the New Process
- Step 7 – Review the Problem-solving Process

## The 7 steps sequence of problem-solving

**Step 1** concentrates on discovering and agreeing the ***appropriate goal*** and on selecting the core team to initiate the improvement cycle. In the interest of avoiding disappointment or even staff resentment, it is worthwhile to have the teams propose a range of at least three solutions to a particular problem, so that the final choice can be selected by a manager. Indeed, it is useful to set the expectation that the final solution can be a combination of the proposed solutions, or even a still newer idea.

**Step 2** entails the collection and ***analysis of data***. The solutions selected should be based on some form of evidence to avoid bias and distortion. Where the data itself produces a compelling conclusion, the cause of the problem will be evident.

**Step 3** seeks the fundamental *root cause of the problem*. If the data from Step 2 did not itself reveal an apparent root cause, the group must brainstorm likely causes. To channel the brainstorming activity, generic potential causes are explored, usually along four dimensions:

> The '4 M' branches prompt the search for root causes along four dimensions that are generally applicable to most situations:
>
> Methods
> Manpower
> Machinery
> Materials
>
> It can be important to dig deep in the search for root cause to avoid superficial fixes. By repeatedly asking 'why', the deeper causes can be discovered. Solutions can then be more soundly based.

**Step 4** When the most likely root cause is finally agreed, the team can move to proposing and project-planning the selected *solutions*.

**Step 5** The loop is closed by *verifying* that the proposed solution actually was effective. This is done by comparing the outcomes here to the data or other evidence available at Step 2 and verifying that true gains were made, without deterioration of other aspects or unintended consequences.

**Step 6** The gains are captured by *institutionalising the changes*, usually into a new formal procedure or new protocol. This newly-standardised process becomes the baseline for any subsequent change efforts, as needed.

**Step 7** *The problem-solving process is reviewed*. This is an important, if often neglected, feedback step, in which the problem-solving routine (and the accompanying team dynamics) is reviewed. It is important to assess, not judge, how each preceding step was handled, asking questions such as:.

- Did we set realistic goals in Step 1?
- Were we good at putting together the initial and final teams?
- Did we capture and analyse sufficient data in Step 2?
- Were we sufficiently rigorous in analysing the actual root causes?
- Did we fail to go below the superficial level in Step 3?
- Were we good at suggesting solutions in Step 4?

- Did we verify the implementation well in Step 5?
- Did we capture the new process, or revert to old ways in Step 6?
- Were we good at maintaining the team in Step 7?

Managers should select only a few problems or projects initially. The main aim is to gain acceptance of continuous improvement as a philosophy, and to teach the methods by doing a few improvement cycles, before progressing to more challenging problems and techniques.

Limit the effort to three problem-solving projects per person per year initially, but expect each team to produce very substantial returns through reliably higher yields, considerably less re-work, fewer returns, lower inventory, faster turnaround, higher morale, or greater teamwork.

Conclude this structured approach to problem-solving by asking each team to present their story in a highly visual fashion, as this both promotes clarity of presentation and generates peer pressure. Consider holding a high-profile event where these achievements are showcased, recognised and rewarded.

## Aids to each of the steps

The skills needed depend on the step involved: analytical ability is needed in Step 2, but creativity can be needed in Step 3. Step 4 demands an aptitude for planning, while Step 5 needs an implementation bias. Step 6 needs procedural skills, while Step 7 needs skill in reviewing team performance. For these reasons, a team approach is preferred, since the diverse talents of the individuals involved can be harnessed at the appropriate step.

The leader of the problem-solving team should understand team members' differing capabilities and be able to avoid inherent personality clashes.

Eventually, a more sophisticated approach will yield results; for example:

- Step 1 – Better goal-setting and team-formation methods
- Step 2 – Statistical process control techniques
- Step 3 – Creative brainstorming tools
- Step 4 – Advanced project planning and decision-making
- Step 5 – Skilled data analysis
- Step 6 – Better change management approaches
- Step 7 – Better feedback and reflection techniques

## 'Lean thinking'

As explained in **Figures 11.1** and **11.2** 'lean' is a subset of WCM. It seeks to eliminate all forms of waste, which is normally defined as anything for which a customer is unwilling to pay. But 'lean' also aims to improve quality and production time, while simultaneously reducing costs. Performed successfully, it can reduce material cost, investment, stocks, physical space and labour.

In one sense, it is a very traditional concept. Industrial engineers have sought to make manufacturing processes more efficient by eliminating unnecessary movement. Initially, time and motion experts, armed with stopwatches, searched for ways to increase the productivity of labour. This, in turn, developed into work study, which was used for job evaluation and pay determination under piecework systems. Such practices were unpopular with the labour force, where they were seen as a means to make work tougher and, consequently, could be strongly resisted by unions.

Lean manufacturing, on the other hand, is firmly rooted in Japanese culture, so the means to achieve greater productivity are very different. Improvements are not imposed by an alien management hierarchy. Rather, they derive from teamwork, involving everyone in the process of making improvements and cutting down unnecessary waste. Invariably, businesses choose the car manufacturer Toyota as their role model. The Toyota systems are set out in detail in the next chapter.

Lean thinking has its origins in manufacturing, particularly in large-scale organisations. Examples include tool manufacturing, wire management systems, aircraft engine and car manufacturing.[8] Lean thinking is now employed in a wide range of organisations, including the service sector. More recent examples include businesses as diverse as ship repair, iron-ore mining, health laboratories and management of nuclear plants.[9] Different companies, large or small, have different reasons for embracing lean thinking to manage the business, and also approach it in a variety of different ways, as the following examples illustrate.

The world-famous Guinness brewery, situated at St James's Gate in Dublin, dates from the 18th Century. For years it was run by gentlemen brewers, Oxbridge educated and often holding sporting blues. At the end of the 1960s, it had over 4,000 employees, who were treated in a paternalistic manner. By 1986, when it took over Distillers, the Scottish whisky business, employee numbers had been reduced to 2,000. In 1997, when Guinness-UDV merged with Grand Metropolitan to become Diageo, a leading global beverage business, of which beers constituted only a small part, the Dublin brewery was operating with less than 1,000 personnel on the back of extensive capital investment and automation. However, based on benchmarking studies, costs were a major concern, and the possibility was mooted that the brewery could be closed and production moved to London.

By 2000, a change plan, including a generous early retirement package, was negotiated, ending demarcation disputes and putting in place 'annualised time contracts', which eliminated overtime and encouraged higher productivity. Production teams were encouraged to learn at work, up-skilling and cross-skilling.[10] These changes provided a platform for the progressive implementation of WCM, lean manufacturing and asset care philosophies, which increased efficiency to Four Sigma levels and reduced unit production costs significantly. Since 2005, following the closure of the London brewery, the Dublin brewery produces Guinness for export to the UK. In 2011, Diageo had about 5,000 employees throughout Europe, of which approximately one-third were based in Ireland. The Dublin brewery continues to reduce its unit production costs every year and operates with a team of less than 150 personnel, a reduction of more than 95% over a 50-year period.

Carton Brothers is a long-established family business, trading for over 200 years, buying and supplying chickens to the Dublin market. Over 50 years ago, it turned to broiler production. It now employs 650 people and contracts with a further 150 farmers, producing 800,000 birds per week. To survive and grow in a competitive commodity market, the company embarked on a 'lean' programme with the assistance of external consultants. It benchmarked its performance globally and embraced measurements to identify market and cost-reduction opportunities.

Colorman operates in a similarly competitive industry – printing – which is well-accustomed to overcapacity and business failure. Its customers included many major multinationals, which insisted on a 'lean' approach from their suppliers. Accordingly, the company espoused a mixture of delegation, teamwork and flexibility to reduce production lead-times, along with a focus on continuous improvement. Such an approach has enabled it to thrive in difficult trading conditions and remain one of the few profitable printing businesses in the region.

'Lean' uses a range of tools, such as process mapping, physical tracking and run charts. But for any enterprise to implement 'lean' successfully, it should fulfil the following four criteria:[11]

- Operate in a competitive, free market environment
- Focus on customers
- Concentrate on waste elimination
- Orient towards the long term, rather than the short term.

Without this mindset an enterprise is unlikely to adopt the necessary rigour entailed in proper implementation of the 'lean' philosophy.

If organisations meet these four criteria, but have limited experience of lean systems and wish to proceed, they may benefit from external assistance. In Ireland, businesses may be able to benefit from State assistance if they wish to embark on such a course.[12]

Of course, adopting 'lean' in itself does not guarantee success. British Airways proclaimed that the planning for the opening of the new Terminal 5 at Heathrow Airport in 2008 was based on using lean techniques for its IT processes. The chaos that accompanied its opening did little to win recruits for a lean philosophy. The following two, very different, businesses demonstrate how 'lean' can be implemented successfully.

## Service industry example – specialist legal practice

Tomkins is an international firm of intellectual property (IP) attorneys. Voted Irish IP firm of the year in 2010, it has offices in Germany, the UK and Ireland, and employs approximately 35 lawyers and 25 administrative staff between the three offices. IP attorneys must possess both a deep knowledge of a technical discipline and an extensive capability in legal matters. Such dual-qualified people are scarce and valuable, so their time must be well spent if they are to be net contributors to the business.

Tomkins's services include IP auditing, IP research and licensing, due diligence exercises, drafting, filing and prosecuting, tax exemption matters, patenting, trade mark protection, copyrighting, agent authorisation, clearance searching, registration services, and the establishment of domain rights – a veritable array of complex services underpinned by the need for stringent administration.

Administrative delays in annual registration in any of a number of countries would cause missed deadlines and could incur the potential loss of a substantial patent. Clearly, there is much to go wrong and much which requires careful coordination across departments.

Traditionally, Tomkins used conventional managerial approaches to fine-tune the system, becoming leading-edge players in terms of software sophistication and the progressive treatment of staff.

The standard processes for the industry could be characterised as fragmented and manually driven, entailing multiple handovers and many opportunities for error or omission. One of the flaws, ironically, was 'false timeliness' arising from the premature closing of files, causing elements to be overlooked and consequently deadlines passing unnoticed. 'False positives' were also potential sources of problems, when items were incorrectly registered as being complete. Other weaknesses included excessive movement of files between departments. Work also tended to 'bottleneck', causing schedule congestion and stresses.

Sensing the possibilities of adapting 'lean' techniques that originated in manufacturing, one of the partners set about selectively applying the Toyota principles to critical administrative processes as follows:

- *Staff involvement and pride building*

First, they shared the practice's overall aims and strategic priorities with staff and explained the underlying purposes of key tasks. An immediate consequence of involving staff and immediately making improvements was a natural sense of achievement. This was deepened when the company won a string of national awards and industry accolades.

- *Mapping the value and ditching the waste*

Secondly, they sat with staff and looked with a fresh perspective at the process defects in the system. To their pleasant surprise, they found there was much replication of data entry, unnecessary logging, and excessive delays, all of which could immediately be eradicated, thus freeing up staff time and streamlining operations.

- *Comparing and contrasting processes with leading practices*

When they compared processes with similar practices, they found that they were in no way inferior. However, when they looked outside the legal profession, they discovered many ripe opportunities that they quickly seized.

- *Eliminating bottlenecks*

The company realised that an optimum way to reduce schedule overload was to manage the bottleneck, rather than the entire system. Every operation has a 'pinch point', which limits capacity, but may be relieved by adding resources or through sharper scheduling.

- *Using 'visual' management of work*

The fragmentation of work caused some tasks to be completed late and others prematurely, causing occasional missed deadlines. Reducing overlap between functions by combining roles helped. But the real breakthrough came from re-organising files according to due date and by providing clarity on which tasks needed to be done next. This was simply achieved by installing a rack of very visible time-ordered folders, organised on a month-by-month basis according to 'need' date, rather than task commencement.

- *Empowering staff*

The sheer eminence of IP lawyers can inadvertently prompt a sense of distance with other staff. The firm was clear in valuing all its employees and demonstrated this with a series of all-staff forums that encouraged inputs from all levels. A little after hours socialising helped lubricate the social joints, too!

Overall, the company was able to report a 30% reduction in standard leadtimes, error reduction to near zero levels, increased customer satisfaction, and a clearly improved working climate. With almost zero expenditure and only a few lost hours in initial meetings, payback was significant, immediate and lasting. This was a novel initiative, which rewarded the risk in a variety of ways, financial and otherwise.

## Combining 'lean' with activity-based budgeting: a North American example[13]

Irving Oil is a family-owned private company which operates in energy processing and marketing. Its headquarters are in Canada, while its marketing operations are based in the US. In 2009, facing difficult economic conditions and demanding environmental pressures, it set about a cost-reduction programme in its three divisions: refinery, commercial, and retail marketing. An external benchmarking exercise indicated that $100 million could be released in the medium term. Initially, Irving focussed on two major cost areas: purchasing and professional services. Purchasing was addressed with the assistance of external consultants, while professional services used an internal study group. Both of these initiatives were necessarily costly in themselves, but they generated significant savings.

To tackle operating costs elsewhere in 2010, the company enlisted the help of Babson College in Boston. The brief demanded, in addition to ambitious cost-reduction targets, that there should be minimal disruption to managers' jobs and the inculcation of a cost-reduction culture into the company's middle managers. The challenge was approached through an initial short workshop, marrying lean thinking with activity-based budgeting to produce lean budgeting. The methodology initially combined online instruction and podcasts to inform managers, with Babson personnel acting as coaches and facilitators. After two weeks, a further interactive session took place for questions and presentations of initial ideas. Finally, two weeks later, Irving middle managers presented their proposals to top management.

By their nature, oil companies have high fixed costs, and budget holders in Irving Oil needed to identify micro-level activities that were not adding value for its customers. Joint operational and financial teams identified 61 projects, which ranged from reducing the number of laboratory tests, improving security clearance for outside contractors and more effective use of the Oracle accounting system to cut down laborious reconciliations. The key was the analysis of these activities, eliminating waste and simplifying the processes, which often crossed departmental or divisional boundaries.

The results were incorporated into the company's 2011 budgets, which evaluated the improved processes. The estimated savings were between $17 million and $30 million per annum from 2012. A further $20 million to $25 million is being sought as part of continuous improvement through lean budgeting. The goal remains $100 million savings by 2014.

## Conclusions

- World Class Manufacturing involves a different approach to manufacturing.
- Central to the adoption of WCM is the use of teamwork and the empowerment of the workforce.
- WCM is a way of obtaining continuous improvement.
- 'Lean' is a WCM technique used to reduce waste with a customer focus and a long-term orientation.

## Management checklist

1. Do you embrace the principles of WCM and 'lean' at present?
2. If not, could you adopt them in your organisation?
3. Are you willing to adopt teamwork and employee empowerment?
4. How do you start and maintain continuous improvement?
5. Would structured problem-solving assist continuous improvement?

# Chapter 12

# Radical improvement

"How wonderful it is that nobody need wait a single moment before starting to improve the world."

*Anne Frank*

World Class Manufacturing (WCM) can provide continuous improvement but, on occasions, this can be inadequate when substantial change is necessary. In this chapter, we will follow the role models of two leading companies, Toyota and Motorola, to probe the demands of radical improvement in the following order:

- Continuous v. radical improvement
- WCM: 'The Toyota Way' – total production systems
- The Toyota Way guiding principles
- Applying the principles to reducing cost and improving quality
- Responding to the recall crisis
- WCM: The Motorola Way – Six Sigma
- Six Sigma and the need for reliability in operations
- WCM (lean and Six Sigma) cost reductions and financial data
- Example: medical devices manufacturer
- Example: national service provider

## Continuous v. radical improvement

When continuous process improvements are no longer sufficient, more radical approaches are needed. Radical improvement is a large-scale, top-down attack on costs that questions assumptions and spares no sacred cows, as summarised in **Figure 12.1** below.[1]

Radical improvement can be understood initially by examining leading global exponents, such as Toyota and Motorola, before illustrating the use of the technique in much smaller companies.

*Figure 12.1*  Continuous v. Radical Improvement

|  | Continuous Improvement | Radical Improvement |
|---|---|---|
| Bases | Sound process | Unsound process |
| Technique | Problem-solving | Reinventing |
| Approach | Incremental | Radical |
| Style | Analytic | Creative |
| Scope | Micro | Macro |
| Goal | Enhancement | Stretch |
| Target | Waste | Non-value-adding work |
| Change | Limited | Holistic |
| Domain | Process | Entire business system |
| I.T. | Secondary | Fundamental |
| Implementation | Bottom-up | Top-down |
| Extent | Widespread | Concentrated |

## WCM: 'The Toyota Way' – Total Production System

Toyota has for many years been a leading exponent of cost reduction, simultaneously improving customer value and product quality. While the company experienced serious problems with the safety features which led to a recall of millions of its cars in 2010 and damaged its brand, it is still regarded as a manufacturing role model. Indeed, while its reputation was damaged, it won respect for the way it tackled the problem without losing sight of its core principles, as described under 'Responding to the Recall Crisis' later in this chapter.[2] The Toyota Way is challenging, relentless and earnest, but massively successful. Elements of the Toyota Way can be applied to almost any business, although its pedigree is in high-volume manufacturing. It has been applied successfully in service industries, professional work and even in governmental work, where costs may be halved with no loss of quality. Indeed, quality usually improves, as the simplicity of running 'lean' actually reduces the opportunity for error.

It is commonly thought that the mastering of tools, such as the 7 Steps or Six Sigma, is the most difficult aspect to replicate from Toyota. However, experience has shown that adopting the Toyota philosophy of learning and experimentation is the most elusive aspect, as it requires a fundamental shift in management thinking, based on deep-rooted cultural assumptions.

It is fundamentally important to stabilise and standardise operations before making improvements, so that true cause-and-effect can be established. There is a corresponding need to make all errors and defects immediately visible so they can be made avoidable. Ultimately, it is a system which strives to produce only what is needed, when needed, as needed; the cost savings and other benefits are enormous. Toyota has accumulated cash reserves of $85 billion, more than the rest of the industry combined, and much of this is attributed to the Toyota way of World Class Manufacturing (WCM).

## The Toyota Way: guiding principles[3]

The 14 management principles listed in **Figure 12.2** guide Toyota's practices and, while most emphasis has been placed on the tools used by Toyota (such as 'kanbans') the deeper lessons lie in the way Toyota learns. This is achieved through a series of connected improvement 'experiments', which are meticulously planned and then corrected, if necessary, through a deep understanding of cause-and-effect.

*Figure 12.2*  The Toyota Way – 14 principles

1. Base your decisions on a long-term philosophy
2. Create continuous process flow to surface problems
3. Use 'pull' systems to avoid over-production
4. Level out the workload
5. Stop to fix problems and get quality right first time
6. Standardise tasks
7. Create visual controls to reveal problems
8. Use only reliable, tested technology
9. Grow leaders who live the philosophy and can teach others
10. Develop exceptional people and teams
11. Respect the extended network of partners and suppliers
12. Go and see the actual situation for yourself to understand problems
13. Make decisions slowly by consensus, and implement quickly
14. Become a learning organisation through relentless reflection and continuous improvement

The 14 principles of the Toyota Way can be enshrined in *four core guiding tenets*:

*1. There is no substitute for direct observation*

Only by seeing the evidence directly, with trained eyes, can true cause-and-effect be established. Managers must get out of the office.

*2. Any change, large or small, must be structured as an experiment*

Improvement alone is not enough; the hypothesis must be proposed and the results observed. For example, a proposal that reduces cycle time by an amount greater than predicted is welcomed, but also investigated to see why cause-and-effect were not well understood.

*3. Everyone should experiment as frequently as possible*

Those learning the Toyota Way should start by making small, bounded, single-factor experiments. This increases understanding of cause-and-effect, develops problem-solving skills and limits failure. Later, more sophisticated changes, such as solving multi-factor problems, can be undertaken.

*4. Managers should coach people, not fix the problems*

Managers should act as teachers, helping students devise these experiments, sharpening their observational skills, developing prototyping capabilities, encouraging experimentation, but not intervening directly. The goal is to develop others to be masters of improvement.

## Applying the principles to reducing cost and improving quality

To gain advantage from the Toyota Way, the philosophy must be embraced in total. The Way is based on deep thinking, and includes many aspects that seem counter-intuitive and even wrong, but which have been shown to work in practice in many situations. The key point is to adopt a learning mode that seeks to understand the system intimately and produces a continuous stream of small and large improvements in a scientific manner.

Linking the 14 principles to actionable items produces the following sequence of disciplines:

## Discipline 1: Standardise the work

Traditionally, this first discipline is perhaps the hardest to accept, as it seems to run counter to individualism and creativity. However, the effect of standardising on the one best way is to provide a baseline for subsequent, planned improvement. Standardisation, in this sense, frees up the mind to make the next iteration in creativity. It produces the familiarity that makes the effort almost unconscious. It is the art that conceals art and is not to be confused with mindless monotony.

Companies such as logistics provider UPS have taken this to an extreme, whereby even the mundane task of drivers safeguarding their keys is minutely specified. While seemingly restrictive, such practices actually free workers up to focus on non-trivial tasks and on other opportunities for improvement. Even at a trivial level, consider how often lost or mislaid keys (or tools or paperwork) contribute to lost time and unnecessary stress.

Smooth, uninterrupted flow of work, coupled with actual customer demand, is achieved by eliminating wastes, by reducing set-up times and using Just-in-Time (JIT) techniques.

## Discipline 2: Balance the work

The Toyota aim is to make the work flow like a metronome and, to this end, the work has to be balanced so that the load is shared equitably. This may involve job redesign and worker flexibility to avoid workload excesses on any particular task. Examples from Denmark[4] include the set-up on meat processing lines, where work is designed to accommodate the flow coming to it, resulting in a saving of more than 10% compared to the next most productive units.

## Discipline 3: Get the rhythm right

This sets the pace of the team, synchronised to actual consumer demand and regulated by the speed of throughput possible at the system's 'bottleneck.'[5] It differs from the common practice of trying to achieve maximum output at isolated stages, even though overall performance is, by definition, constrained by the bottleneck. By analogy, a pipe is constrained at the bottleneck, and adding capacity elsewhere is actually wasteful.

## Discipline 4: Develop flexible, cross-trained workers

The need for flexibility arises from the first two disciplines. Workers with a range of skills and a willingness to use those skills flexibly are required to substitute for each other as may be required. Simple in principle, this degree of cooperation needs conscious culture formation to obtain the kind of collaboration characteristic of the best teams. McDonald's, the fast food chain, have a long history of effective cross-training, with a star-rating system to indicate competences, making it a prime example of Toyota Production System (TPS) (and especially JIT) applied to a service industry. Interestingly, McDonald's approach, which puts all work within two steps of the operator, is now supplanted by one-step processes from Taco Bell and others.

## Discipline 5: Mistake-proof the work

The Toyota system places an extreme emphasis on making sure mistakes cannot happen, often by very simple means, such as templates, guide rails or colour-coded devices. Finding problems before they happen is good practice.

## Discipline 6: Call for help

With the work flow designed to flow smoothly and avoid preventable mistakes, any system deficiencies, such as the introduction of defective parts, need to be signalled immediately. Though it may mean that production is halted, the intention is to solve issues immediately as they arise and where the work is happening. For this reason, there is a signalling system, 'Andon', that each worker can and should use to pause the operation, get help and stop problems arising at source. For service industries also, the ability to recognise, detect and solve problems as they arise is vital in reducing costs.

## Discipline 7: Total preventative maintenance

Maintenance in this system refers to maintaining workplace efficiency. It is aimed at translating the WCM philosophy into a series of practical, worker-managed practices that achieve high levels of overall equipment effectiveness and efficiency. It does this by measuring and monitoring such key elements as system availability, speed of operation and quality of outputs. The underlying measures are combined into an overall measure of efficiency, termed Overall Equipment Effectiveness (OEE). Note that the use of the word 'equipment' in the term is deliberate, as it aims to deflect emphasis from individual culpability to system deficiencies; a blame culture thereby gradually recedes.

Total Productive Maintenance (TPM) and the 5 S system[6] are practical approaches to organising the workplace with extreme order, by having a place for everything and putting everything in its proper place. While such emphasis on tidiness may seem self-evident or trivial, 5 S is one of those simple, rare systems that turn aspiration into reality. TPM and the 5 S System are outlined in **Figure 12.3**.

The 5 S system is a practical, visual, employee-led system which maintains equipment in good order by emphasising simple preventative routines. A by-product of the system is an increased sense of ownership, which has now been extended to professional and managerial functions. Significant cost savings accrue from avoided costs, greater efficiency, higher throughput and decreased downtime. While its shop-floor origins are evident, it has been applied with great success even in management and IT areas in companies such as Hitachi and Motorola.

*Figure 12.3*  Total Productive Maintenance/'5 S'

1. Sort – Remove all unnecessary materials and equipment ('Seiri')
2. Straighten – Make it obvious where things belong ('Seiton')
3. Shine – Clean everything, inside and out ('Seiso')
4. Standardise – Establish policies and procedures to ensure 5 S ('Seiketsu')
5. Sustain – Train, use daily routines, on-going improvement activities ('Shitsuke')

*Discipline 8: Make the measurements visible*

This extends the idea of clear, simple, *visual* management to such activities as the scheduling of work and progress towards targets. The concept is to reduce manual and computerised paperwork by having a short flow of work with a minimum of unnecessary tracking documents, such as works orders and inventory dockets. 'Kanbans' (simple mechanisms such as display cards, special containers or tote boxes) are used to physically indicate what is needed, rather than relying on remote, non-visual systems to generate data.

*Discipline 9: Reduce set-up and changeover times*

Costs can be lowered through economies of scale, whereby ever greater volumes absorb the fixed costs involved. The Toyota Way approaches the cost issue from the alternative direction, lowering costs by reducing set-up and changeover times. For example, in printing books, small runs are uneconomical. Once the set-up is complete, it is relatively cheap to produce subsequent units. Toyota would address such a problem by creatively reducing set-up and changeover times, rather than pursuing economies of scale, which invariably produces surplus volumes.

These disciplines, although not always intuitive or self-evident, are very effective in reducing costs and increasing value. Moreover, they do not actually require specialised approaches or prowess in statistics. In other circumstances with very high volumes, where competition is extreme or where further cost reduction is required, it may be useful to extend the WCM/TPS approach by including a system such as 'ced *Six Sigma*'. Such systems seek to eliminate all wastage by using statistical methods, coupled with advanced project management and problem-solving techniques.

## Responding to the recall crisis

At the end of 2007, Toyota was the dominant car manufacturer globally. It had been continuously profitable for almost 50 years and had an enviable reputation for quality and customer satisfaction. However, in 2008 oil prices had risen dramatically and globally businesses faced recession, while the Yen strengthened against the Dollar, with the result that unit sales fell 15% in 2009, and the company incurred a loss of €4 billion.

Toyota did not react like other auto companies by laying off staff and closing plants. Instead, focusing on the longer term, it embarked on cost reduction and improving efficiency with a view to being profitable at 70% capacity, rather than 80%. Research and development was reduced, falling in 2009 from number one globally to number four, but remained the only auto company in the top 10. Training increased to find cost reductions. Overtime was slashed, bonuses were cut, and management took large salary reductions. Toyota continued to work closely with suppliers and actually speeded up payments. By October 2009 it had returned to profitability.

Just as profitability was restored, Toyota faced a more serious problem. In August a policeman and three family members travelling as passengers in a Lexus were all killed when the car careered out of control. One passenger had complained that the accelerator was stuck and that the brakes had failed. The police investigating the crash found that an incorrect floor mat was in the car and had not been properly installed, causing the accelerator to jam.

As a precautionary measure, Toyota recalled eight models to check the floor mats. However, a rumour spread that Toyota had electronic problems that caused sudden acceleration. The problem was compounded by customer complaints of sticky pedals in certain weather conditions, which was causing customer dissatisfaction. This resulted in a second recall affecting a million vehicles in three months.

The Toyota president was summoned before US Congress, where he accepted responsibility, refused to blame others and promised to restore consumer confidence in the company. However, the public remained unconvinced and the brand was seriously damaged. Nevertheless, Toyota adhered to its core principles, focusing on the long-term issues when reacting to customer complaints by striving for continuous improvement in quality and safety. Searching for the root cause of the problem, they changed their decision-making structures, giving their US operation greater autonomy, while improving responsiveness in engineering and manufacturing.

During the crisis in 2010 the company's performance suffered, with profits, market share and the share price all falling. By the end of the year, Toyota was again receiving awards for quality and safety. Recovery was underway, due in no small measure to its response to the crisis by accepting responsibility and fixing the problems, disregarding the short-term additional costs.

The year 2011 presented a new problem for the company, as it wrestled with the impact of the March earthquake in Japan, which caused a massive loss of power and disruption to the company's supply chain. The result is expected to be a 35% decline in operating profits, as it falls from being the largest automaker to number three in the world, behind General Motors and Volkswagen. It remains, however, a widely respected role model.[7]

## WCM: The Motorola Way – Six Sigma

Six Sigma is a WCM programme in which the emphasis is on achieving perfect quality or zero defects with the aid of statistical techniques, popularised by Motorola, AlliedSignal, GE, ABB and others since 1979. Claimed annual savings for each of these companies exceed $1 billion.[8]

Sigma is a Greek letter representing the standard deviation or variability in a process. Multiples of sigma, as used in statistics, indicate the probability of outcomes. The higher the level of sigma, the lower the probability of defect per unit manufactured. A high level of control and precision can lead to well-managed, defect-free processes.

*Figure 12.4* **Sigma levels and costs of quality**

| Sigma Level | Defects per million opportunities | Cost of quality |
|---|---|---|
| 2 | 308,537 (non-competitive level) | Off the scale: not viable |
| 3 | 66,807 (basic or local level) | 25 – 40% of sales |
| 4 | 6,210 (typical across mature industries) | 15 – 25% of sales |
| 5 | 233 (industry-leading level) | 5 – 15% of sales |
| 6 | 3.4 (world class level) | < 1% of sales |
|   | *Each shift provides 10% net income improvement* |   |

Six Sigma level is achieved when the number of defects is only 3.4 defects per million opportunities for defect – essentially *zero defects*. The term 'opportunities' is employed to normalise relative complexity: making a computer or car versus simpler items such as toys or furniture.

A maternity hospital operating even to a moderate 3 sigma level would experience serious incidents, such as dropping a baby once per day. A large bank processing cheques at such a level would make over 60,000 errors per million cheques each day, even if there was only a single item of information on each cheque! This would have a huge cost impact.

## Six Sigma and the need for reliability in operations

The amount of time that can be compressed out of a process or the degree to which it can be streamlined often depends on how reliably the system performs. If a system is beset with variances, irregular yields, unpredictable stages or uncertain time lags, it is exponentially more difficult to implement a 'lean' system. In this way, leanness (absence of waste, particularly time waste) is inextricably linked with absence of variance (defective parts or errors).[9] A completely just-in-time system is dependent on having perfect and repeatable quality with zero defects.

The achievement of high dependability requires that the best method be obtained and adhered to. This means the process must be made 'standard'. This is not intended to fossilise the process, but actually the reverse, to ensure that it can be systematically improved. Otherwise there are too many aspects ('variables') to manage. Paradoxically, the creativity involved in improvement needs rigid standardisation as a baseline, and often detracts from the appeal of WCM.

156 *Strategic Cost Reduction*

The achievement of zero defects is an aspirational goal, since few systems have zero defects. But this constant pursuit of ever-improving quality provides the energy and focus both for continuous improvement, based on a systematic approach to detecting and eliminating the root causes of product or service defects. In the extreme, Six Sigma may require a proficiency in statistics, but it is perfectly adequate to use simpler means to identify root causes of problems and apply effective counter measures.

It is a basic tenet of WCM that, once a system is properly designed ('in control'), the continuous improvement or maintenance of that system should be routinely managed by those most intimately involved with it, the front line service delivery or manufacturing people. This empowerment provides distributed leadership and a wider sense of involvement. It also promotes the idea, which is often seen as radical, that WCM managers enable a process and empower their staff, rather than dictate to them or otherwise micro-manage an operation. The emphasis on teaching and learning-through-action facilitates a coaching environment, in which the highest standards with the lowest costs can be achieved and maintained. The use of Six Sigma, illustrating the rigour and power of the technique is shown in **Appendix 2**, where an experienced practitioner outlines his approach.

## WCM (lean and Six Sigma) cost reductions and financial data

The table below[10] in **Figure 12.5** indicates the typical cost reductions obtainable within the first year (where there will be a cost of introducing WCM) for a typical manufacturer. The gains are likely to be similar for a service operator, especially in the area of payroll costs.

Note that the introduction of WCM, and the consequent shrinkage of inventory and work-in-progress, ironically can at first appear to make the financial results seem poorer, before the high levels of stock are eventually depleted from just-in-case levels to minimal just-in-time levels.

Lean Six Sigma is not restricted to manufacturing. It can be successfully employed both in the provision of services and throughout the service industry. Illustrations of its use are found in the aero industry, hospitals, banking and local government, which improve quality and reduce costs.[11] Not only is the possibility of significant cost savings there, but also enhanced quality of the service to the customers, which is more difficult to quantify.

*Figure 12.5* WCM value proposition – illustrative cost reduction

| Item | % of Revenue Current | % of Revenue Future | Cost reduction % |
|---|---|---|---|
| Revenue | 100% | 100% | |
| Direct Costs: | | | |
| • Material | 30% | 28.5% | |
| • Labour | 10% | 10% | |
| • Overhead & Quality | 25% | 20% | |
| Cost of Goods Sold | 65% | 58.% | 10% |
| Gross Profit | 35% | 41.5% | |
| General & Administrative | 10% | 10% | 0% |
| Marketing | 10% | 10% | 0% |
| Interest | | | |
| Other | 5% | 5% | 0% |
| Operating Profit | 10% | 16.5% | |

Clearly, while the approaches outlined in this chapter are demanding, the initial investment is largely a mental one: that of embracing the core philosophy. WCM can incur little incremental expense. Costs fall dramatically from a simpler process, visual controls, fewer errors, lower inventory, fewer cash demands, less wastage, higher customer satisfaction and increased staff morale.

## Example: medical devices manufacturer[12]

The company in question produced basic medical accessories for the European market. Union intransigence and docile management had damaged the company, which had high unit costs, declining market share and an ageing product. Management over the years had agreed wage deals that were subject to productivity gains, but these gains were never realised. Facing crisis, the production manager wanted to embrace a new way of working based on TPS, the Toyota production system, in which unions and management would pursue a common ambition and collaborate in reducing non-wage costs. The major barriers were the entrenched positions on both sides, which festered bitterness and a lack of awareness that a different way of working was possible by using TPS.

Ironically, these barriers contained the seeds of redemption. The workforce's frustration was born out of years of neglect of staff development. The majority believed that, given the opportunity, they could yet make a worthwhile contribution. The production manager carved out a negotiation whereby both management and staff would suspend hostilities for an initial six months' trial. Everyone would focus on the issues, not the personalities involved. Cost savings and other gains would be shared. Failure of the trial would result in a return to the old way but, with cost pressures rising, this would lead to traditional cost cutting, focussed on payroll.

Continuous improvement was chosen as the vehicle for change, as it is predicated on mutual collaboration, staff empowerment, and fact-based problem-solving. The areas for improvement were identified by the senior management, but the projects were implemented by small teams, which were given a basic introduction to the 7 Steps method.

These areas, purposefully few in number, were: increasing yield, reducing returned goods, cutting work in progress, and improving machine uptime. Seizing their chance and enjoying the 'ceasefire', the teams progressed quickly. Clutter was removed, the production line was re-arranged into team-friendly work clusters, quality became integral to production rather than an afterthought, customer returns were analysed for root cause solutions and machine uptime was improved dramatically, partially because wilful neglect was eliminated. A sense of pride surged through the teams and a healthy rivalry emerged, with teams competing to achieve the most gains. The management amply rewarded the teams, and the trial became a new way of working. In its first year, the new approach produced over €1 million in hard savings. Cost savings were estimated at €2 million per annum or 8% of total factory costs. Products that other plants had failed to manufacture well were successfully transferred to this site, which ultimately became a showcase for transformation.

## Example: national service provider[13]

A national service provider was facing mounting costs in their consumer cable-laying division. Inventory was ballooning, accounts receivable were seriously overdue, customer complaints were a national joke, cost over-runs were legendary, overtime had become endemic, and absenteeism was rife. The harder the company pressed on costs, the greater was the resistance, creating a vicious cost spiral, with no apparent resolution until an anomaly was noticed. Interestingly, the more remote the region was from central control, the more efficient it was, in spite of longer distances and lower consumer density. One such unit had dramatically lower costs yet higher quality and customer satisfaction.

The local manager of this unit ran his region with surprising autonomy, even experimenting with new ways of working, particularly how work was organised and scheduled. While the company emphasised central planning and had a command-and-control approach, this manager realised this was flawed. It was cumbersome to manage, while generating expensive overheads and spiralling inventory, especially from incomplete work-in-progress in the field operations. Seemingly well-structured, command-and-control was costly and ineffective. While appearing necessary to maintain control, it lessened flexibility, increased job demarcation, disempowered the front line, spawned bureaucracy and obscured the pipeline of priority work.

This renegade manager had created work crews that responded to the autonomy they enjoyed by acting responsibly, collaborating as a team, up-skilling themselves to provide adaptability, actively preserving expensive equipment and costly materials. Most importantly, he introduced a visual management system which scheduled the right work in the right order and could be done in a 'just-in-time' manner.

The local manager also included a seemingly wasteful, but necessary, pre-diagnosis of the work to be performed. To avoid his crews showing up on a site, starting work, discovering shortages, re-instating trenches and leaving 90% of jobs half-done, he arranged for a lead hand to pre-visit the site, make a diagnosis of what was needed and fully kit the crew accordingly.

Curiously, one of the main root causes of problems, he discovered, was termed 'poor paperwork', such as down-revision blueprints, incorrect map references and inaccurate inventory listings. Missing way-leaves and other permits turned out to be the primary cause of work schedule errors. With all this in order, the lead hand returned to the crew, consulted the area manager about commercial priorities and worked with the rest of the crew to agree the most efficient and effective way to meet those priorities. This included factoring in such aspects as logical sequence of work, reduced travel distances, any planned absences of key staff and availability of equipment and materials.

The manager had also managed to find clever ways to reward and recognise his teams, many of which were not in line with company policy. He allowed flexibility for necessary time-off, which the rest of the crew covered, and also provided training opportunities. In return, he received spotless depots, functioning equipment and replacement of missing tools. Most importantly, he never missed an opportunity to catch his teams doing something right. He was open to suggestions and could make the right decisions, as his crews spotlighted the root causes of inefficiencies and cooperated in resolving these issues. The estimated cost savings were 3% of total costs in the first year alone, due to reduced work-in-progress inventory, less wastage and the absence of pilferage.

## Conclusions

- Permanently removing costs requires a well-designed system of work in which all elements are lean.
- The required philosophy of collaboration and teamwork promotes the sharing of a common vision and promotes harmony.
- The techniques can sometimes, but not always, be introduced without any significant training or facilitation.
- Often, cost reductions can be achieved from the very first session, especially if dysfunctional processes are streamlined.
- Increasingly, these approaches are becoming essential for organisations of all sizes, and no serious cost reduction initiative will be truly complete without them.
- Six Sigma provides a discipline to reduce waste and move towards zero defects when operations are repeated on a regular basis.
- The 5 S system provides a practical way to organise the workplace.

Aristotle might have had continuous improvement in mind when he said: "We are what we repeatedly do. Excellence, then, is not an act, but a habit."

## Management checklist

1. What scope is there for radical cost reduction in your operations?
2. Why cannot TPS or Six Sigma be applied in your business?
3. Can you re-design the work so that cost falls away?
4. Can you simplify the work so that it is essentially self-managing?
5. Can you convene a team to immediately find simple cost savings?

# Chapter 13

# Business process re-engineering

"Only in growth, reform and change, paradoxically, is true security to be found."

*Ann Morrow Lindberg, "The Wave of the Future" (1940)*

Business Process Re-engineering (BPR) entails a detailed examination of business processes, and harnesses technology to simplify the structure in a dramatic and fundamental manner. It will be approached in this chapter as follows:

- Introduction
- Designing cost efficiency into the business model
- Planning and implementing BPR
- Phases in BPR
- Waste
- BPR in a life assurance company
- BPR in a pharmaceutical plant

### Introduction

BPR is a technique developed in the 1990s by Michael Hammer, a professor of computer science at Massachusetts Institute of Technology. He found that many businesses were inefficiently structured, and needed to be fundamentally and dramatically re-designed. 'Re-engineering' is defined as the fundamental rethinking and radical re-design of business processes to achieve dramatic improvements in critical, contemporary measures of performance, such as cost, quality, service and speed.

Where organisations are managed on a departmental basis in a way that ideally suited assembly line operations, processes were often fragmented, invisible and unmanaged, without clear overall responsibilities. Once identified, processes can be described in detail by means of flowcharts. By examining and changing business processes, it is possible to combine jobs, change sequencing, devolve decision-making and allow for multiple versions of processes. Checks, controls and reconciliations may be correspondingly reduced. The work units are changed and work is performed where it makes most sense. This normally results in a move from departments to process teams performing multi-dimensional tasks with a greater focus on overall results. Businesses such as insurance companies, where information is passed backwards and forwards across departments, can greatly benefit from a process-focussed reorganisation.

The key to such radical change is the enabling role of technology. Innovations in areas such as personal computers, telecommunications, teleconferencing, wireless, shared databases, expert systems, decision support tools and video linking provide the opportunity to rethink how work should be organised and performed. The starting point is to focus on problem areas, particularly those with most customer impact. Once the wastes and non-value adding activities are identified, creative thinking is employed to identify the best way to eliminate costs. The new mantra for re-engineering became: "Don't automate, obliterate."

Take the example of Ford.[1] In the early 1980s the corporation was seeking to reduce overheads and administrative expenses. In examining its accounts payable department, the company believed that it should be able to reduce staff from 500 to 400. However, when it benchmarked itself with Mazda, admittedly a smaller manufacturer, Ford discovered that the comparable department had a staff of five people. The fundamental reason was that Mazda did not focus on reconciling supplier invoices, where disputes could cause a lot of extra work. Instead, staff were authorised to release payment on checking with the order and delivery of the goods. Supplier rationalisation, just-in-time (JIT) and quality checking by the supplier all helped efficiency. Ford eventually re-engineered its processes and managed to reduce its department by 75% to 125 people.

Unfortunately, in the ensuing crusade to re-engineer, it was found that the majority of such projects failed.[2] Hammer estimated that between 50% and 70% of organisations fail to achieve the dramatic results they intended. He attributed failure mainly to poor project management: insufficient focus on processes, lack of commitment or leadership, insufficient resources, project drift, etc. But he also accepted that failure could be due to the fact that BPR, by its nature, is a top down project and could meet serious resistance from those affected, whether workers or managers. Crude downsizing and de-layering of management can result in serious long-term organisational damage when human resource issues are ignored. Issues around implementation and change management are addressed in **Chapter 19**. However, if properly used, BPR can generate considerable cost savings and can transform a business, or at least certain processes within the business.[3]

## Designing cost efficiency into the business model

Some businesses find that, by the creative design of their systems, they can gain a competitive advantage over their competitors. Essentially, they are using the 'lean' approach to run their business model. To achieve this end, they need to understand the value chain in its entirety.[4] Consider two examples from the retail industry:

**Zara** runs a global chain of fashion stores from the unlikely and remote location of north-west Spain. The company has managed to cut out traditional warehouses by speeding up its distribution process and by only making garments which it can sell immediately, thereby eliminating stock obsolescence. By linking stores directly with production, changes in fashion can be quickly recognised, enabling changes in the company's product ranges to be made almost in real time. As a result, Zara minimises the creation of unwanted stock and avoids end-of-season sales at discounted prices.

**IKEA**, the furniture retailer, is another example.[5] Instead of locating its stores in city centres close to customers, this Swedish chain locates giant stores out of town, where land costs are cheaper and parking is easier. The company's product is flat packed, and customers are responsible for assembly. A powerful computer system controls the operation, while costs of storage, supply and delivery are enormously reduced. IKEA retains only key linkages with its suppliers and customers.

## Planning and implementing BPR

BPR examines existing business processes and usually re-designs them from scratch. BPR can deliver dramatic results, depending largely on one's ability to see these invisible wastes and conceive a new approach. Implementation of BPR is dependent on good change management and excellent communication skills. Good care of staff, at a practical and emotional level, is essential if the cost-reduction effort is to be more than an isolated effort. The main steps are shown diagrammatically in **Figure 13.1**.

164  *Strategic Cost Reduction*

*Figure 13.1*  **Managing the Transition**

| Initiate: | Analyse: | Breakthrough: | Create future: |
|---|---|---|---|
| • Identify weak process<br>• Recruit team<br>• Map visually<br>• Customer inputs<br>• Interview people | • Understand current process<br>• Explore needs<br>• Note all wastes<br>• Stretch goals<br>• Energise team<br>• Show time loss<br>• Show all losses | • Find Eureka idea<br>• Imagine new way<br>• Start afresh<br>• Find new technology<br>• Design new process<br>• Prototype concept<br>• Test for risks | • Develop transition plan<br>• Pilot changes<br>• Gain early wins<br>• Begin next phase<br>• Manage politics<br>• Garner support<br>• Implement<br>• Institutionalise |

*Change Management + Project Management*

## Phases in BPR

Four distinct phases can be identified in achieving BPR results: Initiate, Analyse, Breakthrough Re-design and Transition to the Future, and these are outlined below:

*1. Initiate*

The success of BPR depends largely on identifying which processes have sufficient scope for improvement. These reveal themselves through high cost levels, customer or staff frustration, uncertain outcomes or convoluted workflows.

*2. Analyse*

The analytical second phase hinges on the ability to highlight explicitly the hidden, yet wasteful, elements in the process. The starting point is to make a map of the existing processes, highlighting the waste explicitly. This illustrates the need for change, as well as revealing how the new process should perform.

*3. Breakthrough Re-design*

The third phase needs that elusive '*Eureka*' moment in which the crux of the issue and its resolution suddenly becomes apparent, together with the kernel of the re-design.

## 4. Transition to the Future

The final transitioning or implementation phase depends on project management to complete the detailed re-design. While a rough 'map' is enough to highlight the messiness of the original process, a detailed process design is required here.

BPR, which is closely related to 'lean thinking',[6] is used mainly in information processing, but can be employed equally in manufacturing. It is a natural choice for simplification and, consequently, cost reduction, in all manner of services, such as tendering, procurement, accounting, product development, retailing, distribution, logistics and elsewhere. The key is to identify all aspects of waste, especially time wastes.

## Waste

Waste is any activity or element that adds cost, not value. It is anything that, ideally, could or should be eliminated from a system. Movement, such as transporting items from one part of a factory to another, is regarded as wasteful. A re-designed operation might arrange to have parts closer together, perhaps in a cell configuration or, ideally, might remove the need for movement entirely. The following activities are classic causes of waste:

- Transportation
- Waiting, delays, queues or other time wastes
- Overproduction
- Defective parts leading to re-work
- Inventory or excessive stocks
- Movement
- Excess processing

While a superficial examination may often suggest that a process is operating at maximum efficiency, a more rigorous approach will invariably reveal the existence of waste. For example, in a business process taking, say, four weeks to complete, only a few hours of value-adding (or touch-time) might typically be involved. The rest of the process duration is spent in queuing or waiting for the next activity, with much movement, duplicated data entry, avoidable inspection, unnecessary paperwork, pointless logging, rubber-stamping approvals, signature seeking and double-checking.

If there is a general lack of momentum in the process or it does not 'flow' properly, then it needs streamlining and simplification. If *time* can be compressed out of the process, cost reduction results almost automatically.

BPR is particularly suited for information-intensive services, particularly when those services require the involvement of different departments or the collaboration of tiers of companies. Examples below from the life assurance and pharmaceutical industries illustrate the problem.

## BPR in a life assurance company[7]

Information-intensive processes are prime candidates for cost reduction through BPR, as they invariably require collaboration across various functions, often separated by time or distance. Often, these processes derive from outdated routines, which have never been deliberately re-designed holistically, examining the entire value chain.

In this example, a life assurance company had different sales channels, brokers and in-house sales staff, each working as separate entities. Proposals, queries and other sales information were processed at arm's length by different departments. Each department was optimising its own costs, at the expense (in terms of time, money and effort) of the overall business. Account management, for example, depended on pen-and-paper, with all queries processed centrally and little emphasis on promptness or customer intimacy.

The resulting processes were complex and wasteful, as illustrated by the graphic flow-chart in **Figure 13.2**. This depicts the complicated routing of information, overlaid with a series of duplications, re-work and unnecessary approvals. Quotation requests had to negotiate a maze of internal bureaucracy and convoluted approvals poorly designed to expedite the process.

This traditional approach had worked well in a different era, but was now hampering business and depressing morale, while alienating brokers and customers. The blame game took over and staff quickly learned to avoid responsibility. Improvements decayed, quality fell and complexity multiplied. A new approach was called for. The defining moment was the transition from a task-driven organisation to one that focused on learning and improvement.

The overall value chain was streamlined to produce higher customer satisfaction with simpler systems and a more committed workforce. The system was re-conceptualised, giving more information, power and autonomy to those interfacing directly with the customer. Web-based information technology enabled real-time transactions at source. The new system produced a simpler quotation process and embodied the five key principles of re-engineering:

- Eliminate all unnecessary steps
- Eradicate wastes of all kinds
- Empower staff by delegating authority and re-training
- Envision a better way
- Enable the process, using simple technology

*Figure 13.2* **Traditional Quotation Request Process**

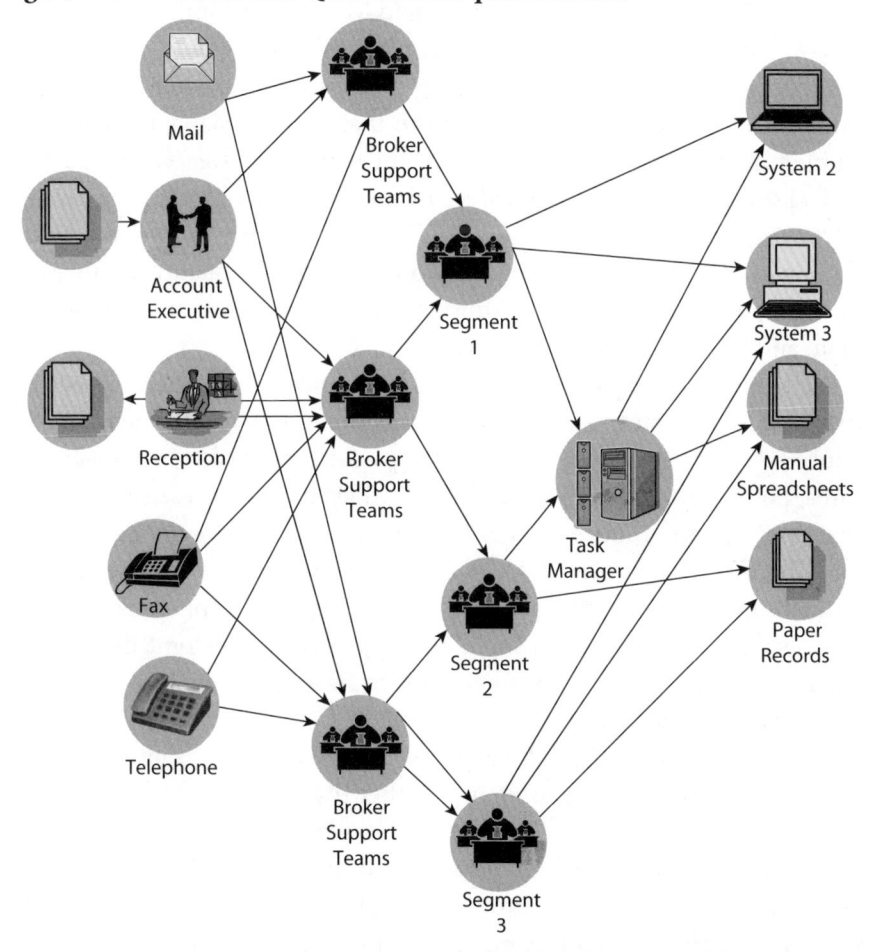

The system was streamlined to avoid duplication, data re-entry and unnecessary approvals, with the clients – not HQ – becoming the focus. After prototyping and proving the concept, the system was Web-enabled, accessible from any location, and protected by passwords and other means.

Surveys and awards testify to the huge changes. Unit costs declined by 50% (a cost saving running to many millions of euro) and profits increased 150% over five years.

## BPR in a pharmaceutical plant[8]

Midco (disguised name) was a pharmaceutical manufacturing subsidiary facing perennial cost issues. The future looked bleak, as the new drugs pipeline contained only low-volume drugs, and Midco's high initial manufacturing costs made the introduction of new products unprofitable.

Midco had a classic manufacturing strategy: step-by-step batching of products led to long lead times of more than a year. Managing costs and maintaining regulatory compliance were the main objectives. Overhead costs were allocated on the basis of direct labour, even though that represented only a tiny fraction of total costs. Large batch size was a goal to capture economies of scale, even though rejection of a batch for quality or other reasons was potentially ruinous. In short, Midco was caught in the wrong paradigm, and fresh thinking was needed.

The solution emerged by adopting a new philosophy, where speed, not cost, was paramount. Set-up and change-over times were dramatically reduced by pre-preparing equipment, performing tasks in coordinated teams, performing tasks in parallel rather than in sequence, using cheaper, smaller vessels to produce smaller batches, and by accelerating documentation. The new system used Midco's existing IT systems to capture and disseminate information, thus avoiding project risk and capital expense, but developed a team-based cross-functional approach to overcome departmental barriers, changing the reward systems to reflect the new WCM philosophy of leanness and agility.

Within a year, and with little expense, Midco was able to introduce new products to manufacturing in months rather than years, and could produce even small lots economically. The newly-available capacity created by processing faster was used to attract many other promising low-volume products and trial quantities into the plant, further offsetting the high fixed costs. No member of staff was made redundant, but natural attrition meant that, within the year, staff costs fell 9%, while throughput rose 20%, resulting in substantial savings.

The new WCM approach was proposed and pioneered by a technical manager, in a traditional industry, where such innovation was considered impossible. Midco credited her – and BPR – with its success.

## Conclusions

- Successful Business Process Re-engineering necessitates a careful and detailed examination of the basic business processes.
- BPR is particularly suited to information-intensive industries, where cooperation is needed between different departments.
- By simplifying processes and eliminating waste and non-value adding activities, considerable savings can be achieved.
- Successful implementation cannot ignore the human dimension.

## Management checklist

1. What scope is there in your business for re-engineering either the entire business model or key business processes?
2. Which business processes would you select to re-engineer?
3. How would information technology assist in the project?
4. How would you implement the project?
5. How would you avoid the pitfalls associated with failed BPR projects?

# Chapter 14

# Benchmarking

> "If you know your enemy and know yourself, you need not fear the result of one hundred battles."
>
> *Sun Tzu, 500 BC*

The comparison of different businesses or even armies is not new. Benchmarking provides a structured approach to making relevant comparisons by adopting an outward perspective, rather than the inward, historical focus of budgeting. The topic is addressed in this chapter as follows:

- Approaching benchmarking
- Benchmarking procedure
- Costs of benchmarking
- Example – newspaper industry

## Approaching benchmarking

Benchmarking is a way of establishing best practice by making comparisons with a relevant external role model. Traditionally, businesses compared their performance only with their own past performance or with budgeted performance. However, if competition is increasing, this approach may not be sufficient.

The logic of benchmarking is clear: "Improve your own business by learning from others." Staying within the business sector of a particular company increases the transferability and relevance of the learning, but the scope for major savings is limited. Greater gains are to be had from a strategic approach to benchmarking, which involves benchmarking from radically different viewpoints. Types of benchmarking include:

- **Financial benchmarking** – a financial analysis and comparison to assess overall cost or value competitiveness.
- **Performance benchmarking** – to assess competitive position by comparing products and services with those of target firms.

- **Product or service benchmarking** – analyzing and even reverse-engineering competitors' products to find strengths and weaknesses or to adopt new ideas.
- **Functional benchmarking** – benchmarking a single function. Because of their intangible nature, functions such as HR, finance, accounting and IT are more difficult to benchmark than physical processes, such as manufacturing, but the gains can be correspondingly greater.
- **Organisational structure benchmarking** – seeking improvements in governance (particularly used for not-for-profit organisations, such as universities). The National Competitiveness Council uses benchmarking to assess the competitiveness of Irish industry.

Benchmarking is a powerful cost-management tool because it overcomes the limitations of one's own singular view. It helps cure 'paradigm blindness', where the prevailing mindset assumes the current way is the best, or even only, way of performing a function or doing business. Benchmarking opens up organisations to new methods, ideas and tools to reduce cost and improve efficiency. By demonstrating the methods used by other organisations, resistance to change may be reduced and implementation simplified.

Benchmarking was originally formalised by Robert Camp of Xerox.[1] The process may be carried out by a company in isolation, by pairs of benchmarking partners or, indeed, collaboratively by groups of companies, such as members of an industry association, a trade association or by subsidiaries of a multinational in different countries. Surveys are usually routed via neutral associations and/or consultants and masked to protect confidential data. Care is needed to avoid allegations of cartel arrangements or price fixing.

For businesses in manufacturing or internationally-traded services in Ireland, the State-owned Enterprise Ireland provides a free benchmarking service, based on access to a global database. Using quantitative and qualitative data, with the help of facilitators, businesses are encouraged to benchmark their performance and improve their competitiveness in the following six areas:

1. Strategy and productivity
2. Finance
3. Marketing
4. Operations
5. Innovation
6. Human resources.[2]

## Benchmarking procedure

To benchmark a process fully, follow these 10 steps:

| Step | Principal activity |
|---|---|
| 1 | Select subject area |
| 2 | Define the selected process |
| 3 | Identify potential benchmark partners |
| 4 | Identify data sources and structure data collection |
| 5 | Collect data |
| 6 | Recruit benchmarking partners |
| 7 | Perform the gap analysis |
| 8 | Target future performance |
| 9 | Communicate the plans and agree targets |
| 10 | Implement and continue to review |

### *Step 1: Select subject area for benchmarking*

Select an area where costs appear disproportionately high or, if business has been lost lately, examine price and cost structures to highlight areas for attention. Focus on areas that have not been overhauled in a few years or where technology is lagging. Other ideas for improvement or cost saving might originate from:

- Informal conversations with customers, employees, and suppliers
- Exploratory forums with focus groups or industry sources
- Market research or other quantitative or qualitative analysis
- Analysis of customer or industry surveys and reports
- Process mapping or re-engineering analysis
- Investigation of quality control variances
- Financial ratios or other comparative analysis

### *Step 2: Define the process*

To enable meaningful comparison, it is important to know your own organisation's processes, which will establish a baseline against which improvements can be measured.

Itemise the specific steps in the process, associating any key costs, such as staff costs, machinery or overheads. Note any special constraints or considerations that may affect true 'apples with apples' comparisons.

## Step 3: Identify potential partners

Look for the very best organisations in any industry and in any country engaged in the particular activity being benchmarked. Consult customers, suppliers, financial analysts, trade associations and magazines to determine which companies merit an approach. Cooperation is most likely where the exercise is mutually beneficial.

Note that nearly all companies share similar processes in areas such as financial processing. Look for companies with evident expertise in less clearly defined processes, such as marketing, selling, employee performance management, recruitment or incentivisation.

The major gains will emerge from different approaches. Sometimes the company visited will have an entirely different approach, such as a particular software application, or will have outsourced an entire function previously seen as a core competence.

## Step 4: Identify data sources

Analysis of one's own process or business will usually demand that the data is structured in a particular way, which can then be used as a template to guide the gathering of relevant data. For example, when seeking to reduce costs in a service activity, the data gathered might initially include direct labour costs, indirect labour costs and associated overheads, both fixed and variable. The degree of automation or information technology will substantially affect performance, as will constancy of demand. The costs will need to be adjusted for volumes processed, for any seasonal or daily fluctuations in demand, producing a ratio or bandwidth of performance, such as orders processed per person or per unit of cost (e.g. per € of direct labour or per € of total cost).

This framework can then be used to drive direct and indirect desktop research, using many of the industry sources, websites, university centres or research institutes available.

## Steps 5 and 6: Collect data and recruit partners

Benchmarking is largely a process of mutual exchange. It is unlikely that leading companies will share actual practice with lesser companies without some *quid pro quo*. Promote the benefits of what is being offered in return, even if it is in a different area of activity. Contacting organisations is made easier if you have prior friendly contact. Ultimately, small or less prestigious companies may have to benchmark with a lower tier of companies with which information exchange is mutually beneficial.

Collaborative group benchmarking, particularly if supported by a recognised authority, such as a university or trade association, is usually a productive approach, as it combines data from many organisations. Companies typically agree to mutually exchange information beneficial to all parties in a benchmarking group and to share the results within the group.

## Step 7: Establish the gaps

From close assessment of the host's operations and any accompanying explanations or presentations, initial lessons may immediately emerge. Explanations could be: a clever new device, a unique method, a different philosophy (such as World Class Manufacturing (WCM)), or a different approach to staffing (such as home-based labour, different shift patterns, or effective incentive schemes).

Gains beyond the immediately evident can be obtained by analysing comparative data, using the template previously suggested in Step 4. This may reveal higher efficiencies in specific activities, more effective purchasing arrangements, better preventive maintenance, or more subtle means of implementing changes.

## Step 8: Target future performance

The new target may be to reach that of the benchmarked company or may indeed be to incorporate lessons learned from other benchmarked situations. This may be influenced by the degree to which those lessons are transferable in practice and the investment required both in time and capital. It is sometimes possible to transcend current performance levels by envisioning future methods or technologies, thereby 'future-proofing' the activities for some time. Imitating other companies, no matter how effective, can be limiting if not accompanied by internal innovations.

## Step 9: Communicate the vision; agree and publish targets

Frequently, the new target is simply to replicate the benchmark level of performance, but consideration should be given to setting higher levels that future-proof the benchmark and, perhaps, create competitive advantage.

It can be useful, and often essential, to include staff from different areas in the benchmarking study, not just for their expertise, but also for their enlightenment. Inclusion can also be expected to facilitate staff acceptance of new targets and in implementing changes.

*Step 10: Implement and review*

Finally, take the best practices and develop implementation plans, which include identification of specific opportunities, funding the project, and selling the ideas to the organisation.

## Costs of benchmarking

Benchmarking is a moderately expensive process, but most organisations find that it has a substantial early payback, particularly if the initial benchmarking effort is extended to other areas and becomes part of a learning culture. If, however, the exercise is misused, as was the case in the benchmarking of public sector pay against private sector pay in Ireland during the Celtic Tiger years, the whole process may become discredited and no real benefits accrue.

The main costs of benchmarking are:

- Staff and opportunity costs: finding worthwhile companies to study and implementation time costs
- Visit costs: hotel rooms, travel costs, meals, token gifts, etc.
- Research costs: subscriptions, fees, books, etc.
- Sustaining costs: maintaining benchmarking, databases of best practices, etc.

The cost of benchmarking can be substantially reduced by utilising the many Internet resources available. This may allow businesses to benchmark best practices much more easily than heretofore.

## Example – newspaper industry

A mid-size weekly newspaper with a circulation of 100,000 per week had a serious cost issue. Revenue, from circulation and advertising, was declining slowly, but relentlessly, at a rate of 5% per year. Costs were rising in line with inflation, while there was little new investment in technology. The managing director decided to benchmark with a smaller, but newer, weekly newspaper, which was growing without a commensurate increase in costs.

Jack, the MD, set up an initial assessment of the apparent cost gap, having appraised his line managers of the proposed benchmarking exercise. He quickly set up an initial discussion with the newer newspaper, whose editor, Frank, was a friend, always interested in learning more about the industry.

176  *Strategic Cost Reduction*

Jack realised that he needed to analyse his own operations first, so he asked each manager to identify the key costs and the main outputs of their respective sections, i.e. editorial, sub-editing (page design), graphics (photography), advertising (large display and small ads), finance and HR. He also roughly mapped the flow of work and formed a preliminary view of where the inefficiencies were.

Jack and his team visited the newer paper's offices and were immediately struck by the open-plan layout, the flatter organisational structure, the lower age profile, the apparent team spirit and use of information technology. Investigating further, the benchmark comparisons revealed major cost reduction opportunities, as set out in **Table 14.1** below.

*Table 14.1*  **Benchmarking Assessment 1: Raw data, not adjusted for different scale operations**

| Area | Original Newspaper (ON) | Newer Newspaper (NN) | Comment |
|---|---|---|---|
| Journalists | 15 | 5 | ON had many star performers |
| Photographers | 3 | 0 | NN used agency instead |
| Sub-editors | 7 | 1 | NN journalists did initial page layout |
| Editors | 7 | 1 | NN had managing editor |
| Small ads staff | 10 | 1 | NN outsourced locally |
| Display ads staff | 5 | 1 | NN outsourced locally |
| Major account mgrs | 3 | 3 | NN – Pro-active selling |
| Structure | Hierarchical, but with key gaps | Flat, egalitarian NN had more united senior team | ON lacked key senior management role |
| Layout | Many cubby-holes | Open-plan room | NN mainly in 1 room |
| Morale | Poor in some places | High, vibrant | Key ON manager not trusted |
| Average age | 48 | 29 | NN – younger operation |
| Incentivisation | Low, some exceptions | Transparent | NN – Team-based bonus |
| Recognition | Good, but ad hoc | Success always celebrated | NN based on verifiable results |
| Technology | Expensive and old | New generation | NN focused investment |
| Contracts | Old, muddled | Clear, collaborative | ON in dispute with largest suppliers |
| Premises | Old, but paid off | Economic rent | |
| Expenses system | Variable, awkward | Streamlined | ON lacked visibility of expense levels |

Even adjusting for 50% lower circulation, the newer paper had a fundamentally sounder base, with less expensive and more committed staff. The newer paper had simpler processes with skilled staff in key areas. For example, in managing major accounts, the older paper lacked a key role in managing newspaper distribution, while the newer paper used IT more astutely. The older paper had a high number of senior editors but, despite their skills, lacked a managing editor with commercial responsibility. The newer paper did not use staff photographers, but had a vibrant, lower-cost, nationwide network of expert freelance photographers.

To compound the cost and quality problems, the older newspaper used a disjointed collection of dated software packages, each good at a particular function, but incompatible with each other. Small ad production needed specialised software, display ads needed manual manipulation, while sales software worked poorly with the accounting package. Even photography, which was digitised, had to be re-processed via an unreliable 'black box' interface.

A key area of difference was in the automation of certain regular information 'feeds', such as TV listings and sports results. The newer organisation had simple but effective software to make this a seamless, automatic process. Similarly, the financial systems were simplified and automated, especially in the high volume area of small ads processing. In addition, the older paper had very fragmented roles, and lacked the multi-skilling that allowed the newer paper better efficiencies and made them less affected if staff were absent. To help complete the picture, Jack had his HR department benchmark staff salary costs, starting with journalists. The results are set out in **Table 14.2** below.

*Table 14.2*  **Benchmarking Assessment 2: Staff salaries**

| Staff salaries | Original Newspaper (ON) | Newer Newspaper (NN) | Comment |
|---|---|---|---|
| Median | 70k | 50k | ON above industry average |
| Maximum | 95k | 70k | Major inequities |
| Minimum | 30k | 30k | Both paid decent junior salaries |

The conclusion was that, while the older newspaper had above-average wage costs, the real issues were the internal salary inequities and productivity. At key moments, some journalists had leveraged their situation disproportionately. It also emerged that the older newspaper had an uneven network of tied journalists who supplemented the outputs of the in-house journalists.

*Table 14.3* **Benchmarking Assessment 3: Journalists' productivity – average weekly output in column inches**

| Journalists | Original Newspaper (ON) | Newer Newspaper (NN) | Comment |
| --- | --- | --- | --- |
| Median | 60 | 80 | 33% differential |
| Maximum | 120 | 100 | ON carried by super high performer |
| Minimum | 10 | 60 | ON had many low performers |

Benchmarking the productivity levels for creative professionals like journalists is necessarily inexact. However, the large differentials raised questions about the wide range of performance. The overall conclusion was that, while the older paper had lower productivity, since much of the writing was covertly placed with freelance staff, this paper had some star performers who actually carried most of the editorial burden, especially the vital front page stories and industry scoops. The same pattern emerged in the page design sub-editing positions, where good, but proprietary, software demanded special expertise to navigate it, necessitating higher salaries and greater ability of staff to extract maximum terms.

Benchmarking the older paper's age profile revealed that there were few staff of middle years, but many at the extremes – either newly arrived or with long service. Some journalists stayed and enjoyed long service, whereas others – though equally capable – could neither assimilate the culture nor adjust to the proprietary systems, and so resigned, thereby generating high replacement and training costs for the newspaper.

With the benchmarking evidence in hand, the management team formulated a plan to reduce costs over a six-month period, with minimal investment and maximum concern for staff. The extended period allowed for adjustment and facilitated early retirement, since the age profile benchmarking revealed that some staff were approaching retirement age. As the pension fund was healthy, and average years of service were high, this was a low-cost option.

Positions were arranged for some sub-editing staff to transfer to the only other newspaper in the area that used similar page-design software. As they, too, had on-going staff shortages, this was another simple and inexpensive transfer. The newspaper moved to cheaper, industry-standard software, which integrated with the accounting software and small ads production.

A few less expensive, less skilled staff were recruited, while some existing staff were re-trained.

Other staff changes were implemented. The newspaper's three photographers were offered freelance options, with guaranteed minimum workloads for the first two years. The key journalistic contributor was promoted to a senior position, and one of the existing editors gradually developed as a managing editor, filling the commercial gap that had existed. A dysfunctional sales executive was released, and morale discernibly improved.

Technological and operational improvements were also made. The digitised graphics were fed straight to a secure hard-drive area, requiring no manual processing. Routine data feeds were automatically processed and formatted for the paper. Where the expense was minimal, dividing office walls were removed, and a more open organisation (in every sense) was introduced.

Total costs, including IT capital costs, staff severance and re-training costs, were 0.5% of revenue. Initial payback was six months, but the real benefit was a reversal in the decline of circulation and advertising revenues, resulting in a return to profits within a year.

## Conclusions

- Benchmarking is a way of establishing best practice by making comparisons with a relevant external role model.
- To be effective, the benchmarking exercise needs to be performed in a structured manner.
- Benchmarking is a moderately expensive process, which can generate considerable cost savings, if properly applied and implemented.

## Management checklist

1. What aspects of the business or processes should be benchmarked?
2. Against which other businesses would you choose to benchmark?
3. How would you approach a benchmarking exercise?

# Chapter 15

# Outsourcing

"Do what you do best and outsource the rest."

*Tom Peters*

Those running businesses have always had to decide what to make and what to buy. Often, these decisions were made on a narrow accountancy basis. Outsourcing, which has grown massively in recent years, is a more strategic way of focussing on the problem. It is approached in this chapter from the following perspectives:

- The development of outsourcing
- The decision to outsource (why?)
- Deciding which activities to outsource (what?)
- On-shoring or offshoring? (where?)
- 10 steps to outsourcing (how?)
- Dos and don'ts of outsourcing

Outsourcing is the retention of responsibility for service or manufacturing operations, but the devolution of the operations themselves to third parties. Activities normally or traditionally contained within a company are subcontracted to an outside organisation, usually for extended periods, governed by a contract that specifies standards, costs, conditions and procedures. Once considered a despicable practice, it is now widely accepted, with subcontractors available to produce almost any type of goods or services across a range of industries.

Outsourcing can significantly reduce costs in a wide variety of activities by transferring the work to more specialised operators who can offer economies of scale or greater depth of expertise. With substantial cost savings available, outsourcing can also be a substitute for adding capacity, overtime, or increasing stock levels. Outsourcing can similarly release working capital through such factors as lower stock levels, and even investment capital by disposing of surplus premises or equipment, resulting in benefits to both the balance sheet and the profit and loss account. It can also act as a catalyst for change, and refresh parts of an organisation that have become lethargic. However, outsourcing also places risk outside the company, and ill-considered outsourcing can put a business in jeopardy.[1]

The major difficulties in achieving effective outsourcing lie in:

- Determining the appropriate activities to outsource
- Selecting the most suitable working partner
- Managing the outsourcing contract

## The development of outsourcing

Outsourcing is as old as society itself. The division of labour, based on specialisation, is fundamental to any community. Sometimes it was deemed desirable that certain activities be undertaken by outsiders. The hiring of mercenaries and explorers was an early example of outsourcing. Trade can always provide advantages for both parties, based on the Ricardian principle of comparative advantage. Outsourcing exploits this fundamental principle.

Business owners have always had to decide whether to sell directly to customers or outsource selling to an agent, and whether or not to outsource transport. They have also considered 'make or buy' decisions, buying the part when the price was deemed cheaper than manufacturing it themselves. Some businesses contracted out some of their manufacturing, but this was relatively unusual. Security, waste collection and canteen services on the other hand have been commonly outsourced for over 50 years.

In the last 50 years, the list of outsourced services has grown dramatically. Recruitment and human resource management, fleet management, facilities, maintenance, engineering and stores, legal services, invoicing, and payroll have all been progressively outsourced by some companies. Manufacturing is now commonly outsourced to China, with IT often being outsourced to India. With a few exceptions, such as supermarkets cutting out intermediaries by using central warehousing or businesses choosing to make their own travel arrangements rather than using travel agents, outsourcing is rarely reversed. Tom Peters' mantra of "doing what you do best and outsourcing the rest" has become increasingly followed.

Many businesses have transformed their structure and shape out of all recognition through outsourcing. Several airlines outsource their flying operations as well as aircraft maintenance. Consumer goods companies often outsource their brand development. Beverage companies outsource drinks production. Hotels sometimes outsource restaurants and staffing. Increasingly, some businesses resemble virtual organisations.

Outsourcing is also an option for the not-for-profit sector, such as education. Traditionally, universities employ a mixture of lecturers on short-term contracts and those who are permanent (having been granted tenure), but such colleges can also use occasional part-time lecturers. Some training organisations have a permanent faculty, but others, such as Management Centre Europe, outsource the running of courses. For many years, the Irish Management Institute (IMI) has operated a hybrid model, with an increasing amount of the training it provides being outsourced to contractors or associates. (This aspect of outsourcing is taken up in the next chapter under the heading 'Shamrock Organisation'.)

Outsourcing can readily cross national boundaries. In this era of globalisation, outsourcing can be near-shore or offshore, as well as on-shore. The limits lie in defining what must remain as core activities and in deciding what activities, though potentially 'subcontractable', cannot be feasibly or sensibly managed through a third party. The remaining activities are all potential candidates for outsourcing. Outsourcing has become a strategic, rather than a financial decision.

## The decision to outsource (why?)

Outsourcing can bring multiple benefits in addition to reducing costs. Delegates attending the 2004 Outsourcing World Summit provided eight reasons to outsource, as shown in **Figure 15.1** below.[2]

It can be seen from **Figure 15.1** that the most important reason is cost reduction. If cost reduction is not achieved, the other benefits are unlikely to be persuasive.

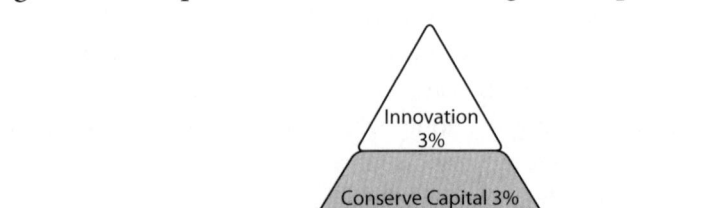

*Figure 15.1* **Top 8 Reasons for Outsourcing – % Respondents**

Innovation 3%
Conserve Capital 3%
Improve Quality 3%
Grow Revenue 4%
Access to Skills 9%
Variable Cost Structure 12%
Improve Focus 17%
Reduce Costs 49%

As well as the perceived benefits, businesses must consider the risks entailed. The decision to outsource, because of its potential impact, particularly on core activities, is generally taken at the highest level and considered strategically. The proposal requires close examination. When outsourcing fails, the client company can be severely impaired, with crippling financial consequences.

While clear and watertight contracts are necessary, they are usually not sufficient to ensure the cooperative partnering needed to resolve all issues which may arise. Fixed cost and defined outcome contracts should be predictable but, invariably, contracts that short-change one partner lead to disputes and impaired performance. Choosing only partners who have demonstrated flexibility and trustworthiness is wise if litigation is to be avoided.

In general, outsourcing should not be undertaken unless the cost reductions foreseen exceed 20%, as these reductions can be eroded by hidden costs. Hidden costs include managing contract difficulties, unexpected logistical costs, employee release costs, and other possibly unforeseen problems with contract surcharges. The decision to subcontract is usually hard to reverse, and power shifts to the subcontractor once the contract is signed.

### Deciding which activities to outsource (What?)

Any activity to be outsourced should meet the following criteria:

- It is a non-core activity that outsourcers can provide more cheaply and more effectively.
- It does not allow the outsourcer to leapfrog the client and serve the market directly themselves.
- It has at least two reliable suppliers available to promote competition, allowing transfer at some future stage to ensure that the contract remains competitive.
- It is capable of having a viable subcontract. The activities can be tightly specified, the product or service is reasonably stable, and demand is sufficiently predictable.

One approach to deciding what internal units should be outsourced is to examine the problem from two perspectives, cost and core competence.[3]

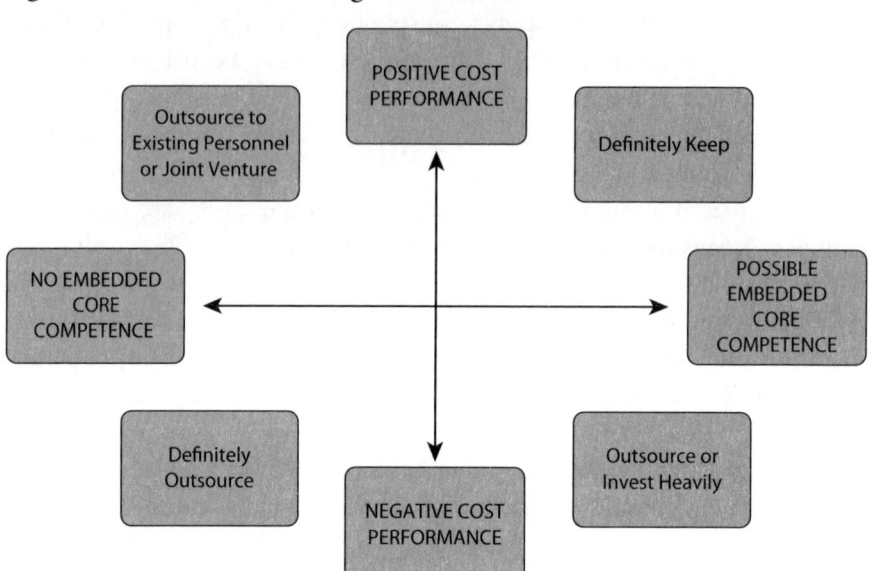

*Figure 15.2* **The Outsourcing Decision Matrix**

A matrix with two axes: vertical axis from POSITIVE COST PERFORMANCE (top) to NEGATIVE COST PERFORMANCE (bottom); horizontal axis from NO EMBEDDED CORE COMPETENCE (left) to POSSIBLE EMBEDDED CORE COMPETENCE (right). Quadrants:
- Top-left: Outsource to Existing Personnel or Joint Venture
- Top-right: Definitely Keep
- Bottom-left: Definitely Outsource
- Bottom-right: Outsource or Invest Heavily

For example, which activities of the finance function would be placed in each quadrant of **Figure 15.2**? A finance department could consider outsourcing several different activities, such as:

- Tax
- Payroll processing
- Asset appraisals and valuations
- Training
- Internal audit
- Sales ledger
- Management accounting
- Treasury

A survey of larger companies in 1995[4] found that the first three activities in the above list were the most likely to be outsourced, and the last three the least likely. Some companies, like Microsoft, have even outsourced the production of local financial accounting, which needs to comply with local regulatory requirements. Given the risks inherent in treasury management, it is not surprising that few companies are willing to outsource that activity.

Smaller companies may outsource many more activities when their in-house resources are stretched. This can include sales ledger management under a factoring agreement, along with management accounting. However, customer relationship management is normally considered to be a core competence, which may explain the growth of invoice discounting, where the company retains control of the debtors' ledger at the expense of factoring.

For the public sector, decisions to outsource are necessarily political. Even large service outsourcers can fail to deliver, as the British Government discovered to its embarrassment when it attempted to outsource security for the 2012 Olympics. Commentators questioned whether such security should have been outsourced to the private sector.

## On-shoring or offshoring? (Where?)[5]

In recent years many businesses have moved their outsourcing offshore, which has become technically possible in a global economy with advanced technology and freedom of capital movement. Enormous savings are possible because of the lower wage rates of developing countries. But with these benefits also come increased risks, which need to be both assessed and managed.

Anywhere in the world the decision to move jobs offshore can provoke a furore with politicians and labour leaders leading the attack, alleging unfair competition and exploitation of third world countries. Even in the US, the hub of free enterprise, politicians are urged to prevent 'unfair' competition and protect domestic jobs. There was a similar outcry in 2008 when the Australian bank ANZ announced the transfer of 500 IT jobs to Bangalore in India, while a comparable reaction greeted the home appliance manufacturer Fisher & Paykel in New Zealand when they expressed their intention to move jobs from Auckland and Brisbane to Thailand. In these circumstances, it is important to appreciate the additional risks that arise from moving offshore.

An obvious risk is *distance*. Most businesses factor in the associated transport costs and the increased time in the supply chain. But there can also be access problems if emergency visits prove necessary, so the location of airports and the regularity of flights should be taken into consideration. Different time zones can be an issue too for personal communication, making control more difficult.

A second issue is *currency*. If pricing is set in the local currency, there is a clear risk if exchange rates move. But even if the outsourcer's own currency is used for pricing, the problem may arise over time. For example, if the Chinese Renminbi was to revalue over time, this would have implications for the price of the country's manufactured goods, and the comparative cost advantage of outsourcing manufacturing to China could be rapidly eroded in such circumstances.

Another concern relates to the *legal system*. A supportive attitude from a government can be a key to success for a project. Some governments interfere more in business than others. Local rules and regulations regarding licences, local taxation, visas, etc., can impose a significant extra burden. In the past, exchange control was a serious potential barrier. While most governments wish to assist their exporters and have reduced the level of bureaucracy, this is not always the case. Intellectual property rights may not be readily protected and appropriate insurance cover may prove either difficult to obtain or very expensive. Loss of intellectual property rights through illegal counterfeiting or copying is a real risk in some jurisdictions. In the case of disputes, local courts may not look kindly on foreign multinationals. Successful outsourcing requires a good understanding of the legal implications at home and abroad.[6]

In some countries, *political or economic instability* may be a factor. In the case of an unexpected regime change, the outsourcing company may face the confiscation of its assets or serious disruption to its supply chain. Rampant inflation in an unstable economy also complicates the conduct of business and, in extreme cases such as Zimbabwe, makes normal trade virtually impossible. Most businesses would also be reluctant to become involved with countries that cannot guarantee the security of foreign businesspeople.

*Quality and reliability of services* can be problematic. The availability, skills and education of the local workforce are fundamental in deciding on a suitable location. Many call centres that moved offshore have experienced serious customer service issues. It is also important to assess the relevant infrastructure, especially power and telecommunications. For information technology, data security, backup and disaster recovery need to be evaluated. To ensure quality equivalent to the level available onshore, additional costs may be incurred.

*Language and culture* can provide barriers. For some businesses it may be essential to conduct business in English. The use of interpreters and translators, as a minimum, imposes an extra cost, but may also slow down the resolution of problems. In addition, the enforceability of contracts can vary in different jurisdictions and cultures. Many businesses will avoid countries where bribery is part of the culture.

Finally, there is the risk of *damage to the brand*. Goods manufactured in 'sweat shops' might provide cost savings, but may be unacceptable to the values espoused by shareholders. Labour issues, such as the conditions of the workplace and living quarters, can become problems, as can the length of the working week and the use of child labour. The fact that the factories are run by middlemen does not mean that the multinational shareholders will approve, as Nike discovered in 2004. The exposure of the dreadful conditions in some of the Asian free-trade zones, where much of the world's garments, shoes, electronics and machinery are manufactured, has shocked Western consumers and obliged multinationals both to set and enforce minimum standards.[7]

In view of the risks associated with offshoring, some businesses prefer to choose a destination closer to the core business or market. Canada and Mexico have grown in popularity for many US businesses. Within the EU, certain Eastern European countries can provide an acceptable compromise. Wage rates are much lower than Western Europe, which can compensate for lower productivity in many cases. In such cases, *near-shoring* is preferred to offshoring. Whatever the destination may be, the business should be set up in such a way that it can be properly managed and controlled.[8]

It is inadvisable to choose an offshore location purely from a cost standpoint. It may be sensible to consider the options from the outsourcing experience based on the country's share of the outsourcing market. In the field of IT outsourcing, India is the most popular destination, followed by the Philippines. India rates highly on cost, quality, available skills, language, infrastructure and experience. The Philippines rates highly on language, infrastructure and cultural compatibility, but has fewer skilled individuals, a slightly higher risk profile and less experience as an outsourcing destination.[9]

Since outsourcing abroad can prove controversial for the domestic workforce and politicians, it is imperative that businesses have a clear understanding both of the savings and the risks involved. Where the risks are high, as is usually the case in offshoring, the expected savings need to be substantial to justify the decision. The benefits of lower wages can easily be eroded by lower productivity and additional costs incurred elsewhere. A survey by the global management consulting firm McKinsey & Company in 2008[10] found that over a five-year period labour savings from products sourced in China had actually disappeared. When the increased logistical costs were factored in, the total savings were reversed. Returning manufacturing on-shore after a period of years, however, is a difficult process. Nevertheless, some American companies are beginning to invest domestically, rather than in the Far East, thus starting a 're-shoring' movement.[11]

## 10 Steps to outsourcing (how?)

For any business considering outsourcing, it is advisable to have a clear plan. The following is a recommended approach:

### Step 1: Establish the outsourcing project team

Treat the outsourcing proposal like a project, even for a small organisation. Apply the principles of sound project management, such as selecting a project leader and team, agreeing a method of working and an action plan.

### Step 2: Review your current strategic position

Ensure you are not outsourcing those competences that create your strategic advantage, now or in the future, as outsourcing is often difficult to reverse. Conduct a strategic and operational review of your organisation's processes and activities. In particular, assess the following:

- The risks of outsourcing core processes, and the costs of failure.
- Processes that could impinge seriously on customer relationships.
- The effect on overheads of the remaining activities. Do not create a doom loop where activities become progressively uneconomic.
- The vision of where the business needs to be.
- The suitability of the employee plan towards that vision.

### Step 3: Develop a people plan, for those leaving and those remaining

The understandable anxiety that people will experience will not be confined to those immediately affected. Those remaining may suffer from a form of post-trauma stress. If staff are not treated fairly, morale will suffer and management's credibility may be undermined.

### Step 4: Benchmark

Neither the business nor the intended supplier may be the best or cheapest performer. Benchmark widely the activities to be outsourced.

### Step 5: Decide whether to proceed – final analysis

Make the final strategic and financial appraisal, bearing in mind total costs, including initial investment costs, current stock write-offs, employee transfer costs, travel expenses and miscellaneous costs. The cost of monitoring the contract should be included, as well as any consequential costs for which a business may become liable, even if the fault lies with the subcontractor.

## Step 6: Canvass the potential supply base

Identify likely providers at home or abroad, and work with them to create the conditions for a long-term relationship, starting with the initial tender or similar opportunity.

## Step 7: Tender the package

The tender is both an objective document, detailing the services, activities and targets required, and a selling document, which serves to attract those who can add to your organisation's capability. Outsourcing is not just a matter of getting rid of problem areas.

Once an acceptable package has been defined, send an outline specification and request for information from those organisations likely to be interested. The outline specification should contain the broad intention of the outsourcing proposal and the timescales that the organisation has in mind. The request for information is a questionnaire-type eligibility test intended to establish the level of the sub-contractor's competence and interest. The second stage is the invitation to tender, a precise document which spells out exactly what agencies are required to bid.

## Step 8: Choose a partner

At this stage, the organisation should be looking for a partner with which it can share objectives and values, have regular senior management meetings, and disclose otherwise confidential information. Harmony of management styles is a key requisite for success. The organisation should also look for:

- Evidence of quality management.
- A proven track record, a flexible approach, and financial viability.
- Experience in handling the sensitive issue of staff absorption, if needed.
- An understanding of how important the contract is for the outsourcer.

Finally, bear in mind the following important warning about reliance on the wrong partner from the father of modern political theory, Niccolo Machiavelli (1469–1527):

> "Mercenaries and auxiliaries are useless and dangerous; and if one holds his state based on these arms, he will stand neither firm nor safe..."

While it is always important to check out carefully the financial strength of any supplier, it is critical for an outsourcing partner, since the impact of failure can be catastrophic for both parties.

## Step 9: Engage ALL the staff

It is essential that the outsourcer meet its prospective new staff before any contracts are signed. Allowing concerns to be aired and questions to be asked may help to reduce existing staff's feelings of being cast aside. Conflicts in style and personalities may emerge that can have an important impact on the contractual stage. Many other issues covering terms and conditions of employment will need to be addressed, including appropriate compensation where further employment is not available or not required.

## Step 10: Draw up the contract

If the project team draws up the contract, it will be bound by the laws of the particular jurisdiction, which may prove to be onerous. Within the EU, employees have considerable protection under regulations such as the UK's Transfer of Undertakings (Protection of Employment) Regulations (known as TUPE). Contained within the contract should be:

- Minimum service levels that the outsourcer will provide, together with checks and controls that these are met – perhaps via a liaison manager – and clauses including remedies or financial compensation if they are not.
- Demarcation of service responsibilities and boundaries so that the organisation and provider are clear on their respective responsibilities.
- The identity of who owns what in terms of equipment, hardware, software and intellectual property.
- Treatment of staff to be outsourced and their terms and conditions.
- Allowance for change, e.g. if business volumes increase or reduce.
- A contract term, with a review date and provision for the outsourced function to revert to the organisation.
- A honeymoon period before the contract becomes fully enforced.

The contract should be tested to ensure that it will stand up to the complexities of the operation in practice. Decide what to do in the event that the partnership does not succeed. Schedule and hold regular 'open book' reviews of costs. Define means of achieving mutual cost savings as the contract progresses. Wage inflation and other costs can significantly change the economic landscape very quickly.

## Dos and don'ts of outsourcing

Do:

- Outsource the activity, but not the responsibility for it.
- Understand the risks, scope and complexity of outsourcing.
- Have a clear vision of what outsourcing should achieve.
- Have an effective partnership arrangement and escape clauses.

Don't:

- Let the goal of cost savings dominate everything else.
- Think that outsourcing is a panacea.
- Outsource strategic, customer or financial management.

## Conclusions

- There are few limits to the activities that could be outsourced.
- The decision as to what activities are suitable for outsourcing should be taken carefully at a high level, since mistakes can be expensive and hard to reverse.
- Outsourcing is now commonly undertaken offshore, but this does entail extra risks.
- Careful consideration should be given to the risks involved and how they can be mitigated.

## Management checklist

1. What activities (if any) are currently outsourced?
2. What further activities could be outsourced?
3. What activities are core competences and should not be outsourced?
4. Can the activities be off-shored or near-shored?
5. Does the selected partner meet the key criteria?
6. What are the risks, and how can they be minimised?

# Part IV

# Implementing cost reduction successfully in a strategic manner, while preserving core values and avoiding financial failure

# Chapter 16

# Structuring and rewarding the labour force

"Two things are infinite: the universe and human stupidity; and I'm not sure about the universe."

*Albert Einstein*

Tackling the cost of labour is never an agreeable task. Given that it is likely to lead to a reduction in the living standards of employees if wages are reduced or redundancies occur, it is also likely to meet considerable opposition. For top management, this opposition may seem to be sheer stupidity, but for those affected it is simply self-protection. Yet, if the cost of labour is ignored, the consequence may be loss of employment for everybody. In service industries, labour tends to be the largest cost and, therefore, cannot be omitted from any credible cost-reduction programme. This chapter touches on the rewards system and its impact on costs. It does not, however, attempt to deal with the legal requirements relating to the termination of employment, since this varies between different jurisdictions. The issue will be addressed under the following headings:

- Hidden costs of the labour force
- The 'Shamrock Organisation'
- Five approaches to reduce labour costs
- Redundancy
- Example from the electronics assembly industry
- Influence of the rewards system
- The rewards system and the sub-prime lending crisis
- Wipro: an Indian IT model

## Hidden costs of the labour force

Traditionally, as businesses grew, so too did their labour forces. Employees might initially be recruited on a short-term contract but, providing they performed satisfactorily, they would become permanent, obtaining the rights of tenure in the same way as academics in universities. Security was granted, while loyalty and commitment were expected in return. Unfortunately, the cost of such employees was very high, not only in terms of salaries and bonuses, but also pensions and other benefits.

It is commonplace for chairmen to describe their staff as the 'greatest asset'. Although incorrect in the accounting sense since they are not owned by the company, it is easy to accept the statement in a looser sense. Staff can be expensive to hire and train, but they should generate a return to the company over time through their skills and application. If, however, they need to be dismissed, they may then become a liability, measured in terms of redundancy cost. In either case, the balance sheet does not record the cost of this important intangible 'asset', which, nevertheless, has to be managed.

A hidden cost associated with labour is the rate of turnover. In some industries, rates of turnover have drastically increased, as the idea of a 'job-for-life' fades. Younger workers, having experienced only years of economic prosperity, may not have the same fear of unemployment as their elders and are more mobile as a result. So, for many businesses, a rising labour turnover is a fact of life. If, on the other hand, labour turnover has increased because of declining employee satisfaction, a more serious long-term problem may exist. For a service industry selling the unique skills of its employees, such as major investment banks or professional practices, being unable to retain its key employees may make it difficult to survive and prosper. Employee climate surveys in these circumstances are just as valuable as customer satisfaction surveys elsewhere.

A high rate of labour turnover has advantages when it comes to reducing numbers through a process of natural wastage. It also permits the infusion of new blood and new ideas through external recruitment. On the other hand, it has its dangers. However highly companies pride themselves on their information systems for capturing organisational learning, it is commonplace for businesses to discover that the loss of certain employees can leave a serious gap. Filling the void may necessitate considerable recruitment and training costs in finding a replacement. It can also result in these expensive assets being recruited by competitors who may pay highly for their knowledge, skills and connections.

## The 'Shamrock Organisation'

Rather than accepting the costs implicit in the natural turnover of staff, it may be possible to manage the cost by structuring the workforce in a different manner. Twenty years ago, Charles Handy, a well-known writer on management topics, likened the ways in which the labour force was structured in modern businesses to a shamrock (see **Figure 16.1**).[1] The shamrock consists of three leaves within one leaf and was used, it is told, by Saint Patrick to illustrate the Christian concept of the Trinity.

*Figure 16.1* **Composition of the Labour Force: The Shamrock Organisation**

Core Employees

Subcontractors     Temporary Workers

The first leaf of the shamrock denoted by 'core employees' in **Figure 16.1** represents the professional workers, managers and other professionals who are pursuing a career. They tend to work hard and need to be highly rewarded by salaries, bonuses and other benefits. The second leaf represents subcontractors, who are employed only for the duration of their contract. They have a specific function to perform and are rewarded with a fee when their work is satisfactorily completed. They may be former employees and may not be located on site in the case of 'teleworkers'. The third leaf represents the casual temporary workers, who may be part-time and will not necessarily have a long-term commitment to the business. They expect fair pay for their contribution when they work.

Such a model has been commonplace in the construction industry for many years. Formerly, builders employed a large full-time workforce, but in an industry which has always been notoriously cyclical, lay-offs could not be avoided. A more effective alternative was developed, which required only a very small permanent labour force. Most work duly became undertaken by subcontractors, while casual labour was recruited for a particular contract. The resulting flexibility meant that a construction business could shrink to a minimum in times of recession and expand rapidly when contracts were won. While not all practices associated with subcontracting are perfect, such as periodic tax evasion by subcontractors or forced renegotiation of terms after the start of a contract, the model has nevertheless endured in that industry.

This type of model has also been adapted effectively in many service industries. Software companies, for example, may find it high risk to retain a large full-time workforce when contracts are uncertain. The core expertise will probably need to be retained full-time, but programming, for example, may be undertaken by self-employed contractors, often operating from their own homes, while peaks in demand may be met by short-term employees. IBM, facing competitive pressures over 20 years ago, adopted the shamrock concept.

The terms on which the full-time professional workers are employed have also changed over time. Employees nowadays do not expect a full or lifetime career with one company. Defined benefit pension schemes frequently are being closed to new employees, being replaced with defined contribution schemes, where the employee bears the risks. Bonuses in good times loom larger in the overall remuneration package, but can be cancelled or reduced in a downturn. In an increasingly uncertain world, it may become necessary from time to time to 'downsize' the labour force.

The relative size of the three leaves of the shamrock varies enormously across different businesses and different industries. Many organisations have decreased the size of their core employees in recent years, thereby significantly increasing the flexibility of their labour costs. Many others would have a very different shaped shamrock if they were to start today, but reducing core employees in a recession can prove very difficult. So, how can labour costs be reduced in a downturn?

## Five approaches to reduce labour costs[2]

Naturally, transforming a traditional organisation into a shamrock organisation cannot happen overnight. If labour costs must be reduced quickly, more surgical tools are appropriate. Occasionally, it may be possible to improve productivity by better training or removing obvious inefficiencies, such as excessive absenteeism and overly-restrictive work practices. But such opportunities are comparatively rare in the private sector. Typically, businesses facing the necessity of reducing costs heavily and quickly will have to choose between unpopular alternatives.

Facing such a dilemma, any given organisation is likely to consider not only the legal situation in making its choices, but also organisational values and the severity of the crisis. The legal situation varies enormously between different jurisdictions, but will also be impacted by agreements with trade unions, staff associations, trade associations and individual employment contracts. Corporate values may prescribe employment terms, but may mean that the cheapest solutions are vetoed. Unfortunately, many organisations now face a more severe crisis than at any other time in their history.

In the current recession, many organisations have been obliged to re-examine their attitudes to employment norms. In Ireland, the minimum wage rate has come under scrutiny, while in the case of public sector remuneration, where salaries typically exceed those of their UK counterparts,[3] pay and pensions have also been targeted. Defined benefit schemes, once considered sacrosanct, now come under the microscope.

Fundamentally, businesses may decide to choose from a mixture of five distinct routes. The more voluntary the choice for the individuals concerned, the easier the change will be. The list of alternatives set out here will vary in their acceptability to any given organisation. Some may already be in place, others would not be considered, while some might be possible candidates for change.

*1. Enhance natural wastage*

- Ban recruitment
- Introduce an early retirement scheme
- Introduce voluntary sabbaticals or unpaid leave
- Introduce a voluntary severance scheme

Each of the above courses of action aims to reduce the size of the labour force voluntarily, whether by eliminating entrants or encouraging exits either on a temporary or permanent basis. Unfortunately, the inducements required may be substantial to achieve the desired reduction and, therefore, while they should not be strongly opposed, may prove inadequate as well as expensive.

*2. Reduction of non-pay elements in remuneration*

- Change pension scheme contribution rates and defined benefits
- Abolish company cars
- Cancel fee subscriptions (e.g. health insurance payments or clubs) or subsidies (e.g. canteen)
- Tighten discretionary expenditure (e.g. travel and entertainment or attendance at conferences)

Pension schemes have proved to be an expensive imposition for many organisations, so many are now closed for new employees, while rates of contribution are introduced or increased for existing employees to reduce the deficits.

Some of the remaining perks are no longer tax advantageous and are regularly targeted by financial controllers. Increasingly, businesses are considering flexible benefit packages, which assess the total cost of benefits and permit employees to choose their desired mix.

3. *Change individual workloads*

- Flatten the organisation with greater individual responsibility
- Introduce mandatory job-sharing
- Introduce mandatory sabbaticals
- Introduce short-time working (shorter week or month)

Flattening organisations is often seen as a way of permanently taking out costs by removing one or more layers of supervision and delegating greater responsibility. Naturally, this course of action needs to be approached with care to ensure that neither quality nor key controls are sacrificed. The remaining methods aim to spread more thinly the existing workload in preference to dismissing employees. The restructuring plan may benefit from social welfare benefits available to employees from short-time working.

4. *Reduce the price of labour*

- Change mix of pay between fixed and variable elements
- Eliminate or reduce bonuses
- Cancel payment for overtime
- Freeze promotions and automatic increments
- Freeze or reduce rates of pay

Reducing core salaries, while allowing employees to earn commissions or bonuses (dependent on performance), enhances flexibility. However, any attempt to reduce overall pay is likely to attract strong opposition from sectional interests. Bankers may consider that large bonuses are vital to retain their peculiar and supposedly rare talents. Irish judges insist that, whatever about the remainder of the public sector, their remuneration can only be reduced on a private, voluntary basis. Nevertheless, this approach remains central to efforts to reduce costs in the Irish private sector, being adopted by approximately three-quarters of companies.[4]

5. *Radically restructure the labour force*

- Target redundancy on a selective basis
- Introduce general redundancy on statutory terms

- Relocate the labour force to a cheaper destination
- Convert to a shamrock organisation

The last set of measures is both radical and involuntary, often meeting serious employee resistance and facing legal obstacles. Accordingly, redundancy with minimal compensation may only be chosen in an extreme crisis, such as a restructuring under the control of the courts to ensure solvency. Relocation, however, need not be undertaken purely with statutory termination payments. Many multinationals may choose to pay generously and offer retraining or employment elsewhere in the group. Moving towards a shamrock organisation can be achieved gradually over time, as various activities are outsourced, and is now a more acceptable practice than in the past when many workers expected a job for life. New recruitment can also be made on a casual, rather than permanent basis.

Different organisations respond to these options in contrasting ways. Some measures may lead to unwanted side effects. Frequently, effective short-term economies can have serious adverse longer-term repercussions, affecting employee morale, which ultimately impacts the ability to recruit and retain first class people. Devising an appropriate strategic plan will require a mix of skills from human resources, operations and finance as a minimum.

## Redundancy

In an ideal world, there would be no redundancy. Change could be introduced by natural wastage. More often than not, however, some redundancy in a major cost-reduction programme is inevitable. At its most benign, this change can be effected through early retirement or voluntary severance packages. Any such plan needs to protect against the loss of skilled, key personnel. Too often, in both the private and public sectors, employees have been made redundant only to be re-hired when it was discovered that nobody else could perform their function. Where these inducements fail to produce the desired workforce reduction, only then is the possibility of involuntary redundancy likely to arise.

Involuntary redundancy, a last resort, may be subject to negotiation. It can be treated as a capital cost, as in any other capital project, except that management can determine its price and, therefore, the scale of the outlay. As mentioned above, the terms of such a package may be influenced, if not governed, by the gravity of the current situation, legal agreements and the company's espoused values, particularly management's perceived responsibility to the workforce. It should be borne in mind that redundancy and the way it is handled may have a significant effect on the morale of the survivors. A company that dismisses long-serving employees on purely statutory terms may find it hard to attract the best employees later on. If it is carried out on a drip basis, it will engender a culture of fear, which may result in a deterioration of the overall corporate performance. If, on the other hand, it can be conducted at a single stroke in a humane fashion, then it should be perceived in a better light. The provision of an outplacement service and retraining may also soften the blow.

As recession spread in 2008, businesses were forced to consider the unpalatable option of redundancy as a matter of urgency. In Ireland, redundancies rose at a rate of over 50% in 2008[5] and continued to grow thereafter. Sometimes a crisis in an industry is well-publicised, as in the case of US car manufacturers but, more usually, it comes to notice when layoffs are announced. Globally, financial services and manufacturing were particularly prominent. Other industries have included a very diverse group: Pepsi bottlers, law firms, retailers, media companies, chemical companies and technology firms.[6] In the recession which followed 2008, few industries have been able to avoid redundancies. Investors appreciate such action. When British Telecom axed 10,000 jobs in 2008 the share price rose by 9%.[7]

Management should be aware of the average cost of taking on a new employee, the costs of dismissal and the natural rate of labour turnover. If they wish to retain good staff, they should also try to ensure that the rewards system helps, rather than hinders this objective. An example from the electronics assembly industry below illustrates the benefits of careful HR planning.

### Example from the electronics assembly industry[8]

Well established in their location in Ireland for over 20 years, the management of this business recognised the plant was incapable of competing with labour rates in Asia. Having collaborated on an outsourced project, local management benchmarked the costs and identified very significant cost savings for the group if the entire business unit was relocated to Asia.

Ignoring their self-interest, the management brought forward a plan to HQ that saw the phased closure of the facility in Ireland over a two-year period. To facilitate the orderly closure, the Asian facility needed to be fitted out with Irish located equipment, supported by an intensive skills transfer programme. To assist with this task, the management retained a consultant.

The consultant was first requested to research the 'market' for phased closures: what were the normal retention deals put in place; what were the typical payment triggers; was payment best held to the end? After a number of companies were identified and contacted, a comprehensive survey was prepared before a report was presented to the CEO and the HR director, together with recommendations on the most appropriate retention plan. This report was agreed initially at plant level, then by the corporate executive and, finally, with senior management at global level.

Satisfied with the work done, the retention plan for the management team was referred to as 'Tier 1'. This group was given responsibility for the overall execution of the plan. However, it became clear that technical considerations would be crucially important. As a result, the consultant was asked to propose a retention plan for 'Tier 2'. This would include the key technical personnel needed to support the technology transfer from Ireland to Asia.

The critical element for both plans was to decide what were the most appropriate criteria for the payment of the retention bonuses and what payment release triggers would apply. Much debate was properly generated on these aspects. In particular, care was taken to align every action with the closure strategy, to foster cooperation both within and between the various teams, and to meet planned deadlines, which were actually surpassed.

The selection criteria also generated much discussion. A number of different factors were considered and every potential entrant was assessed against them. These included qualifications, experience, importance to the programme, etc. Each employee, whether in Tier 1 or Tier 2, had to consent to the terms of the skills transfer agreement.

All of this took place in a long-established plant with a strong industrial relations culture. However, the unity of purpose demonstrated by the management team in particular ensured that whenever resistance surfaced it met a tight group, always with the same message. The manner in which the communication process was managed contributed significantly to the success of the programme and its timely implementation.

## Influence of the rewards system

The field of rewards is a wide area, far beyond the scope of this book. Yet, it cannot be overlooked and should be reviewed in any cost-reduction programme. A rewards system is designed to motivate employees to produce high performance. The overall package may include not only a salary and possible bonuses, but also benefits-in-kind, pension schemes, general working conditions, and possible longer-term sharing of the business success, such as share incentive schemes. What is critical is that the rewards system has regard to the type of employee the business wishes to attract and the length of time they are expected to stay.

A basic consideration is whether or not employees are to receive the lowest possible remuneration or whether the business should pay more to attract and retain the employees it needs. Paying the minimum, as required by statute, may be cheaper in the short-term, but inadvisable in the longer term, since it is unlikely to attract the most skilled and motivated recruits where there are more attractive employment alternatives. Certain businesses in the services sector, however, have chosen to go down that route. The fast food industry is largely staffed by young people earning low wages who are quickly trained into the job. Shipping companies may elect to operate under flags of convenience in countries with little regulation to lower the costs of their crews. Conversely, management consultancy companies are most unlikely to adopt such a policy, since their business is generated from selling advice that requires a high level of skill and expertise. The starting point for setting salary levels is to clearly understand the salary norms in the industry and to decide whether the business wishes to pay more or less than the norm.

Many businesses have changed their overall policy on pay over the years. Fifty years ago, professional service practices recruited apprentices, who could sometimes expect to pay, rather than be paid, for their apprenticeship. Their cost could be recovered many times over by the rate charged to clients, and their performance was closely monitored by time sheets. Nowadays, many such firms pay salaries necessary to attract graduates and the brightest of school leavers. Banks, on the other hand, have tried to reduce the costs of some of their lower level jobs. They may recruit employees on lower pay scales and with limited job prospects to perform the more routine functions. At the same time, they have offered 'hello money' on joining to attract those believed to possess rarer skills, as well as 'golden parachutes', which provide generous termination payments for enhanced job security.

Another consideration is the split between *pay* and *non-pay benefits*. For many businesses, the tendency has been to reduce non-pay benefits. Some benefits-in-kind, such as company cars, have diminished in popularity due to tax changes. Others, such as non-contributory pensions, have had to be reduced or eliminated, because of their high cost. Workspace, in some cases, has been reduced to the statutory minimum due to the high cost of city centre space. Even subsidised meals and other perks have been attacked from financial necessity.

An often-crucial consideration is the split between *fixed pay* in terms of salary and *variable pay* in terms of potential bonuses. Many businesses have sought to reduce the proportion of fixed pay, particularly when it has associated pension costs. The extreme example of this is sales organisations offering big commissions and minimal salaries, as commonly existed in the past in businesses such as encyclopaedia sales organisations. This balance in favour of variable pay is particularly attractive to cyclical industries, which may need to reduce their costs quickly when faced with a business downturn. More emphasis is then placed on bonuses, which are sometimes guaranteed in the short-run, to attract and retain staff. The bonuses may be paid on an individual or team basis and may be paid in cash or shares with restricted rights of sale. Frequently, where bonuses are set at high levels, such as in financial services, they will have a very big impact on the way managers behave, although this may not be in the manner that the business intended.

Finally, there is the issue of sharing in gains or increases in productivity. To this end, some businesses, especially those wedded to the concept of continuous improvement, have introduced a system of making some payment for suggestions adopted throughout the organisation. This can be a flat payment or a share of the savings, possibly capped at some figure. Others have adopted a more formal system of profit-sharing with the workforce as part of a major cost-reduction initiative.

Naturally, where rewards are offered for increased productivity, there should be some way of checking on the delivery of the increased productivity. In Ireland, large pay increases were granted to public servants, based on a benchmarking comparison with private sector peers, in return for productivity improvements. This led to much adverse comment, since the pay increases were granted, but the promised productivity increases were not monitored. Similarly, incentives may be provided, not always effectively, to align the rewards of the senior management to the long-term profitability of the business through share options or share incentive schemes.

Every organisation needs to ensure that the overall rewards system is aligned to its overall strategy.[9] The example of how budgeting can affect the behaviour of salesmen through the commission calculation has already been discussed in **Chapter 2**. A company that experiences declining gross margins and rising bad debts may find that changing the basis of the commission to sales for which cash had been received and the margin obtained may dramatically improve its results in terms of credit control and enhanced gross margins. If elements of the rewards package are reduced, it is likely to impact labour turnover in the short or longer term if alternative employment is available. Sometimes economies may be made without obvious harmful side effects, as in times of high unemployment, but the impact on morale and, therefore, motivation should not be underestimated. The impact of a misaligned rewards system is illustrated by the sub-prime lending crisis, which led to devastating consequences for global banking.[10]

## The rewards system and the sub-prime lending crisis

In financial services, profits can be difficult to measure. The only time a bank knows its profit on a loan with certainty is when it has been repaid, so great care and skilful judgement is required in providing for impaired loans, where losses are anticipated. Insurance companies are similar. The provision for bad debts or insurance claims has traditionally been made on a conservative basis. It is always easy to grow business by offering cut-price loans or insurance. Eventually, under-provisioning catches up with the institution, as it did in the UK in the tertiary bank-lending crisis in the 1970s or the problems of Lloyds of London in the 1980s and cut-price motor insurers.

Another important aspect in financial services is the reliance on confidence. The word 'credit' is derived from the Latin word 'credo', meaning trust. Without trust it is difficult to manage credit and, without credit, it is difficult to carry on trade. Without trust also a fractional banking system is ultimately vulnerable to a run on deposits. Damage to a bank's reputation from breaking the rules, whether by rigging LIBOR interest rates or laundering money, is potentially very serious, since it undermines public confidence. So too are reckless lending and weak risk management.

Banks in the US lent aggressively to the American sub-prime mortgage market over recent years. By definition, sub-prime borrowers, receiving 100% mortgages with initial 'teaser' rates of interest of 1%, would be likely to experience repayment difficulties when rates were reset, particularly if property prices were to fall. 'NINJA' loans were made to borrowers with 'No Income, No Jobs and No Assets'. 'Liar' or self-certified loans were made to people who were asked to fill in their own financial details, which were not checked by the lender. Documentation was limited, and 'no doc' loans became accepted. Unfortunately, independent checks by internal or external auditors and regulatory authorities either failed to highlight effectively the dangers and risks involved or else were ignored.

How could such foolish lending happen in the staid world of banking? Essentially, it happened because of the way bankers were rewarded and the fact that a bank making a loan did not intend to retain it, but pass it on to a third party (who was a greater fool than the bank itself) through the process of securitisation. If the bank disposed of all its loans to investors, it carried no risk of incurring losses, however poor the underlying credits were. Mortgage brokers could offer finance on terms that no bank would accept, if the loans were to be retained on its books. When the rating agencies, such as Standards & Poor's or Moody's, provided the packages with an AAA rating, indicating minimal risk of default, all parties appeared happy and were well rewarded in the short run. The loans were administered by a third party for a modest fee. The banks made enormous profits and paid out large bonuses to their staff, usually in cash.

There thus existed every incentive to advance high-risk loans, which could be packaged together with many other such loans in bundles that few people could understand due to the complex slicing and dicing of the loans to provide different levels of risk. These complex packages turned into deadly toxins, spreading their poison widely throughout the financial system, whenever they changed hands, which could happen easily under securitisation. The system of paying large cash bonuses to individuals who originated the loans actually encouraged the growth of securitisation in the sub-prime industry, creating an unsavoury culture of greed which exacerbated the property bubble and ultimately led to the global credit crunch.

The rewards system clearly had an important role in the creation of this bubble. A former senior investment banker explained the traditional model as a kind of joint venture between shareholders and employees with revenues divided roughly evenly between them. The shareholders bore the costs of the business and the remainder was the profit. The employees were paid their share largely in the form of bonuses.[11] Lavish entertainment expenses added to the culture of greed in the financial services industry. Several practitioners both in the UK and the US have exposed a culture where dubious practices were condoned in pursuit of profitable business with the interests of clients being subordinated to those of the bank, broker, or individual trader,[12] just as had been described some 20 years earlier in Salomon Brothers.[13]

Banks today might ponder on the success of Handelsbanken, described in **Chapter 1**. This Swedish bank avoided both the Swedish banking crisis of 1992 and the international banking crisis of 2008. Bonuses at Handelsbanken are only made when profits exceed the industry average and are divided equally between all employees with payment deferred until retirement.

A prominent strategist explains the crisis in terms of poor strategy.[14] The financial engineers had overreached themselves in designing the systems. The risks were not understood because bankers assumed that property prices could not decline. The incentives of both organisations and individuals were not aligned with successful strategic implementation, resulting in massive risk taking. The strategy was not questioned largely because of social herding, which encouraged 'groupthink', while data was ignored on the naïve assumption that this bubble was different.

It may be instructive to see how such greed and recklessness can become an epidemic, which can threaten the global economy. The spread of social epidemics was set out some time ago in the popular American book, *The Tipping Point* by Malcolm Gladwell.[15] It has been used to explain the spread of sexual diseases, consumer fashions, and even the start of the American Revolution. Only a few parties need be involved, but if the message is 'sticky', or easy to pass on, and the context favourable, the 'disease' may tip into an epidemic.

There were a few key parties involved in the spread of the sub-prime crisis, although the amounts of the loans involved were large. First, there were the banks, which originate, package, and distribute the loans; they acted as 'persuaders'. Occasionally, they held on to a portion of the loans in incestuously-related hedge funds, termed 'conduits' or 'structured investment vehicles', which were not consolidated in the banks' accounts, were off balance sheet and out of sight. These funds act as 'connectors'. The other parties that facilitated the transactions were the rating agencies that provided a stamp of quality to the loan, certain insurers that underwrote some of the debt, and the brokers who assisted in the distribution. All parties benefited from the boom, since their fees, conveniently paid by the banks, grew correspondingly. These parties acted as 'evaluators' because their involvement was likely to influence other parties.

Loans were 'sticky' or readily transferable. Innovations from securitisation had transformed the traditional relationships between borrowers and lenders. Banks want to pass on their loans, rather than raise extra capital and hold them. Investment funds wanted to hold these bonds, which they considered to be low risk investments generating a steady stream of income. The fees involved encouraged the transmission between the various parties. Doubtless, too, the momentum was reinforced by the tendency of banks to adopt a herd mentality, encapsulated by Chuck Prince, CEO of Citicorp, who remarked at the height of the boom in July 2007: "As long as the music is playing, you've got to get up and dance. We're still dancing." With only a few major financial centres and modern electronic technology, it is easy to transfer loans around the market without being stopped at national boundaries.

The context of the sub-prime industry was supportive in an opaque world with low levels of disclosure, high financial gearing or borrowing and often little regulation.[16] The siren voices warning of the regulatory flaws in the system were ignored.[17] In the US the goal of universal home ownership was lauded, so there was little political will to curb the boom. The lessons of the somewhat similar problems faced 20 years earlier by the Savings and Loan Institutions or 'thrifts', together with the excesses of the mortgage trading departments of the investment banks, which gave rise to enormous subsequent bailout costs, were forgotten or overlooked. Monetary policy provided an era of sustained low interest rates which enabled banks to set attractive initial mortgage repayments.

The policy of light touch regulation discouraged intervention by the authorities. The regulator believed in the invisible hand of competition, assuming that the banks would always act in the best interest of their shareholders, which meant managing the risks effectively. It was assumed that market forces would inhibit banks from taking undue risks, because the share price would suffer if they did. The complex technical risks inherent in derivatives, the technical instruments employed, often were not well understood by those responsible for managing the system. Indeed, Alan Greenspan, Chairman of the Federal Reserve and the doyen of the industry, advocated a policy of laissez-faire, relying on competition between the banks and the expectation that bankers would act in the best interests of their shareholders.[18] Restrictions were strongly opposed by the banks on the grounds that it would put America at a competitive disadvantage in what had become a global industry.

Many believed that the economic policy of 'the Great Moderation', which featured low inflation, high growth and mild recessions, had brought an end to economic volatility, so permitting higher levels of risk-taking. Small wonder then that the deadly toxins can be transformed into financial weapons of mass destruction, to use Warren Buffett's phrase, contaminating all who come into contact with them.

It was only a small step then from 2007 onwards, when it remained unknown how badly affected various financial funds and institutions were, before confidence in the entire financial system evaporated and several long-established banks collapsed. In the ensuing crisis, blame was laid at many doors: the rating agencies, the hedge funds, the regulators, and those who serviced the loans. However, the problem could not have started without the banks and the way in which they remunerated themselves. Where bonuses were paid in cash or shares which could be sold immediately, the incentive to disregard longer-term problems was exacerbated. Massive bonuses and termination payments sometimes continue to be paid, although, in many cases, the banks' shareholders have lost most of their wealth. The interests of employees and shareholders can diverge when incentives are provided to reward short-term performance.

Alan Greenspan, testifying to Congress in 2008, admitted he was in a shocked state of disbelief and that he had made a mistake in believing that the banks would do what was necessary to protect their shareholders and institutions. He admitted that there was a flaw in the model and that regulation had not worked.[19] Perhaps the key to the flaw was the remuneration system and its impact on motivation? As the surviving banks have since been obliged to raise massive amounts of extra capital from their impoverished shareholders and increased the costs to borrowers, the bystander can be forgiven for wondering what has changed to prevent a recurrence of the problem. Many might also agree with Paul Volcker, another former Chairman of the Federal Reserve, who, in 2009, stated that the most important, useful financial innovation in the preceding 20 years was the invention of the automated teller machine. For most businesses, unable to pass on their problems to others, there is no alternative to remunerating their employees in a way that prevents antisocial behaviour. If managers are rewarded on the basis of short-term profits, which can be created by imprudent cost cutting, there is no reason to expect them to resist that temptation. Where large bonuses based on short-term performance form the main element in a rewards package, the entity may be vulnerable to abuse. When businesses succumb to moral hazard, where large risks are taken by parties who can avoid their consequences, the results can be devastating.

The challenge for all organisations, especially in the service sector where the customer is purchasing the skills of employees, is to motivate employees, while still keeping a rein on total costs. Occasionally, this is done using a stick, but usually it is by way of a carrot. GEC, the leading US multinational, under Jack Welch, would regularly dismiss the bottom 10% of its managers, which doubtless encouraged the survivors. In countries outside America, such a policy would tend to find less favour. The human resource policies of a successful Indian IT outsourcer may provide a better role model than the financial services sector.

## Wipro: an Indian IT model

Wipro[20] was a small family business, whose management was inherited by Azim Premji in 1965. It diversified into IT and, following the success of many Indian programmers dealing with the problems of Y2K or the Millennium Bug in the year 2000 developed into a major IT outsourcer, servicing many leading global companies. From its base in Bangalore in southern India it can pay its workforce salaries far smaller than those paid in the US. With employee costs comprising approximately 50% of total costs, it has a competitive edge but, nevertheless, operates in a cost-conscious industry.

To win international business it needs more than low costs. The business must be innovative, adopt best practice, be totally customer focused and adopt a policy of absolute integrity. To attract and retain top engineers it must pay mid-market salaries or marginally more. It does pay minimal perks and is generally parsimonious with expenses, but it has a key value in rewarding employees, treating them with recognition and respect. It encourages criticism and suggestions, while always keeping a sharp focus on training and education. Promotion is largely internal, with outsiders and non-nationals hired as necessary. The result is a well-motivated workforce and a profitable company.

## Conclusions

- The structure of the labour force has considerable effects on the cost of labour. The chosen mixture of full-time 'permanent' employees, sub-contractors, and casual or temporary workers is of crucial importance.

- Cost cutting in the rewards area must be made with the hidden costs of labour turnover, recruitment, and loss of core skills in mind.
- The cost of labour can be reduced through enhanced natural wastage, reducing non-pay costs, spreading the workload more thinly, cutting the price of labour or radical restructuring.
- Redundancy, when necessary, needs to be applied with fairness and, ideally, on a once-off basis, rather than repeatedly.
- The rewards system should be aligned with the human resources policy and overall strategy. Ill-considered rewards based on short-term performance may undermine the longer-term growth of the business, or even its survival.

## Management checklist

1. What would be your ideal labour force configuration in terms of the 'Shamrock Organisation', and how does the present structure compare?
2. Can and should any moves be made to change the configuration?
3. What is the current rate of labour turnover, and how does this compare with the norm in the industry?
4. What ways to reduce labour costs in your organisation have already been tried, and what further ways might be considered?
5. In the event that some redundancy is required, how would this be approached and on what terms?
6. Are your employees motivated to reduce costs in the way you desire?

# Chapter 17

# Strategic cost reduction – the critical links

> Turning and turning in the widening gyre
> The falcon cannot hear the falconer;
> Things fall apart; the centre cannot hold;
> Mere anarchy is loosed upon the world…
> 
> *W.B. Yeats, "The Second Coming"*

If a strategic cost reduction plan is to succeed, it is important that it fits in with all parts of the organisation so that the centre does indeed hold and anarchy is avoided. It will involve mobilisation of resources from across different functions and, therefore, has the potential for conflict if not properly managed. Cost reduction plans should not take place in isolation, but rather form part of an integrated strategy, linked in to other key success factors from the start. These will include the effective operation of the existing costing and budgetary system, the activities of the head office for a group, together with the strategy and values of the organisation, including the desired quality of the product or service. A way needs to be found to monitor these features of the system throughout the cost reduction project. These linkage issues will be addressed in this chapter under the following headings:

- Budgeting and costing systems
- Head office
- Strategy, values and quality
- The 'balanced scorecard'
- Loss of core values in Irish property lending

## Budgeting and costing systems

As has already been stated in **Chapters 1** and **2**, budgeting and strategic planning are inextricably linked. It is unlikely that a major cost reduction exercise will fall into one accounting year. If it involves redundancies, there may be a significant extra cost in that period and a material downturn in reported profits for the year in which it occurs. Once a cost reduction plan has been adopted, the interface with budgeting needs to operate smoothly. What frequently happens is that budgeting has a lesser role for the duration of the plan and needs to act in a supportive way to the greater end.

In many businesses, there can be a clash between strategists and financial controllers. Each group tends to have different timeframes and different cultures. The annual budget tends to follow a well-established routine. Reporting structures reflect the current organisation structure. However, if a radical change in the organisation structure is required, budgeting responsibilities will need to be realigned. It is also important that, in adhering to a rigid budgetary timeframe, sight is not lost of the greater strategic goals. Budgeting needs to be the friend and not the foe of strategic cost reduction. To achieve this end, it is usually helpful if a formal review of the cost reduction plan is undertaken at the outset of the budgeting process.

Given that the plan may not coincide with the accounting year, one way to assist the process of change is *rolling budgeting*. Rolling or continuous budgeting adds one new period on at the end as each period finishes. Often, it is rolled on a quarterly basis, but it can be done on a monthly basis. This almost continuous discipline forces companies to constantly review the future and is invaluable in times of great uncertainty. During a cost reduction plan it is not unusual for the timings of initiatives to change as a result of negotiation. Therefore, rolling budgeting, which is growing in popularity irrespective of cost reduction, is a useful tool. It is interesting to note that the EU and IMF have adopted a similar quarterly review in the provision of sovereign loans to ensure adherence to national budgetary targets.

Naturally, effective budgetary control requires an effective underlying costing system, which will enable managers to detect and remedy variances. Many traditional systems centre on departmental costs, so that those mangers can be held responsible for meeting budgetary targets. While such systems may achieve short-term financial control, they can create problems where cost savings do not fit readily into departmental silos.

Perversely, some costing systems may, in practice, hinder cost reduction, undermining rather than underpinning strategic changes. Many businesses have developed *standard costing* systems to underpin their budgeting systems. Standard costing was developed in the first half of the twentieth century before computers were available to process costs. The variance between actual costs and standard costs became central to financial control. In manufacturing, variances are traditionally broken down into volume, efficiency, and price for both material and labour. The standards, however, are usually based on past experience, which may be less than optimal. While, of course, these standards should be updated on a regular basis, this may prove to be a time-consuming and, therefore, expensive task. If the standards themselves are not challenging and not signalling adverse variances, they may generate complacency, thus allowing inherent inefficiencies to be ignored.

Another costing system often associated with Japanese manufacturing, target costing, reverses the normal process of building costs from the bottom up. It starts with the desired selling price and deducts a profit margin to establish the target cost. It becomes the task of management to achieve this target cost, generally over the product life cycle. Cost reductions may be achieved through the careful coordination of production, engineering and research & development. Such an approach keeps cost reduction to the fore and avoids building up standards based on past inefficiencies. Though its adoption is not widespread, such an approach could prove beneficial to many businesses in a time of recession, whether in manufacturing or services.

Costing systems can also inadvertently discourage rational decisions to reduce costs when they are misused. A capital investment may be justified for the savings it will bring. However, sometimes managers may be reluctant to dispose of existing equipment if it will show a book loss and possibly reflect poorly on their performance. Sunk costs, which have already been expended, should be ignored in weighing up the options. Capital investment projects should be assessed on their projected cashflows on an opportunity cost basis, which considers how else the funds could be deployed.

Lastly, in some circumstances, managers lose faith in accounting systems as an aid to decision-making. After the first oil crisis in the 1970s there was a period of rampant double digit inflation, which caused doubts to be expressed on the reliability of the depreciated historic cost basis. Profits tended to be overstated, due to the rising replacement cost of stocks. The problem of adjusting accounts for inflation was never satisfactorily resolved, but receded as inflation abated in most economies. If accounting systems fail to help managers to identify costs for reduction, management accounting could again be accused of irrelevance.

## Head office

Four questions for head office:

- What is the role of head office?
- How does it add value?

- Does it provide value for money?
- Has it any involvement in divisional cost reduction?

The focus of cost reduction in this book has been at the level of the business unit and, to a lesser extent, the department. It can equally be applied to the head office of a group of companies. In some cases, the head office may be the instigator of the change in the business units, and the way it conducts its own business will have a powerful demonstration effect around the group by the example it sets. A call from head office with plush accommodation, large staff, and high salaries is likely to evoke the same cynical response from the business units as might an owner–manager with his or her Rolls Royce when belt-tightening is demanded. Similarly, in 2008, leaders of the US car manufacturers cannot have helped their cause for a Federal bailout of their industry by flying in their corporate jets to Washington.

## What is the role of the head office?

The first question to ask is: what is the role of head office?[1] Some head offices are mainly coordinators. In a diversified group the business expertise lies chiefly with the divisions. Head office will monitor and review the results, ultimately sanction capital investment proposals and, where appropriate, seek divestment. Other head offices will adopt a much more hands-on approach. Strategic plans from the divisions will be meticulously reviewed and may be sent back for revision. They will try to generate synergies between different subsidiaries and attempt to influence the group's overall profitability. The second type of head office will require greater resources than the first type. Some will provide a range of central services, such as legal, information technology, internal audit, etc. In other groups, the head office rules by diktat, virtually running the divisions from the centre.

## How does head office add value?

The second question to ask is: how do the head office functions add value? Can the often substantial costs of the head office be justified in terms of the benefits they provide? Frequently, head office performs functions which are not greatly valued by the divisions and do not add significant value. Often, there exists unnecessary duplication between head office and the divisions. Given that their costs are allocated out to the divisions, there is little that dissatisfied managers of the business units can do. If the head office wishes to lead by example it is sensible to review the service it provides and establish whether these functions are necessary. Given that the head office staff will have a strong vested interest in the result of the process, there may be benefits from employing independent outside assistance. In a recessionary climate, an exercise of overhead value analysis, comparing the head office with peer groups, may provide considerable benefits.

## *Does the head office provide value for money?*

The third question to ask is does the head office provide value for money? Sometimes impressive-sounding systems, such as risk management in banking, seem to fail miserably. While some services may be required for regulatory purposes, there can be a tendency for head office to become a self-perpetuating bureaucracy. Could some of the services, for example legal services, be more efficiently outsourced? A rigorous application of the three 'Es' mentioned in **Chapter 2** can lead to substantial savings. Like any business unit, head office should be subjected to tests of economy, efficiency and effectiveness.

It can often be that there is greater scope for headcount reduction in support operations than in manufacturing. In 2008, as part of a worldwide plan, Dell announced the loss of 250 jobs in Ireland.[2] It employed 4,500 people in Ireland, of whom 1,500 were engaged in customer support across Europe. This latter group in sales, marketing and general customer support was expected to bear 180 to 200 job losses, more than 10% of the operation. Rather than tinker with the manufacturing labour force, however, in 2009 Dell decided that the entire manufacturing operation would be moved to Poland, with the loss of 1,900 jobs in Ireland as a consequence.

## *What role will head office play in divisional cost reduction?*

The final question for head office is to decide on the role it will play in a cost reduction plan conducted at divisional level. It may instigate the process and await the recommendations. It may provide assistance in the way of staff, or it may just adopt a monitoring role. There can be no single right answer. It depends on the basic role of the head office and the expertise at its disposal.

## Strategy, values and quality

### *Strategic implementation*

In the 1970s, McKinsey, the management consultancy firm, popularised the implementation of strategy through their '7 S' model.

*Figure 17.1* The '7 S' Model

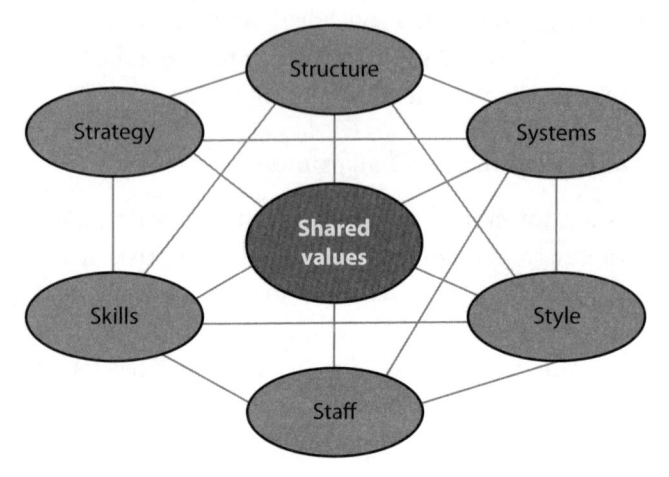

In this framework, they outline three 'hard' elements and three 'soft' elements, linked together by 'shared values'. The three hard elements are 'strategy', 'systems' and 'structure'. *Strategy* formed the basis of **Chapter 6**; operational *systems* underpinned **Chapters 11, 12** and **13**; and *structure* was addressed in **Chapter 15** with outsourcing and under 'head office' in this chapter. The soft elements are 'style', 'skills' and 'staff'. *Style* was covered in **Chapter 6**; functional *skills* arose in **Chapter 7**; and *staff* issues were covered in **Chapter 16**. This leaves *shared values*, which is the critical topic, a kind of glue, which holds all the others together.

Shared values are fundamental to success in business. Authors who identify great companies that can act as role models, as visionary or excellent businesses, invariably emphasise core values, which are part of the corporate culture and carefully guarded by CEOs.[3] Products or services may have a finite life, but values are a key and enduring aspect of the strategy, often highlighted in mission statements. They cannot solely guarantee success, as evidenced by the many casualties shown in the lists of great companies a decade or so after they have been proclaimed to be role models. But when important values are abandoned, failure can follow quickly, as demonstrated below by the Irish banks in their property lending from around the year 2004 onwards.

*Values*

The shared values of an organisation should provide direction to areas where costs may be cut, but should also establish boundaries to protect the longer-term future of the business. These values will almost certainly have an impact on the capital cost of the plan, since they will provide guidelines on such sensitive issues as the cost of any redundancy package. In the company's own best interest, it may pay to be generous with redundancy terms, since if it restricts payments to the statutory minimum, it may damage industrial relations and make it difficult to attract the right kind of employee at a future date when the company wishes to expand again.

It may also be that fundamental values need to be rethought. Michael Porter, the eminent strategic thinker, has suggested that a new form of capitalism is emerging in leading companies.[4] The zero sum game approach, in which a gain to one party incurs an equal loss to the other, may enable a powerful customer to lower prices from suppliers in the short term, but also damage the interests of society and consumers in the longer term by creating unpleasant environmental side effects. Instead of the adversarial approach, it is more beneficial to seek mutual advantages to create wealth for both parties in a way that transcends the traditional approach to corporate social responsibility. If, for example, fair trade arrangements are such that farmers learn to enhance productivity while protecting the environment, their profits can increase in a way which benefits both parties over time. Porter indicates that normal fair trade pricing increased farmer incomes by between 10% and 20% but, by increasing productivity and building supplier clusters, it was possible to increase their income by 300%. Each element of the value chain should be examined to see if shared value is being increased to maximise long-term profitability.

## Quality

One value which needs particular attention during a cost reduction programme is the quality of the goods or service. There are numerous cases where a loss of quality, whether caused by cost reduction or oversight, has resulted in catastrophic additional costs. In the extreme case, where health or safety is affected, the product may need to be withdrawn. When the problem is in an intermediate product in the supply chain, as has happened recently in the pork industry in Ireland, this can have devastating consequences for the entire industry. For outsourcers, the cost of manufacture may be lower in China, but this advantage can easily be nullified if quality is lost, as happened in the toy industry due to defective products.

It can be easy, when cutting costs piecemeal, to overlook the impact on the customer. However, if valuable business is lost in the process, it may completely negate the benefit of the costs saved. Everyone should be on the lookout for the straw that breaks the camel's back or the last cut, since the process can inadvertently lead to the death of the business by one thousand cuts.

The first essential step in protecting quality is to understand exactly what it means in relation to the product or service. It can relate to functionality, aesthetics or product features. It might be speed of response, reliability, durability or lack of defects. Quality is best regarded as what the customers perceive as value, which may differ from what the business itself sees as quality. Once quality is understood fully, it is important to keep track of it during a cost reduction programme and, in particular, to monitor customers' complaints.

## The 'balanced scorecard'[5]

The problem facing many businesses in the course of cost cutting is just how to recognise when damage is being done elsewhere in the business by a side effect of some cut. If the surgery is to work, the right balance needs to be found. One approach is to monitor various non-financial metrics. A more comprehensive approach is to employ a balanced scorecard.

The balanced scorecard, originally a performance management tool, has now been developed into a popular tool for monitoring the implementation of strategy. Its justification lies in the limitations of financial measures, which tend to be both short-term and historic in their focus. They can also mislead. If all discretionary expenditure is cut, the profits may be satisfactory in the short term, but the seeds of long-term destruction have been sown. What is needed is a system of warning signals which indicate where there are problems which could have an impact on future business. Very often, the mere measuring of an activity leads to the solution. The old maxim, 'What gets measured gets done,' should ring true.

The concept is easy to grasp. Once the strategy is agreed, the key success factors are identified. A measure is then devised for each key success factor and assembled into a customised scorecard under four headings.

It can be seen that financial measures are still monitored, but are supplemented by customer-oriented measures, efficiency measures and by learning and growth measures. Cost reduction measures should be reflected in the efficiency measures, but they are balanced by measures around customer and staff satisfaction.

A simple illustration may clarify the usefulness of the balanced scorecard. A small Irish manufacturing subsidiary of a US group experienced a record month of sales and profits. Congratulations were received from headquarters

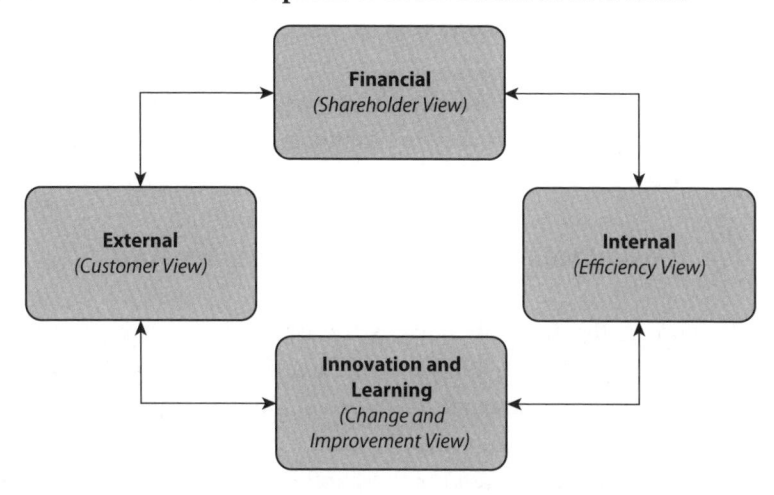

*Figure 17.2* **The Four Perspectives of the Balanced Scorecard**

```
                    ┌──────────────────┐
                    │    Financial     │
              ┌────▶│ (Shareholder View)│◀────┐
              │     └──────────────────┘     │
              │                              │
              ▼                              ▼
    ┌──────────────────┐           ┌──────────────────┐
    │     External     │           │     Internal     │
    │  (Customer View) │           │ (Efficiency View)│
    └──────────────────┘           └──────────────────┘
              ▲                              ▲
              │     ┌──────────────────┐     │
              │     │  Innovation and  │     │
              └─────│     Learning     │─────┘
                    │   (Change and    │
                    │ Improvement View)│
                    └──────────────────┘
```

in the US. On checking the scorecard, however, it discovered that the overall score actually fell. Orders were incomplete and late, so customer satisfaction measures signalled a problem. If this were allowed to continue, customers would be lost. The problem was easily resolved by putting an extra person into despatch, where costs had been excessively reduced.

The scorecard is designed to meet the requirements of an individual strategy. If all the key success factors are properly identified, then there should be a measure to monitor that factor. If measures are carefully selected, there should be a mixture of lag measures (e.g. customers lost), and lead measures (e.g. customer satisfaction ratings). Attention can then be focussed on the longer term and steps taken to address the problems. Sight should not be lost of quality declines, which should appear under the operational quadrant, or labour problems, which should appear under the learning and change quadrant. Naturally, scorecards are not set in stone for all time and should be modified as the strategy evolves.

An example from a US chain of garages with convenience stores[6] illustrates the model. In this case, financial measures are selected to trace asset utilisation, running costs, high-margin revenues and new sources of revenue. Customer measures centre on the customer shopping experience around petrol price, cleanliness, safety, speed of service and friendliness. Internal processes focus on fuel costs and the store operating processes. Learning and growth measures include measures around employee knowledge, commitment and communications.

If a good scorecard is in place and reviewed monthly by senior management, it should be possible to identify both the success of cost-cutting measures in terms of increased efficiency and the wider impact on the business. It should, therefore, provide a balance against foolish cost cutting, which undermines the long-term success of the business. It is not a major undertaking and, often, the measures are already in existence. If well communicated and properly used, it can be the key to monitoring continuous improvement.

## Loss of values – Irish bank property lending[7]

A theme running through this book is the importance of respecting core values when cutting costs. In a large group it can be expected that such values will be treasured by the head office and senior management. Strategies may evolve over time, but core values should be more permanent. They form the basis of how value is created for shareholders, which is the central, fundamental tenet of modern capitalism. If they become neglected or corrupted in the interests of short-term management rewards, the ultimate business objective is placed in jeopardy. In the '7 S' model at **Figure 17.1** above, the shared values remain at the centre, linked to everything else, forming the glue which holds the business together. When they are broken, in the words of the poet W.B. Yeats, the centre cannot hold and anarchy ensues.

For over a century, Irish banks had lent in a traditional, conservative and prudent manner to ensure that credit was only advanced when the prospects of repayment were reasonable. At the start of the 21st century, the Irish banks were considered to be amongst the strongest in the world. Yet these lending values were abandoned a few years later, leading to the virtual collapse of the Irish banking system in an orgy of widespread reckless lending to property developers. Although the underlying reason seems to have been to increase profits by competition to grow loan books, rather than by cutting costs, the consequences are the same.

The problems of the Irish banks in recent years have been widely reported. While many bankers chose to attribute the difficulties to the global banking problems in the aftermath of the collapse of Lehman Brothers, this interpretation does not stand up to scrutiny. The sub-prime housing crisis barely affected Ireland and the collapse of the Icelandic banks too had only a marginal impact. The Governor of the Central Bank, Professor Patrick Honohan, attributed about three-quarters of the downturn to local factors.[8] José Manuel Barroso, President of the European Commission, stated bluntly in the European Parliament that the problems of Ireland were created by the irresponsible financial behaviour of some Irish institutions and by the lack of supervision in the Irish market.[9] The institutions directly providing the finance were not purely indigenous, but also included the overseas subsidiaries of UK and continental European banks. Perhaps some blame too must ultimately be laid at the door of those foreign banks which provided the unrestricted funding to the Irish banks, without which the banks could not have expanded their balance sheets so rapidly.

## The boom

To understand the behaviour of the banks, it is necessary to understand the property bubble and the role of financial institutions. One economist, who had warned of its dangers at the time, explained the background.[10] Ireland in the 1990s experienced enormous economic growth, based on improved competitiveness in the heyday of the Celtic Tiger. However, from 2000 onward, growth continued solely based on a boom in construction. Ireland went from deriving a normal 4–6% of its national income from housebuilding in the 1990s to 15% in 2006/2007, with a further 6% coming from other construction. Bank lending to the non-financial private sector rose from a modest 60% of GNP in 1997 to 200% in 2008 (or around 270% if securitised mortgages are included), while deposits only amounted to 125%. Irish banks were more exposed to commercial real estate in 2007 than Japanese banks were in 1989 at the height of their property boom.

Ireland went from completing around 30,000 housing units in 1995 to more than 60,000 units in 2007. Traditional mortgage finance rose from up to three times the main family income to 10 times for a new house in 2006, or 17 times for a second-hand house. Traditionally, building societies advanced between 65% and 75% of the cost of a new house but, in 2006, only 24% of first-time buyers had loan-to-value ratios of less than 80%, while 64% exceeded 90%, including 30% which had 100%. The term of mortgages increased from a traditional 25 years to 35 or even 40 years in some cases. Clearly the banks had enormously increased the riskiness of their housing loans and would experience big problems with negative equity when house prices had fallen by over 50%, as they often had by 2011. The problems were exacerbated by the fact that the banks had offered a large volume of unmatched 'tracker' mortgages, which they were obliged to fund at a significant loss as soon as their funding costs exceeded the low rates offered on such mortgages.

Commercial property development has different risks. It relies on finding a creditworthy tenant, who is willing and able to pay the required rent over the period of the lease. If institutions do not wish to purchase the completed developments and market rents fall, despite upward only rent reviews, the developer may face vacancies and be unable to repay loans. Speculative buying and building to let are high risk strategies.

## The bust

From March 2007, in the light of the international property slowdown, house prices in Ireland started to fall. To finance their enormous growth, banks increasingly came to rely on overseas sources through the inter-bank market and bond issues. When these markets dried up in the international financial crisis following the sub-prime collapse in the US, Irish banks suffered serious liquidity problems.

With Anglo Irish Bank, a bank considered to be of systemic importance, on the verge of failure in September 2008, the Government took the unprecedented step of guaranteeing all the deposits and senior capital of the six leading Irish financial institutions, amounting to €440 billion, or approximately €100,000 per head of the population. Its proud boast that this was a cheap solution to the problem proved hollow as ever-increasing demands for capital were made. Eventually, the Government set up a 'bad bank', the National Asset Management Agency (NAMA), which took over the large property loans of five financial institutions financing the developers at 'economic value', an amount generally in excess of their market value.

As NAMA took on these massive loans, becoming in effect the world's largest property company, the true horror of the fall in lending standards started to emerge. The average discount on the face value of the €15 billion loans amounted to almost 50%, reflecting how poor the lending had been. NAMA's chairman accused the banks of "reckless abandonment of the basic principles of credit risk and prudent lending", describing a "litany of horrors" in documentation, which he was unsure whether to attribute to fraud or incompetence. Later, he stated that he was "extremely disappointed and disturbed" at the behaviour of the five institutions. These institutions were not using the full range of legal options open to them to secure income in respect of their troubled loans. [11]

The NAMA CEO pointed out that some borrowers had free cashflow over which the banks had not established a charge. Some had not been pressed to pay interest. Surplus funds were returned to developers on sale of surplus assets, despite unfulfilled commitments elsewhere. He stated that major developers operated on a divide-and-rule basis, where they did not disclose the full level of cashflow to each of the lenders. The Honohan Report (referred to above) revealed that in December 2007 inspectors for the financial regulator, examining the five largest exposures of each of the five institutions participating in NAMA, had found some serious deficiencies in credit assessment and an attitude of complacency at the banks.

## *The values around credit*

Traditionally, bankers spoke of the four *'Cs' of Credit*: The *Character* of the borrower, the *Capital required*, the *Capacity to repay* and *Collateral* or security. A few extra 'Cs' within these broad areas are added here to amplify basic credit considerations.[12] Lending should be a relatively simple function, if executed in a traditional, prudent manner.

In assessing the *character or culture of the borrower* banks historically considered property development to have been a cyclical business, where large fortunes were often made and lost as high-spending developers moved from boom to bust, without always adopting best practices – all of which suggested a cautious approach to lending. A *competent* developer is more than a builder and must buy the property in the right location at a reasonable price, obtain the appropriate planning permission and manage both the risks and the funding, making allowance for the fact that sales might be slower or at a lower price than expected. Many building groups are complex legal entities, often comprising a myriad of associated companies for different developments, so it is imperative to understand the *corporate constitution* of the group. Funds can rapidly move around a group, so a *consolidated* picture is required.

The *credibility* of the business model is questionable, where developers build more houses than their *customers* want to buy, where they have inadequate ability to *contract* operations in a downturn and where they lack proper *controls over cash and costs*. When the risk is *concentrated* in terms of the number of developers, the property sector and the geographic spread, these risks are increased. The numerous ghost estates around the country testify to developers' lack of skills in these matters.

In deciding on the scale of a loan, banks need to be satisfied that the *capital in total* is adequate and that the *capital contribution* of the borrower is reasonable. It appears that developers frequently provided minimal capital contributions, often in illiquid assets and unrealised profits, which were used for their contribution to subsequent developments under unwise equity release schemes. Where the *cause or purpose* of the loan is land speculation without planning permission or building finance in place, it is extremely imprudent to offer large loans with minimal capital provided by the developers.

The key to good lending is comfort around the *capacity to repay*. Capitalisation or rolling up interest does not solve the problem, but may disguise difficulties. If banks are unable to obtain a full picture of the borrowers' *commitments* and, therefore, lack the full *cashflow forecasts*, it is impossible for them to be assured that cover has been made for all *contingencies*.

Finally, the *collateral* or security was inadequate, particularly in view of the weaknesses in documentation. The publicity periodically emerging in the media about developers transferring properties to their wives indicate that available assets were not grasped by the banks. The *conditions* for loan drawdown were insufficiently rigorous, as were the *continuing covenants*, which were sometimes unenforced or waived in 'covenant-lite' loans, which had minimal conditions attaching to the credit.

Anglo Irish Bank, though the largest, was arguably not the worst offender. It is often bracketed with Irish Nationwide Building Society (INBS), which was also run by a long-standing chief executive, whose generous remuneration package was excoriated by the media. It had morphed from being a traditional building society to an extremely risky financier with over 80% of its €10 billion loan portfolio for property development or investment. A press story[13] indicated that reports prepared for the Financial Regulator and Department of Finance disclosed numerous irregularities and a remarkable lapse of corporate governance, whereby the board permitted the CEO to circumvent the credit committee in making loans and setting terms.

By 2011, the Government had to inject €5.4 billion into INBS, and provisions for impairment amounted to 50% of the loan book. A significant proportion of the NAMA loans had no recourse to clients. The €8.9 billion loans transferred to NAMA attracted a 64% discount, which was 'worst in class'. The new management deplored the appalling files and documentation, as well as the fact that there was no orthodox management structure.[14] Sustaining heavy losses on its mortgage book, as well as its commercial property, it reported catastrophic losses of €3.3 billion for 2010, following a loss of €2.5 billion the previous year.

Traditional lenders would accept these lending values outlined above as routine. But it is difficult to avoid the conclusion that practically every one of them was breached by lenders in the Irish property bubble. The Nyberg Report,[15] which was set up by the Government to investigate the causes of the banking crisis, emphasised the herd instinct of banks, together with a tendency to 'groupthink'.[16] But to explain the deterioration in standards merely as the herd instinct of banks trying to compete with Anglo Irish Bank and Irish Nationwide is inadequate. Perhaps a better analogy is lemmings, diving from a cliff. The decline in lending standards became hopelessly contagious, with bad lending driving out good lending in even some of the most conservative banks. Anglo Irish Bank was estimated to require almost €30 billion funding, and the reasons for its downfall are examined in the next chapter.

*Root causes*

The problems could and should have been largely avoided. Property bubbles are not new but, formerly, they did not imperil the banking system. When the vast Gallagher property empire collapsed into insolvency in 1982, this did indeed severely damage confidence and Irish property prices. But banks had adhered to their traditional values, thus limiting the aftershock. Loans to individual developers, together with any connected parties, were capped at prudent levels, while reasonable loan to value limits were observed. Risks were spread and exposure to property limited. Security was usually ample and put in place strictly prior to credit availability, with only occasional reliance on solicitors' undertakings for short periods. Above all, further drawdowns of the loans were prevented until certain sales targets were achieved. Accordingly, when markets tightened and property sales declined, funding under revolving credit facilities was withdrawn, so that both banks and borrowers stayed out of trouble.

The problems have been compounded by the banks poorly funding their own growth, failing to raise equity when stock markets were firm, over-reliance on the short-term inter-bank market and a reluctance to tackle their inflated cost base. To address these challenges, one further 'C' is required: *Culpability*. The spin of economists and estate agents in predicting a 'soft landing' was exposed by a former property practitioner.[17] A prominent journalist and independent politician[18] identified many parties collaborating to inflate the bubble: banks, developers, stockbrokers, estate agents, the Government and the media. Remarks by a leading politician that "the boom was getting 'boomier'" and advising moaners to commit suicide encouraged the hype.[19] But the Central Bank Governor pinned the primary responsibility on the directors and senior managers of the troubled banks. Lesser blame was placed at the door of brokers, auditors and accountants, as well as the regulator. But no party was totally innocent. The Central Bank itself had repeatedly reassured the public that the Irish banks were well capitalised.

Part of the explanation for the lack of public debate about the mistakes made might be what a former CEO of the Bank of Ireland[20] terms "the culture of silent dissent". In Ireland, there has been a longstanding distaste for whistleblowers and informers. Pressure can be brought to bear on directors holding unpopular views not to express them publicly lest they damage confidence or the share price. If directors and dissenting managers can be 'persuaded' to remain silent, proper discussion of relevant problems can be suppressed and difficult decisions avoided.

Even so, it is hard to understand why non-executive directors did not challenge the credit policies of bank management more effectively. There were dire warnings from sources such as *The Economist* and some independent economists that Irish property markets were overvalued. One key may be the composition, as well as the culture, of the bank boards. A former governor of the Bank of Ireland stated that banks were reluctant to appoint directors whom they did not know for fear that they might endanger the cohesiveness of the board.[21] Such a policy must encourage 'groupthink'. Even after the bust, criticism of the banks by senior business figures remains singularly muted.

It is perhaps surprising that more changes were not made within the senior echelons of the Irish banks, those people who must accept ultimate responsibility. Certainly the chairmen and chief executives of the five banks participating in NAMA were replaced. But many of the directors and senior managers remained in situ some 30 months after the Government had come to their rescue by guaranteeing the liabilities of their banks. Niall FitzGerald, formerly CEO of Unilever, posed a challenge to them: "If you knew what was going on, were you complicit; if not, were you competent?" No answer was forthcoming, except to urge the public to move on, though many of them ignored this advice in relation to their own positions. Professor Honohan, speaking in Washington, stated that keeping in place the management that had made poor decisions had prolonged the tendency to remain in denial about the problems.[22]

## Prudent financial management

Sound financial management in financial institutions has always been complicated, given the problems in measuring profits and the obligation to protect depositors. Greed and recklessness has always existed in banking. In bygone times, imprudent banks, which competed unwisely, seeking short-term profits and growth at the expense of sound risk management, were allowed to fail. But in the era of globalisation and interconnected global capital markets, central bankers are loath to permit banks to fail. The first line of defence should be the banks' own controls, such as internal audit, credit and risk committees. But reckless executives in pursuit of growth should still be restrained by non-executive directors on effective boards and diligent external auditors. Further removed are the regulatory authorities, who should set and enforce the rules. They must never be captured by the banks, and their independence must be fully supported by the authorities.

When all these checks and controls fail in a bubble, inflated by the many interested parties, including the Government, bankers can be tempted to sin. Lured away from traditional conservative values and behaviour, they sin by seeking growth at the expense of prudent risk management, so that catastrophe ensues with devastating social costs. Ireland's case has been particularly serious, but the same issues arise in many countries. Simply observing Basel requirements for capital adequacy is necessary, but in itself does not guarantee sound banking. New international guidelines may eventually emerge but, in the meantime, after bailouts, bankers remain vulnerable to moral hazard, taking risks which may ultimately fall on the taxpayer if they believe the banks cannot be allowed to fail.

Internationally there has been much talk of 'regulator capture' by the banks. In Ireland, there seems to have been an element of 'bank capture' by developers. The old adage that if you owe the bank £100 the bank owns you, but if you owe the bank £100 million you own the bank, has a worrying echo of truth. If the burden on the taxpayer is to be minimised, the accusation of crony capitalism rejected and the unpleasant charge of being the 'wild west of European banking' refuted, property oligarchs cannot be indulged. Traditional credit values and sound financial management must be restored.

## *The consequences*

With the recapitalisations of the Irish banks in the spring of 2011, the enormous cost of the banking bailout became clearer.[23] The banks' centre could not hold and, to some extent, Yeats's financial anarchy had indeed been loosed on the world. The capital required to recapitalise the six Irish banks amounted to €70 billion, which was double the estimate a year earlier and equated to more than two years' tax revenues. Including the overseas banks, the losses exceeded €100 billion. It was, in the words of the governor of the Central Bank, one of the most expensive crises in history.

All of the six Irish banks were heavily dependent on life support from the European and Irish Central banks, which provided funding of €140 billion. The one bank, Irish Life and Permanent, which had eschewed financing developers had lent aggressively in the housing market, was heavily dependent on inter-bank financing and mismatched its funding in offering 'tracker' loans. They all fell under varying degrees of State ownership, with two of them being wound down, a third merged and the bond ratings of the remainder severely reduced by Moody's.

In 2008, the World Economic Forum ranked Ireland's banking system as the ninth strongest in the world. By 2010, this rating had fallen to 139th, the weakest of all countries surveyed, trailing even Iceland and Zimbabwe, a ranking which did not improve in 2011. The Celtic Tiger is now a corpse, slain by the recklessness of its banks. The abandonment of traditional values and the collapse in lending standards of the Irish banks to the property market has come at a very high price indeed. The results have been felt not just by the banking industry and the taxpayer, but also throughout the European Union and international currency markets. Risks to the banks' funding position and risks to sovereign financial health remain (as an IMF report elegantly stated) "elevated and highly correlated".

## Conclusions

- A cost reduction project which is not integrated into the budgetary system is doomed to fail.
- Traditional costing systems may hinder strategic cost reduction.
- Head office needs to review its role and lead by example.
- To succeed, the project must be grounded on the business's strategy and values.
- To ignore the impact on quality risks destroying the business.
- The wider impacts of the project are best monitored by some form of the 'balanced scorecard'.
- Abandonment of core values can prove fatal to a business or even an industry.

## Management checklist

1. How will your budgeting system interface with cost reduction?
2. Would a system of rolling budgets be helpful?
3. Does your costing system need adaptation to support cost reduction?
4. What are the functions of head office, and does head office provide value for money?
5. Which key performance indicators need watching to ensure that cost reduction does not impair performance elsewhere?
6. Can cost reduction be linked to continuous performance?
7. Do you have a comprehensive strategic performance monitoring system, such as the 'balanced scorecard' in place?
8. Is the cost reduction plan consistent with corporate values?

# Chapter 18

# The fundamental causes underlying business failure

"Success breeds complacency. Complacency breeds failure. Only the paranoid survive."

*Andrew Grove, Chairman, Intel Corporation*

The subtitle of this book is 'Cutting costs without destroying your business'. It would, therefore, seem sensible for managers to be aware of the symptoms of business failure. In recent years, during an era of prosperity, little research was aimed at identifying the causes of business collapse. Except for the extreme case where liquidation is chosen to release the value of hidden assets, survival is the most basic objective, without which shareholder value cannot be created.

Business failure can also affect the business indirectly through its stakeholders. For most companies, the sudden collapse of a major customer can lead to a bad debt problem, which can prove fatal for the business. Equally, the collapse of a major supplier can cause significant disruption to a business. Yet, UK research at the height of the credit crunch[1] shows that 75% of organisations did not know how their suppliers were faring in the economic crisis, and 80% had not met with them to discuss the situation. If businesses are to avoid bad debts and disruption costs, they would be well-advised to watch out for potential failures.

This chapter will approach the issues as follows:

- The seven deadly sins
- An SME example
- Lehman Brothers
- Anglo Irish Bank
- Early warning signs
- The public sector

## The seven deadly sins[2]

In an ideal world, businesses would be able to obtain recent accounts from customers or suppliers to analyse their financial strength. Indeed, some businesses with strong negotiating positions may insist that such information be provided to them. Others may have to rely on what is publicly available to them, which may be limited in its usefulness.

In Ireland, companies that offer unlimited liability to their creditors are not obliged to file annual accounts. Unfortunately, many who avail of this exemption are owned by limited companies, which are often domiciled in jurisdictions where they in turn do not need to file detailed accounts. So, the ultimate shareholders are protected from the unlimited liability, while keeping their accounts out of the public domain, thus defeating the purpose of the filing exemption. While this loophole may be closed sometime in the future, meanwhile it is essential to find other means of monitoring the health of these businesses.

In recent years, perhaps due to strong economic growth, there has been little research conducted into the causes of business failure. Much of the earlier work relates to failures of at least 20 years ago, particularly in the US and the UK. Drawing on the common features of failure in this research,[3] an Irish academic researched nine publicised Irish corporate failures.[4] Four of these failures were rapidly-growing 'adolescent' businesses, while the other five can be described as 'mature'. Many classical signs of failure were evident in both groups, although overtrading was generally absent in the mature group. Some of the signs overlapped, and the academic's list of 20 signs has been condensed here to seven, which can be likened to the biblical seven deadly sins. More recently, Jim Collins has researched American business failures and identified five stages on the road to collapse, which have close parallels to the seven deadly sins.[5]

### 'Pride' – autocratic management

Pride does indeed come before a fall. A business rarely fails with its management's reputation intact. Often, an entrepreneur with drive, but without the full range of management skills, is reluctant to delegate responsibility. Autocratic managers rarely mend their ways. In 1971, UK government-appointed inspectors described Robert Maxwell as: "Not being a fit person who can be relied upon to exercise proper stewardship of a publicly quoted company." Twenty-five years later he was raiding his company's pension scheme, while his sons (as managing directors) later protested in court that their father did not keep them informed about company business.

## 'Sloth' – ignoring change

Many businesses fail to spot changes arising from new competitors or technological innovations, often becoming complacent, rather than being vigilant. If the company has no strategy or long-term plan, it is likely to experience unpleasant surprises in turbulent times. Without investment in technology, new products or people, survival is threatened. In a rapidly changing world, paranoia may not be misplaced. Charles Darwin's adage that, in nature, it is neither the strongest of the species that survives, nor the most intelligent, but the one that is most responsive to change, applies equally to business.

## 'Anger' – lack of control

In times of a recession or credit crunch, control over cashflow is critical. Thoughtless or reckless expenditure must be curtailed, with prudent financial management to the fore. This necessitates sound credit control, working capital management, rigorous budgeting and timely management accounts. The tightening of trade credit, accompanied by the withdrawal of bank credit facilities, has made the discipline of control imperative for survival.

## 'Gluttony' – overtrading

After more than a decade of growth at the start of this century many businesses assumed that sales growth would continue indefinitely. The accompanying growth of overheads, spread over a wider base, all too often did not attract the attention it merited. With profits growing, banks obligingly financed cash shortages, so businesses were not obliged to tackle inefficiencies in their cost bases. Overtrading from unplanned and undisciplined expansion often went unpunished as a result, but is unlikely to be tolerated in a credit crunch.

## 'Covetousness' – overborrowing

The desire to have something belonging to others is the financial equivalent of high gearing or, to use American terminology, high leverage. High property valuations allowed businesses to increase their debt to equity ratios to levels which, historically, would not have been considered prudent. Secured bankers have the power to appoint receivers and, thus, precipitate the failure of businesses.

## *'Lust for power' – the big risk*

The danger of big uninsured risks has always been a hazard that company boards are keen to avoid. Even risk-conscious businesses succumb periodically. The banks have been caught out by rogue traders. But they have also taken on toxic risks by failing to monitor adequately their exposure to various derivatives, which frequently are complex financial instruments, with consequences that, on occasions, have proved fatal.

## *'Envy' – creative accounting*

The US accounting scandals of recent years have shown that, even in highly regulated markets, companies have resorted to dubious accounting policies and practices to bolster their reported performance. The purpose was either to enhance the income statement by aggressive income recognition or understatement of costs, or the balance sheet by overvaluing assets or understating liabilities. While international accounting standards, where they are adopted, have closed some loopholes, others remain to be exploited. Banks, in particular, have recently come under scrutiny for their accounting policies for loan impairments.

## An SME example

To evaluate 'the seven deadly sins' as a model for describing corporate failure, it needs to be applied to business failures, where there is adequate information in the public domain. It is rare for a failed business person to provide an objective account of mistakes which led to the collapse of an enterprise, since pride and reluctance to admit to mismanagement are likely to intervene.

An exception to this rule is an SME account of a regional Irish car dealer, where the owner–manager candidly described the factors underlying the collapse of his business and the personal trauma involved.[6] Having joined a family business, he pursued with his brother a policy of rapid expansion for over a decade up to 2006, opening up new premises, investing in showrooms and taking on new dealerships in a thriving marketplace. Overruling the more cautious approach of his father, and driven by his strong ego, the business initially thrived as car ownership grew in an economic boom. He also took up day trading on the stock market. When the car market suddenly imploded in 2008, the business was unprepared. Its costs were out of control, and the business was overstocked and overborrowed. Fortunately, the story had a reasonably happy ending. Following a programme of redundancies, the closure of surplus premises and a dramatic attack on all costs, closure of the business was averted. This was achieved by retaining only a single dealership, and by implementing a new business model centred on second-hand cars, tight controls and much lower borrowings. He had committed most of the seven deadly sins, but by contritely repenting, he survived to manage a much reduced business.

Do the seven deadly sins equally apply to larger businesses? Many of the most spectacular and notorious collapses of the international recession relate to the world of banking. Below we have selected two well-documented examples, both very different but highly significant in their own markets. Lehman Brothers was a prominent US investment bank, one of the best known on Wall Street, famous for its deal making. Anglo Irish Bank was a bank which specialised mainly in Irish property lending. Both failures had catastrophic consequences for their respective countries.

## Lehman Brothers

Lehman Brothers in 2008 was the fourth largest investment bank in Wall Street. During the 150 years of its illustrious history, it was associated with advising many of the greatest businesses in America, such as F.W. Woolworth, Macy's, Campbell Soup and TWA. In the 1980s it changed its emphasis from traditional corporate finance advisory and fundraising to trading. In late 1983, there was an internal coup, which resulted in the senior trader, Lew Glucksman, being appointed CEO of the banking partnership. After a period of infighting during difficult trading conditions, the partnership, facing a crisis, was forced to seek extra capital. Eventually, after some trading losses, it merged with Shearson American Express in April 1984[7] before being demerged in 1994 with Dick Fuld, a close associate of Lew Glucksman, as the chairman and CEO.

The investment banking industry changed fundamentally in 1999 with the repeal of the Glass–Steagall Act of 1933, which had prevented investment bankers from merging with commercial banks and gaining access to their substantial deposits. In the era which followed, businesses developed on a global scale with financial innovation being the order of the day.

With the development of the swaps markets and securitisation, which permitted the transferring of loans from banks to investors, risks were freely moved from one institution to another. Wall Street came increasingly to resemble a casino, as had been revealed a decade earlier in a description of Salomon Brothers[8] where the players made large bets, generating vast profits for shareholders and executives alike.

In due course, derivatives with strange-sounding acronyms were created for such purposes as enabling US citizens to avoid capital gains tax, Mexican banks to bypass exchange control regulations and Japanese banks to defer recognition of trading losses, all the while generating massive fees for the investment banks which devised them. These complex instruments contained obscure, arcane risks, which were hard to assess for fund managers buying them to obtain the higher income they offered, but were all too real. Derivatives, designed to reduce risk, could equally be used to increase risk with devastating consequences, as rogue traders in banks have demonstrated. Bets could be made in any direction, since stocks could be shorted (whereby stocks were sold even though they were not owned) when a fall was anticipated. If it was thought that borrowers could not repay debt, it was possible to profit through dealing in credit default swaps. The world of banking was dominated by large and highly interrelated institutions, which many people believed were too big to fail.

In September 2008, however, with the spread of the sub-prime mortgage crisis, described in **Chapter 16**, the future of many venerable financial institutions was in doubt. With varying degrees of US government support, Bear Sterns, Fannie Mae and Freddie Mac, AIG, Morgan Stanley and Goldman Sachs survived. Lehman Brothers, however, did fail and was forced to file for bankruptcy, generating catastrophic repercussions for the industry and causing major ripples worldwide.

Larry McDonald, a trader at Lehman Brothers, has written an insider's account of the collapse of the bank.[9] He portrays Dick Fuld, CEO since 1994, in a most unfavourable light, describing him as a poor listener, a recluse, greedy and a bully who had never had a powerful deputy. The Board was considered irrelevant, with only two of its 10 members having banking experience, nine being retired, and four aged over 75 years old. The executive committee was also accused of being unwilling to challenge Fuld.

Did the bank fail to anticipate the property bubble? The housing collapse had been foreseen by some traders in June 2005, some 18 months before the collapse, when it was likened to an athlete taking steroids. These views were, however, ignored, despite the resignations of several senior executives, while the bank continued to create sub-prime securitisations, being caught in the end with a $2 billion sub-prime portfolio deal on its books.

Did the bank overtrade, over-borrow and lack controls? From the first quarter of 2005, when they amounted to $7 billion, revenues expanded steadily every quarter until they reached over $13 billion in the last quarter of 2006. Gearing increased from 20 times net worth in 2004 to 32 times in 2006. By the end of 2007, it was reported to be 41 times, while early in 2008 a senior managing director protested that the multiple was estimated at 44 times net worth and had to be reduced.

What about controls and risk management? In response to the complaints about high gearing, the company president was reported to have criticised the conservative attitude and affirmed that the aims of the company were growth, risk and major deals. The bank took on an enormous exposure to commercial-mortgage-backed securities, estimated at $30 billion, which was considered to be a hedge against any weakness in the residential market. Real estate acquisitions continued. When the Treasury Secretary, Hank Paulson, urged Fuld to deleverage (or reduce its borrowings) the bank and consider its sale, he apparently deemed Fuld's response to be something between arrogance and disrespect.

Investors were critical of Lehman's accounting policies and questioned the value of its assets, even though it was still reporting profits. Concern was expressed over the exposure to derivatives in arcane special purpose vehicles.

Another account by an outsider, a well-known financial journalist, broadly paints a similar picture.[10] Fuld's behaviour was variously described as confrontational, bullying, aggressive and hectoring. A senior colleague accused him of having a blind spot for weak people who were sycophants. It was suggested that, in part, he selected his deputy because he was a non-threatening individual.

The board saw little wrong when, shortly before the end, an octogenarian member delivered a ringing endorsement of the executive: "I want everyone in the room to know that I know that you guys have done a good job. This is just bad luck. We are a hundred per cent behind all of you."

Fuld was reported to consider the bank as too conservative. The treasury secretary was reported as regarding him as a reckless risk taker due to mistakes made in 1995 over exposure to the Mexican Peso. Fuld was said to have little understanding or interest in the risks contained in complex derivatives. The risk officer's role was virtually non-existent and she was eventually removed from the executive committee. The bank had an enormous exposure to property, and it was stated that the bank was turned into an all-in, un-hedged player on the US real estate market with which it was inextricably linked.

Accounting practices were also heavily criticised. Property assets were overvalued in the accounts, sometimes not being marked to market so that write-downs could be deferred, since current market valuations were not employed. Window dressing was employed at the end of the quarter to reduce the amount of gearing reported through the use of repurchase agreements ('Repo 105'), whereby assets were sold just before the period, but repurchased shortly afterwards. The bankruptcy examiner was critical of these practices and indicated that there could be civil claims for filing misleading reports against certain members of management and the auditors.

Based on these two accounts, one by an insider and one by an outsider, it appears that Lehmans committed most, if not all, of the seven deadly sins. Perhaps the failure of the bank was best summed up by Larry McDonald in the naming of his book, "*A Colossal Failure of Common Sense.*"

## Anglo Irish Bank

In 1980, Seán FitzPatrick was appointed general manager of Anglo Irish Bank, a small bank with assets of less than IR£500,000, and which could be described as a mixture of a finance house and a merchant bank. In 1986, it merged with City of Dublin Bank, and FitzPatrick was appointed chief executive. For the next two decades, the bank expanded rapidly, growing organically and making occasional acquisitions.

The bank began to challenge the two more apparently staid market leaders, Allied Irish Bank and Bank of Ireland. It rewarded performance and, by 2001, FitzPatrick, affectionately known as 'Seánie', was the highest-paid banker in Ireland. A heavy emphasis was placed on knowing the customers, taking decisions quickly and usually obtaining personal guarantees. It had well-established relationships with the leading property developers and provided finance for them not only in Ireland, but also in the UK and US. In 2005, FitzPatrick stood down as chief executive, having been at the helm of the bank for almost 25 years, but stayed on as chairman. The new CEO, David Drumm, who had run the bank's US operations for several years, was a surprise appointment. The rapid growth of lending continued.

The bank had many admirers. It was awarded the Grand Prix by the prestigious *IR Magazine* first in 2003 and subsequently for the next five years. In

2006, a leading global management consultant firm, Mercer Oliver Wyman, named it as the world's top-performing bank, based on its returns from 2001 to 2005. The following year at Davos it proclaimed Anglo Irish Bank to be the best of the 170 banks worth over $10 billion surveyed, given its average growth rate of 35% over 10 years. In 2007, Standards & Poor's rated it strongly with an 'A' long-term and 'A-1' short-term ratings.

In September 2008, after the collapse of Lehman Brothers, Anglo Irish Bank experienced severe funding problems and was facing imminent collapse, initially attributed to liquidity issues, rather than solvency. The Irish Government reacted by guaranteeing the main liabilities of the Irish banks, which amounted to a massive €440 billion on 30 September 2008, the date of Anglo Irish Bank's year-end. On radio shortly afterwards FitzPatrick attributed the problems to a systemic problem worldwide, denied recklessness and refused to apologise.

In December 2008 the bank announced its results, with profits down by 37% from 2007 to €784 million. The bank remained confident in its business model and its stringent risk management, predicting profits for each of the next three years. However, that same month, both FitzPatrick and Drumm had resigned. In January, the Minister of Finance stated that the funding position of the bank had weakened and that 'unacceptable practices' had damaged the bank's reputation. The bank was then nationalised. Having been valued at more than €13 billion at its peak, it had become worthless.

It transpired that FitzPatrick had undisclosed loans of €87 million from the bank, which had been temporarily transferred or 'warehoused' with Irish Nationwide Building Society over the year-end. Over €7 billion had also been placed with Anglo over its year-end by another financial institution, which controversially was treated as a deposit. Finally, the bank had loaned €451 million to 10 major customers to purchase shares in the bank with personal recourse limited to a maximum 25% of the borrowings, a serious exposure to the bank if the shares fell in value.

The decline in fortune continued for all involved. The fraud squad and other regulatory authorities were called in; FitzPatrick was arrested, but released without charge. Later, in what was the biggest such case in the history of the State, he was declared bankrupt, while Drumm filed for bankruptcy in the US. The Government's newly created bank, the National Asset Management Agency (NAMA), took over the large property loans of Anglo and five other banks at a large discount to their book value. Finally, Anglo Irish Bank's efforts to provide a survival plan failed, and its run down commenced with its deposit book being sold in 2011.

To judge from the accounts for the year ending September 2007, published in the year before the collapse of Lehman Brothers, all was well at the bank. It had just delivered its 22nd year of uninterrupted earnings growth which, in terms of assets and profits, had averaged 35% over the past 20 years. Pre-tax profits had grown by 46% to €1.2 billion, with a similar growth in deposits of 46%, while assets amounted to almost €100 billion. The 'high quality' growth in customer lending of €18 billion had grown 37%. Overall, the bank proclaimed an improvement in its cost to income ratio, 30% return on equity, earnings per share growth of 44% and a 20% dividend increase.

Shareholders were advised of its prudent credit policy, its strong capital position, its focussed and disciplined business model, together with its stringent risk management. The bank boasted that impaired loans amounted to only €335 million, being 0.5% of its customer loans of €67 billion, significantly less than that of its peers. The bank stated that it did not engage in speculative lending, and the group risk management review completed in November showed that the bank was not experiencing any stress. The bank operated to the highest ethical standards and governance, aspiring to be a model corporate citizen. Looking ahead, the chairman expected growth in the UK and Ireland, with earnings per share growth in excess of 15% and confidently expected above market returns in subsequent years.

Not everyone would agree with FitzPatrick's confidence in the years that followed nationalisation. The report by the governor of the Central Bank, Professor Patrick Honohan, stated not only that the bulk of the crisis could be attributed to local issues, but that both Anglo Irish Bank and Irish Nationwide Building Society were well on the road to insolvency at the time of the collapse of Lehman Brothers.[11] In 2010, Anglo Irish Bank announced a loss of €12.7 billion with impairment charges of over €15 billion for the 15 months to December 2009, a new Irish corporate loss record. It also had outstanding loans of €155 million to former directors, much of which is not expected to be repaid. The new chief executive of the bank castigated the previous management over their governance, risk management and managerial processes.[12] Finally, in 2011, Anglo Irish Bank announced 2010 losses of over €17 billion, requiring substantial further Government assistance.

To what extent had Anglo Irish Bank committed the seven deadly sins? (Readers may be assisted in answering this question through information contained in a book written by two journalists, Brian Carey and Tom Lyons, to whom Seán FitzPatrick granted interviews, presenting his side of the story.[13])

Seán FitzPatrick was a much more amiable man than Dick Fuld in Lehman Brothers. One account describes him as a hard worker, a delegator, a fast decision-maker and a virtuoso salesman.[14] Another calls him a "quick-fix banker" who got things done.[15] He saw himself as neither technically a good lender, nor someone who involved himself in credit committees, but an entrepreneur and a businessman. For a long-standing CEO, as FitzPatrick had been, to become chairman did not constitute good corporate governance and, with the benefit of hindsight, his chairman's report in the 2007 accounts (see above) contained more than a hint of hubris.

Did the bank ignore changing conditions in the property market? A decision was made around 2005/2006 to stop development lending in Ireland, but the bank incredibly continued to support developers with a good track record, permitting them to gear up through equity release, a policy which FitzPatrick believed led to the bank's collapse. So, if the bank did understand the property bubble, it failed to take the appropriate action.

Did the bank overtrade, over-borrow and lack proper controls? Average growth of 35% over 20 years sounds distinctly like overtrading. The Central Bank Governor, Professor Honohan, indicated that rapid balance sheet growth is a very simple warning sign for regulators. Despite the confident statement about the bank being adequately capitalised, the massive capital subsequent injections required by the State would indicate otherwise. The *Nyberg Report*, referred to in **Chapter 17**, indicated that there was a weakness in enforcement of controls.

Did the bank manage risk as well as it asserted? FitzPatrick claimed that Anglo was a very "solid bank, making very good profits, well diversified geographically, well diversified in terms of that our property lending was for investment property and some development". The bank's rule of thumb was that loans to any one customer should be limited to 1% of its loan book. It had, however, lent more than €1 billion to six customers, with an exposure of over €2 billion to the troubled Quinn Group. By the end of 2008, 15 of the bank's customers owed more than €500 million. The bank had a massive exposure to the Irish property sector in particular. Spreading into the risky UK and US property markets hardly constituted good geographic diversification. The bank also had another rule of thumb, limiting its exposure to development lending to 15% of its loan book, but this figure rose to 25% when, in 2008, it reclassified a further 10% of the loan portfolio as development loans.

Anglo Irish Bank's claim that it adopted a prudent credit policy and stringent risk management is open to question. As described in **Chapter 17**, most, if not all, banks had lowered their lending standards in the period that led up to the international financial crises in 2008, but Anglo seemed to lead the way in this regard. An Irish developer claimed that obtaining loans from the bank was easy.[16] The credit committee, whose role is to apply lending standards, comprised mainly associate directors, who headed up the different lending teams. Nobody worried about the head of risk, because he was believed to have no power. An unnamed former Anglo lender in the US was reported[17] as stating that credit checks could have been stronger and more rigorously applied.

Finally, did Anglo Irish Bank want to be or present itself as something it was not? Seán FitzPatrick has admitted that the warehousing of his loans, which he considered to be perfectly legal, was inappropriate and unacceptable.[18] There are plenty of loose ends remaining. For example, there is the question, still not satisfactorily explained, as to why weeks before nationalisation Anglo sold off its Austrian subsidiary, which contained €570 million in deposits and less than €35 million in lending to a Swiss group for €141 million, even providing a loan to assist the purchaser, at a time when it was critically short of deposits.

In 2012, many investigations into Anglo continued, such as those by the Garda Fraud Squad, the Director of Public Prosecutions, the Director of Corporate Enforcement and the Chartered Accountants Regulatory Board, so judgement on any matters under investigation is premature. Even if and when the results of these various investigations eventually become public, the effects of the Anglo saga is likely to continue for many years. It announced losses of €17.7 billion for 2010, the worst financial results in Irish history, surpassing its own previous record. Over a two-year period the bank accepted State assistance amounting to almost €30 billion. It is little wonder that the *New York Times* in 2010 posed the question: "Can one bank bring down a country?" or that the subtitle of the *FitzPatrick Tapes* is "The rise and fall of one man, one bank, and one country". As in the case of Lehman Brothers, its fall could be ascribed to a lack of common sense.

It would seem that, in hindsight, both Lehman Brothers and Anglo Irish Bank had committed most, if not all, of the seven deadly sins. The fact that they were not recognised in the marketplace at the time is perhaps most surprising. The share price was slow to react to the warning signs. Admittedly, business failures were rare in times of strong economic growth and failures of major banks had not occurred for many years. Many 'experts' rated the banks highly, and few security analysts predicted disaster, despite the fact that a careful examination of the accounts would uncover signs of weakness. Maybe in times of recession businesses will probe more thoroughly for evidence of the seven deadly sins in their trading partners and take appropriate action before it is too late.

## Early warning signs

Businesses cannot afford the luxury of waiting for the collapse of a stakeholder to analyse the causes of its failure. There are usually several signs of difficulty before a business collapses, evident in the marketplace long before weakness appears in the accounts. Some parties are better placed than others to spot and interpret the clues. Normally, the closer the party is to the afflicted business, the more obvious are the symptoms. The reader of the accounts, the bank manager, the trade creditor, the employees or visitors can all spot the signs of trouble.

There may be signs evident in the public domain for a normal manufacturing or service business. Any concerned party can seek credit references, and larger businesses may have their debt graded by rating agencies. For listed companies the share price is likely to weaken and dividends may be cut. Any party – customers, suppliers or employees – anticipating business failure may try to protect themselves by leaving or terminating their contracts.

### *The reader of accounts' perspective*

The unavailability or delays in the production of a company's accounts can be a warning sign. The directors have to state and the auditors accept that the going concern is applicable to the business. With banks unwilling to give adequate reassurance regarding renewal of facilities, audit qualifications in this respect may become more common. Changes in auditors, year ends or significant accounting policies merit explanation.

The vigilant reader can also check the cashflow statement, borrowings and the payment of taxes. Ratios can be calculated to assess profitability, liquidity, gearing and working capital. These ratios are all likely to deteriorate when problems commence.

### *The bank manager's perspective*

The provider of the clearing account is especially well-placed to spot problems. Abnormal payments, round figure payments on account to suppliers, declining lodgements and the kiting of cheques, where funds are moved around group accounts to inflate lodgements, are warnings. Overdrafts tend to become permanent, and excesses or requests for 'temporary' increases commonplace. Cheques or direct debits may bounce, financial information falls behind and communications may be ignored.

## The creditor's perspective

Creditors may find payments are delayed, sometimes with payments on account and requests for extended trade credit. The business grapevine will provide more information and rumours. Banks may increase their security, or borrowings may have to be refinanced at greater cost. Some creditors may register judgments through the courts or initiate legal proceedings. Tax audits may be initiated, and both trade and bank references will be weak.

## The employee's perspective

Employees may notice changes in managerial behaviour. Management will probably be under permanent stress or, indeed, become genuinely ill. There will likely be endless meetings and a major drive on cash collection. Traditional perks may disappear and expenses may be curtailed. Redundancy or short-time working may be mooted. Creditors may be pressing and stock late in arriving. Key employees may give in their notice and trading partners may break off relations.

## The visitor's perspective

A visit to the workplace may prove instructive, revealing management under stress, pressing creditors and worried employees. The premises may be badly run down, with offices becoming empty and equipment poorly maintained. Stock levels may rise, and the quality of products or service fall.

Some warning signs are nearly always apparent when a company runs into difficulties. If they are ignored, there can be a nasty increase in costs, whether from a bad debt or a disruption of supply.

# The public sector[19]

At first sight, the signs of difficulty in government finances may seem to have nothing in common with the private sector, since governments are not run for profit and can always raise cash from additional taxation. Yet, increasingly, politicians fear that countries may default on their loans and effectively bankrupt themselves if they lack either the political will or the ability to address the difficult aftermath of banking collapses in different countries. Countries cannot be placed into liquidation, but the workout imposed by institutions such as the International Monetary Fund (IMF) or the European Central Bank (ECB) may, in many ways, resemble cost-cutting in a commercial restructuring. The European Commission has even raised the possibility of some form of 'administration' for weakened sovereign states. At least one journalist has likened the Irish government's progress down the slippery slope to insolvency in the aftermath of the collapse of the property bubble, bank bailout and sovereign debt problems, to a 'bust'.[20]

The challenges facing finance ministers confronted with rising interest costs and lack of available credit do not differ greatly from those experienced by finance directors of failing businesses. In this troubled time, they may seek bailouts by creditors or 'bail-ins' from reluctant bondholders, who may be asked to share the burden and avoid total collapse through debt restructuring. Changes in top management are likely to occur, whether from creditor pressure, as has happened in Greece and Italy, or by the national electorate, as happened in Ireland, Portugal and Spain. **Chapter 17** viewed the Irish property bubble from the perspective of the banks. In dealing with the problem, politicians exhibited many of the signs of corporate difficulty found in the private sector.

Politicians in democracies worldwide can be guilty of hubris in their claims to the electorate in search of votes, generally preferring to cast themselves more as a bountiful Santa Claus than a miserly Ebenezer Scrooge. Many welcomed the benefits of economic growth, which enabled them to finance popular spending programmes, but failed to see the dangers of uncontrolled growth. The electorate in Ireland has never taken it kindly when it detects any hint of arrogance in its representatives, particularly if they are seen to favour their cronies. To blame the crisis on the loss of international confidence following the collapse of Lehman Brothers, as many bankers did, was not credible, while suggesting that 'moaners', who forewarned of trouble ahead, should commit suicide contained more than a hint of arrogance.

Irish politicians were slow to recognise changes underlying economic growth, as measured by GNP or GDP.[21] There existed many different parties who benefited from the bubble and were ready to believe in a 'soft landing', including: economists, brokers, estate agents and the media. But some did warn of approaching hazards, in particular *The Economist* magazine and Professor Morgan Kelly. Instead of curbing growth in the changed environment, the Irish government took no action to control the excesses, which arose from reckless lending and inadequate regulation.

After years of Celtic Tiger growth, the public finances seemed to exude good health. But, if expenses were benchmarked against our European peers, some worrying weaknesses and lack of control might have been detected. Many welfare benefits exceeded European norms by a wide margin. Expenditure on health services was growing rapidly despite many complaints and warnings of inherent inefficiency. The remuneration and expenses of politicians seemed high by international standards. Irish public servants, enjoying job security, numerous special allowances and generous pensions, were also paid not only more than their private sector counterparts, but more than their equivalents in other EU countries. Such expenditure is difficult to reverse quickly and creates serious structural problems when the underlying tax revenues dry up in a recession.

Neglect of change, accompanied by lack of control, naturally leads into overtrading. Well-founded economic growth, based on foreign direct investment wishing to locate businesses in Ireland allowed the country to spend heavily on upgrading its infrastructure, improve its services and even provide some funding for public sector pensions. Many groups sought to take the credit for the birth of the Celtic Tiger: the EU for funding and providing the wider market, governments for their fiscal leadership, the Industrial Development Authority (IDA) for attracting foreign businesses, unions for maintaining industrial peace, and teachers for creating an educated workforce. Fewer claimed responsibility for its subsequent failure. Most commentators would now accept that growth came at a very high cost to the country and the taxpayer, once the bubble burst.

Jim Collins in the US emphasised the danger for private sector businesses in 'grasping for salvation' through taking a major risk. Governments too, in the face of a crisis, can find themselves taking big chances in search of salvation. With Anglo Irish Bank, a bank considered to be of systemic importance, on the verge of failure in September 2008, the government took the unprecedented step of guaranteeing all the deposits and senior capital of the six leading Irish financial institutions, amounting to €440 billion or approximately €100,000 per head of the population, a colossal commitment by any standard. Its proud boast that this was a cheap solution to the problem proved hollow as ever increasing demands for capital were made.

Ireland entered the financial crisis of 2007 with its national balance sheet in excellent shape and was envied by many European competitors, whose borrowings as a percentage of GDP greatly exceeded Ireland's modest debt levels. As a small island nation, Ireland avoided the cost of a large defence budget and was able to reduce the national debt by many successive budget surpluses. But overtrading and the recapitalisation of the banking system quickly reversed the situation. Since debt exceeds 100% of GDP, the country is now heavily indebted and, as a result, locked out of international capital markets. With the rising costs of funding loan repayments, in 2012 the country faces many years of austerity before prudent levels of borrowing can be restored.

Many businesses, wishing to compare their performance favourably with their competitors, resort to dubious accounting practices to inflate their profits or disguise balance sheet weaknesses. Given that accounting errors overstated the deficit, Ireland is not vulnerable to this accusation of creative accounting. Nevertheless, when setting up NAMA, a structure was openly chosen to try to keep the liability off the national balance sheet, though this device ultimately proved unsuccessful when Eurostat ruled that they must be included in national borrowings.

Ireland is, of course, in no way unique in falling for many of the seven deadly sins. Both Greece and Portugal failed to undertake structural reforms to their economies, allowing public sector costs to grow with insufficient controls. Greece itself has been accused of creative accounting in presenting its finances to gain access to the Euro. Italy is generally considered to be over-borrowed, with debts amounting to 120% of GDP. Spanish banks were reluctant to recognise their losses in property lending. All were slow to respond to change.

Just as in the private sector, early warning signs of trouble may be in evidence, but they are sometimes too easily ignored in a world dominated by spin. The quality of many services, especially health, may deteriorate. Public dissatisfaction may be expressed both at the ballot box and in the opinion polls, showing declining support for a government by their customers. Senior political figures may resign or opt for early retirement. As the problems deepen, the situation increasingly resembles a private sector collapse. Creditor concerns lead to declining ratings from the credit agencies, increased costs of borrowing and, finally, the closure of the primary bond markets in a currency crisis. Unemployment and emigration surge. Moral transgressions can exact a heavy price.

Tackling a crisis in public finances may superficially appear totally different from a business failure, since a country cannot cease to trade. Yet the process does bear many similarities. If the country must rely on overseas creditors to provide finance, it has little bargaining power in settling the terms. However regrettable or unpalatable it may be, loss of sovereignty is an inevitable outcome. The broad parameters are set by the financiers, leaving politicians with the task of selecting policies to achieve the financial targets. If the plan to save the Euro through tighter central fiscal policy is adopted, Ireland may have little more freedom than any restructured business attempting to regain competitiveness.

Controls are now being restored to avoid financial collapse. A plan is required to reduce the cost base in a strategic manner. If, however, politicians succumb to short-term pressures and strong sectional interests to tackle the problem in a haphazard way, the painful surgical process could result in long-term debilitation, if not the destruction of the body politic. While politicians and economists may differ as to the best remedies, if early action is taken to reduce costs in the public sector, the problem is more readily addressed. How this might be approached is discussed in the next chapter.

## Conclusions

- It is important to recognise signs of business failure in your own business and that of customers and suppliers.
- Early warning signs may be evident to readers of accounts, bank managers, creditors, employees or visitors.
- Signs of difficulty may exist in the public sector, as well as the private sector.
- When difficulties are detected, action is required.

## Management checklist

1. Does your business display any signs of collapse and, if so, what can be done to remedy the situation?
2. Do your major customers or suppliers exhibit any signs of business failure and, if so, what action is required?
3. Have you a robust system for tracking early warning signs of failure?

# Chapter 19

# Managing the change process

> "Change is not made without inconvenience."
> *Dr Samuel Johnson, 18th Century English essayist*

Successful change of anything may entail considerable inconvenience and requires careful planning. However good a cost reduction programme may be, without effective implementation it is probably doomed to failure, whether in the private or public sector. Even the best plan can be consigned to the wastepaper basket if it is not properly executed. To succeed, change must be organised and managed as in any good project. But also, in light of the fears it is likely to engender, it must be handled with the right mix of firmness and understanding. This chapter is prescriptive, drawing on the experience of the companies set out in **Appendix 1** to establish best practice. Their amalgamated advice on successful implementation is described under the following headings:

- Project management
- Force field analysis
- Managing change
- Communications and negotiation
- Monitoring progress and continuous improvement
- Eight steps in leading change
- Application in the public sector

## Project management

The guidelines for successful project management suggest that clarity is required in assessing the scope of the project, its timing and its cost.

### Scope

The starting point for the project team is the terms of reference provided by the Board to the CEO or other project leader. This will normally set out as a minimum the overall objective in terms of savings, the time allowed and the reporting procedures. It is also likely to lay the boundaries of where to look and the values to be respected. If the brief is both clear and feasible, the work of the project team is made much simpler. Without full support of the Board, success is improbable.

The project leader will need to decide on the composition of the team, if this has not already been established in the terms of reference. In particular, it is desirable to let members know in advance the likely time commitment, which may vary from member to member. As well as selecting the members of the team, thought must be given to who else needs to be consulted and who needs to be informed of the project. If there are staff or union agreements in place, the appropriate procedures need to be observed. In most cases, absolute secrecy will prove impossible and a controlled information flow is preferable to rumours, which may prove disruptive.

The project manager may act as secretary and convenor or may delegate this function. In any event, meetings will need to be scheduled, minutes taken and information distributed. The leader will allocate responsibilities for the various tasks which may be on an individual or joint basis. In simpler cases the steps involved and ordering may be obvious. In more complex cases the team may use techniques such as critical path analysis to control progress.

A key factor in managing the process is determining what information is required. If the project involves a significant investment in fixed assets, for example the automation of a brewery, the level of data will be substantial. If the project is focussed on downsizing, the information may be readily available from the human resources department. Even then the information required will differ for a voluntary redundancy or compulsory redundancy programme.

### Time

The total project time can be divided into two elements:

1. The time required to come up with the cost reduction proposal.
2. The time required to implement the changes.

For the proposal time the Board will likely determine the limit which, in turn, may be influenced by shareholders or financiers. The longer the delay the longer will be the uncertainty and disruption in the workplace, as employees fear for their future. The tendency to seek ever more information and delay the decision must be resisted. In an emergency, such as the collapse of turnover in a recession, the desirable time may have to be curtailed and decisions taken quickly. In these circumstances, it is particularly important that members commit their time accordingly.

Once the information is gathered, the team will need to devote their energies to ascertaining the options and selecting the most desirable course of action. Brainstorming can be employed to identify the alternatives. Where the business is to be restructured or layers removed, this stage should not be rushed if the best solution is to be found.

The time required to implement change will be largely determined by the amount of consultation and negotiation involved. The culture of the organisation may help or hinder the process. Suffice it to say this tends to be much longer in the public than the private sector. Clear but realistic deadlines will considerably assist the process.

*Cost*

The Board will need to sign off on the business case for the project. In order to do so they will usually look for a clear statement of costs, benefits and risks. While major investment proposals will entail a discounted cashflow analysis, either employing net present value or internal rate of return, simpler headcount reductions may be justified by payback time or return-on-investment criteria. The important factor to bear in mind is a realistic allowance for severance terms. Other costs, such as training and any transitional or disruption costs, should not be overlooked.

An assessment of the risks will need to address the likelihood of resistance, including the possibility of strike action. In the case of any voluntary redundancy or early retirement scheme, the risk of loss of skills must be evaluated, which may curtail the availability of the scheme to selected groups.

## Force field analysis

Assessing the risk of a major strategic cost reduction programme failing is not simple. An approach favoured by some companies is to employ a general psychological model to assess the likelihood of any social change occurring, namely the force field analysis propounded by Kurt Lewin.[1]

To apply force field analysis, it is necessary to identify those forces that assist change and those forces that inhibit change. It is normal to weight the strength of these forces subjectively. If the forces inhibiting change are greater than those promoting change, then change is unlikely to occur and vice versa.

Once the forces have been identified and assessed, the next step is to try to weaken the inhibiting forces and strengthen the assisting forces.

*Figure 19.1* **Force Field Analysis**

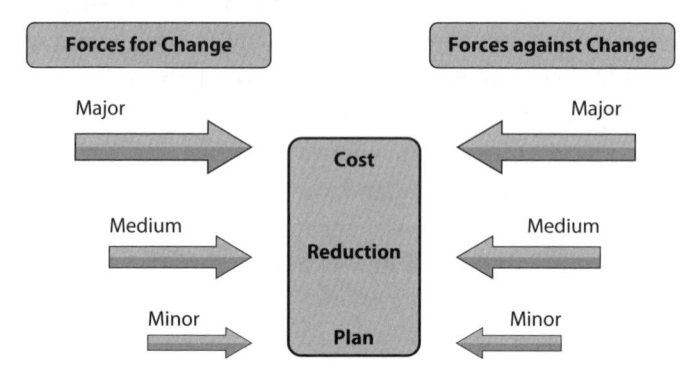

One particularly common inhibiting force is a belief that cost reduction is unnecessary and can be avoided. If there is no crisis, it is difficult to generate the energy needed to create the change, and apathy may prevail. So, an initial task is to persuade the workforce of the danger of inaction. In the private sector, with declining sales and rising unemployment, this task has become easier for many companies. However, in the public sector, where job security has been guaranteed in the past, the challenge may prove much greater.

Another inhibiting force may be the attitude of any diehard trade unionists, who may consider any job losses or extra workload as anathema. To this end, some companies, such as Ryanair, strongly resist the introduction of unions. Certainly Ryanair can reduce costs more quickly than its highly-unionised competitor, Aer Lingus. As a minimum, the pace of change is likely to be slower when union resistance is encountered. It is also necessary to assess the likelihood of industrial action and the management's response to same should it occur.

## Managing change

The majority of companies presenting at the Irish Management Institute (IMI) found resistance to change to be normal but, nevertheless, felt that it required careful management. Fear, uncertainty and doubt can be expected from employees facing an uncertain future. The threat of job losses naturally induces fear, particularly to those with heavy external commitments. Many employees worry that the plan may be the first of several, so any reassurance which may be reasonably given on this score may help alleviate this concern, though some doubt may still remain. Whenever possible, it is prudent to present a single cut, rather than a constant drip of job reductions.

The reaction of employees is likely to be heavily influenced by whether the cuts are voluntary or compulsory. Where a voluntary scheme – particularly if it contains generous severance terms – is introduced, resistance should be limited. Some employees who already intended to leave will welcome it and urge their more reluctant colleagues to accept it. The key issue is restricting eligibility to those whom the company wishes to see depart. A compulsory severance scheme will face tougher opposition.

Napoleon Bonaparte once proclaimed that those who have changed the universe never did it by changing officials, but always by inspiring people. Given that cost reduction is not a topic which readily inspires people, selling the idea may well present a real challenge to the leadership and persuasion skills of management if they are to transform their corporate universe. Persuasion may entail both carrot and stick. The stick is spelling out the consequences of failure and its impact on employment in the medium term. The carrot is describing the vision of the business future after the implementation of the scheme. The exercise may need to be repeated many times and the doubts expressed, however misguided, must be addressed.

## Communications and negotiation

One aspect of change management that was stressed by practically every company that succeeded in its cost reduction programme was the importance of good, clear and regular communications. Problems may arise at any stage of the process, so a willingness to listen to genuine concerns is fundamental to success, which must be balanced with firmness in ensuring that the plan's objectives are achieved. A carefully planned communications strategy will include the most appropriate medium to be employed, as well as the appointment and briefing of the relevant spokespeople.

When the change is announced to management and staff, it is helpful to emphasise the benefits of the plan. If there is a real threat of closure, staff may accept the painful cuts as a necessary evil and appreciate the enhanced job security for those remaining. It may be more difficult to persuade public servants to cut costs in the interests of reducing the national budgetary deficit or for the greater public good. In addition, there needs to be clarity on the timetable for implementation and a medium for clarification of issues and the resolution of problems.

Not only must internal communication be conducted effectively, but external communication to stakeholders must also be assiduously planned. Customers and suppliers need to be assured that trade will continue without loss of quality in the level of service, which may require letters or visits. The general public and local community should not be overlooked and, to this end, several companies advocated a proactive public relations exercise, identifying the relevant spokesmen at an early stage.

As mentioned already in **Chapter 3**, skilful negotiation can greatly enhance purchasing decisions. Clearly, this applies similarly in selling cost reduction projects to employees, since some parts of the package may be open to negotiation. Successful practitioners emphasised the need for careful preparation, which includes clarity around the goals and the assembling of relevant benchmarking data, particularly regarding rates of pay and redundancy deals in the industry. The ability to compromise will naturally be affected by the severity of the crisis and the time available to resolve the situation. Part of the plan should establish timeframes to avoid negotiation degenerating into a ruse to defer change.

## Monitoring progress and continuous improvement

It has already been stated in **Chapter 6** that many cost reductions fail in either the short or the long run. Sometimes the plan is good, but the execution poor. Sometimes serious collateral damage is caused to the organisation's growth or the quality of its products and services. Sometimes, after a period, the costs bounce back, returning like a rubber ball. Given these dangers, the monitoring of true progress cannot be overemphasised.

A 'balanced scorecard', as described in **Chapter 17**, provides the most comprehensive monitoring of all relevant features. However, if a scorecard is not in place, it is unlikely that it can be introduced alongside a cost reduction programme. In these circumstances, it may be possible to monitor progress through key performance measures, which many companies report with their monthly figures.

In the longer term, several companies found it important to measure employee morale. The guilt of survivors is a well-known phenomenon in organisations that have downsized their workforces and may seriously adversely affect morale. Some organisations check the situation with regular climate surveys, which, of course, are only valuable if the problems lead to action.

Continuous improvement is an aspiration for most companies, but will only occur in a supportive culture. The Japanese emphasise this concept, and their 'kaizan' is envied by many Western businesses, but is based on trust and teamwork, which may be damaged where mandatory redundancy is introduced. Changing a culture towards genuine and effective continuous improvement is a Herculean task for most businesses. In a McKinsey global survey of 300 operations, while nearly 75% of respondents believed that cost reduction would remain a top priority, some 40% believed that some proportion of the costs saved since 2008 would return.[2]

## Eight steps in leading change

Many companies that set out on a major cost reduction exercise for the first time have found that a formalised approach to change management provides useful guidance. A particularly useful approach that was adopted by several companies presenting at the IMI has been provided by Professor John Kotter of Harvard Business School,[3] who breaks down the process into eight steps:

### 1. *Establish a sense of urgency*

Without urgency it is difficult to mobilise the energy necessary to undertake what is rarely a pleasant task. Since employees are fearful of change and its potential impact on them personally, it is to be expected that the status quo is preferred. Accordingly, many justifications may be advanced to avoid action and an atmosphere of complacency created. Serious losses may get attention, but that may be too late. Leadership is required to persuade everyone that a continuation of the status quo is likely to lead to disaster.

### 2. *Create a guiding coalition*

If the cost reduction process is not to degenerate into political infighting or turf battles, it is important that key personnel from different areas give their backing to the project. A single individual, however competent, is unlikely to succeed in overcoming the obstacles which will emerge. To be effective, the team must comprise people in the right positions, with the relevant commitment, expertise and credibility to lead the process. They will need to develop a common goal and operate on a basis of mutual trust.

## 3. Develop a vision and a strategy

Successful plans require strong leadership, which may make the difference between ultimate success and failure. A test of leadership is the creation of a clear vision which is readily understood and to which employees can subscribe. If the vision is to inspire, it must paint an attractive future, which is both realistic and desirable. This is rarely achieved by diktat or micromanagement and is unlikely to be generated instantly. A powerful vision can provide a focus, which can be communicated throughout the organisation and adapted to changing circumstances.

## 4. Communicate the change vision

Too often while at boardroom level there is a clear understanding of what needs to be done, the message is wildly distorted by the time it reaches the factory floor. If communication is to be effective, it should be simple and consistent, using imagery understandable to everyone. Questions and discussion must be encouraged to avoid misunderstanding. It should be repeated time and again, using whatever media are appropriate. Above all, management must lead by example if the message is to be believed.

## 5. Empower employees for broad-based action

If change is to occur quickly, as many employees as possible should become involved in a co-ordinated manner. This may sound trite and most managers pay lip service to the idea. But, in practice, there may be many barriers and vested interests opposed to true empowerment. Structures may need to be changed, training provided and information more widely disseminated if empowerment is to be embraced effectively across the organisation.

## 6. Generate short-term wins

There are few greater boosts to morale than being able to see at least some signs of success at an early stage. Any short-term win, if well publicised, can do much to bring doubters on board and confound the cynics. If, on the other hand, the benefits seem never to come any closer, then the project can easily become derailed or run out of momentum. A suitable balance between long-term transformation and short-term gains provides a recipe for success.

## 7. Consolidate gains and produce more change

The early triumphs must be extended into a series of victories if the campaign is to achieve ultimate success. Many projects can falter after the initial sense of urgency has faded. Resistance to change can then reassert itself and ultimately lead to failure.

## 8. Anchor new approaches in the culture

Culture change is never easy, but building cost reduction into the mindset of managers is critical to produce continuous improvement. The values which businesses espouse and behaviour norms are notoriously difficult to change. Very few companies outside of Japan achieve continuous improvement of their cost base as part of the organisational culture.

One company which undoubtedly has adopted a cost reduction ethos is Ryanair, as described by one of their managers:[4]

> "The root to being a low cost airline is to start with a new or renewed focus on operating costs. You need to look from the top to the bottom on an airline's cost. You need to cut out anything you don't need and be as close to a train as possible… If you cut a Ryanair person down the middle like a stick of rock, you would see cost control written all the way through."

Many organisations would not be willing or able to effect a transition to such a culture, particularly if their values around customer and staff relations differ from those of Ryanair. Nevertheless, many would like to inculcate the spirit of continuous cost improvement into their staff at every level. Whether or not this culture exists, if managers adhere to the basic principles inherent in good change management, they stand a better chance of implementing successfully a strategic cost reduction programme.

## Application in the public sector[5]

### The problem

Achieving radical reforms in the public sector and cutting expenditure are the goals of many governments worldwide that are in fiscal difficulties arising during the recession. Serious diseconomies of scale have been permitted to develop, often with minimal managerial attention. In Ireland, previous attempts, such as that when large pay increases were granted under a benchmarking exercise in 2002, proved remarkably unsuccessful. As discussed in **Chapter 8**, the Croke Park Agreement between the Government and public sector representatives envisaged radical change in work practices, centralisation of services and increased productivity through greater use of on-line services.

Yet, more than two years after the agreement was signed on 1 April 2010 (appropriately perhaps 'All Fools Day'!), a survey showed that 86% of senior Irish executives expressed dissatisfaction with the level of reform achieved.[6] A consultant's report in 2011 revealed that average pay in the public sector had grown to 44% more than the average private sector pay.[7] The average pay in the ESB (the Irish electrical authority) in 2010 was €85,000, which was more than double its Northern Irish counterpart, while numerous extra allowances could add a further €6,000.[8] Could the next attempt led by a new minister, who has been given specific responsibility for reform, benefit from some of the approaches to implement change in the private sector?

## Accounting systems

It is difficult to attribute the failure to bring about change in the public sector to a lack of information or ideas. Admittedly, Ireland does not have a particularly sophisticated accounting system. Some countries have adopted an accruals-based accounting system, as is commonly found in the private sector, in place of the traditional cash-based system, to provide better management information for public finances. Ireland, while initially espousing the concept as part of the 'New Public Management' discussed in **Chapter 8**, failed to implement it for Government departments, although it was adopted by local authorities.

The UK has adopted such an accruals system since the beginning of this century and, although it experienced some teething problems, it is now fully operational. A study by Chartered Accountants Ireland has compared Northern Ireland, where an accruals system in place, with the Republic of Ireland, which still uses the cash basis, together with some minor additional accruals-based information.[9] The results question the usefulness of the information provided in Northern Ireland, with many continuing to use cash-based data and complaining of the cost incurred and resources required to provide accruals data. The authors conclude that, in view of the Northern Ireland experience, the non-adoption of accruals accounting in the South was "not unwise". If this is so, it would seem that the Republic of Ireland is not significantly disadvantaged by relying mainly on cash accounting.

While cash accounting may not be disadvantageous, there can still be gaps in the information system. There is no central personnel and skills database, making it difficult to identify gaps and overlaps. A central procurements database could highlight purchasing inefficiencies. A property and facilities database could ensure that expensive facilities are being utilised effectively. While such deficiencies can hinder progress, they cannot explain adequately the lack of progress in reform.

Nor can the blame be laid at a lack of ideas. An independent report commissioned by the Irish government, published in July 2009, identified potential savings of €5.3 billion in a full year, together with a reduction in 17,300 public sector jobs.[10] But politicians, who had deferred action prior to its publication, then decided to ignore many of its recommendations.

## Accountability

There are, of course, major differences between the public and private sectors in accountability. In the private sector there is usually the opportunity to hold the management to account for their performance at an annual general meeting following the publication of the annual accounts. Though this right may at times prove ineffective, it can sometimes lead to changes in management. The equivalent power to remove top management is absent in the public sector, except through periodic elections of politicians. Where there are boards in semi-state organisations, their members may be appointed on political grounds, rather than competence, so that they can lack the ability or interest to control costs. Politicians too, nominally in charge of spending departments, may baulk at cutting costs which they believe, rightly or wrongly, will lose them the votes of sectional interests.

There is also a problem with the accountability of public servants who implement policy. Given the security of their employment, those responsible for massive cost overruns in projects are unlikely to be penalised. When, in extreme cases, they are forced into early retirement, they are likely to part on generous termination terms with substantial future burdens on the public purse from their considerable pensions, which can eventually substantially exceed their final salaries. In their defence, departmental heads may protest that they do not have the authority vested in financial controllers in the private sector to control costs and attribute cost increases to decisions of their political masters. While the Department of Finance has traditionally had responsibility for the national budget, it too lacks the power of financial control commonly found in the head office of large corporations.

But some blame can also be laid at the door of obstructing public servants, opposed to any change. Absenteeism, such as the 'blue flu' epidemic in the security forces first appearing in 1998, can severely impede progress. Sick leave is reported to cost over €500 million a year.[11] Another report indicated that they were unable or unwilling to operate performance management systems rigorously for fear of a backlash from the unions.[12] Under the Performance Management and Development System in 2011 only 1% of staff was awarded one of the two lowest grades on a five-point system. More widely there has been criticism of the management culture, which has been described as "dysfunctional" with a lack of individual responsibility.[13] The reply of "Yes, Minister" from a civil servant to reform proposals may not produce the necessary action, especially when the interests of the various departments are perceived to be adversely affected.

## Work practices

For all these reasons, necessary changes can be deferred for long periods. It is not merely that absenteeism rates in the public sector are high in comparison with the private sector. In Ireland, work practices which seemed alien to the 21st Century have been revealed. Employees were given time off to cash salary cheques, even though they were paid by direct debit. County managers were entitled to 42 days' annual leave, and some employees in the Central Bank operated a 32-hour week. In FÁS, the State training authority, it was disclosed that some employees were entitled to 70 days annual leave in the two years prior to their retirement. Elsewhere, the Government tried to cancel 'privilege days', whereby – from a throw-back to British rule – civil servants were entitled to two days' holiday to celebrate Empire Day and the King's Birthday. However, even though the country has been an independent entity for over 90 years and annual leave is generous, the change was strenuously opposed. Attempts to standardise local authority working hours to a 35-hour week met similar resistance while, overall, the numbers employed throughout the public sector increased dramatically in times of prosperity.

Finally, facing unprecedented financial crisis, with pressure from external creditors, an attempt is currently being made to reform the public sector and reverse the growth in the number of its employees. The Government has committed itself to reducing the 23,500 jobs in the public sector by 2015, but rejects compulsory redundancy. While termination terms may prove costly, this should generate annual savings of over €300 million. Accordingly, at the outset, the scope and timing have been determined, but not the important matter of the net cost. Given that Ireland became locked out of the bond markets and has been obliged to accept financial assistance from the EU and the IMF, who will be monitoring progress closely, there is little leeway. In addressing the challenges ahead, the question arises: Can the public sector learn from the experience of the private sector in implementing cost reduction plans?

## Implementing change

Force field analysis for Ireland would show a very powerful force against change – the opposition of the public sector unions. But there are also some positive forces. A strong political mandate was created following the 2011 election. There may be reduced tolerance for public sector obstruction in view of numerous reports which have indicated that public sector employees are significantly better paid than their private sector counterparts, while receiving security of employment, long holidays and generous perks, especially pensions. Another force for change could be the threat of introducing less palatable ways of reducing labour costs, as described in **Chapter 16**. The clause protecting civil servants from further pay cuts or compulsory redundancy over four years is subject to there being no further budgetary deterioration.

The leadership of the process will entail daunting challenges, but sticks may have to be employed as well as carrots. The minister responsible for the changes has indicated[14] that the approach will be based on partnership and will seek to avoid confrontation, but whether this will produce the changes in time and within budget remains to be proved. Other countries, such as Greece and the UK, have experienced real confrontation when attempting to impose severe public sector cuts and the patience of European creditors may be limited. If no sanctions are available to deal with recalcitrant public servants, a traditional partnership approach may be found wanting.

In Ireland, the broad outline of a plan was unveiled quickly in April 2011[15] by the new Government, so that ministers would not be 'captured' by their departments. Plans for spending cuts were to be available by June, with a view to agreement by September to allow for implementation in the autumn before the annual estimates process starts. Some State assets would be sold and various quangos would be merged or abolished to achieve savings of €2 billion. Outsourcing of non-essential activities would be considered. Failure to achieve the savings could result in further public service pay cuts. To succeed, the Government must risk short-term unpopularity from affected parties and remain steadfast in pursuit of savings.

The success of the plan will be judged, not only by the extent of the achievement in obtaining the savings, but also by the impact on the quality of the service provided. After implementing a voluntary redundancy scheme in March 2012, it was reported that dozens of senior civil servants were being re-hired.[16] There has been widespread dissatisfaction with the levels of service in certain areas, such as the health sector. Where a programme is based on maintaining levels of pay, while cutting numbers employed, there is a real danger that reforms and enhanced efficiencies may not materialise, with consequential deterioration in levels of service provided. The Governor of the Central Bank has argued that greater emphasis should be given to cutting levels of pay, rather than numbers employed.[17] Perhaps the public sector could copy the private sector and monitor progress through some form of balanced scorecard?

Some other countries place a strong emphasis on efficiency. New Zealand, ranked in 13th place for the strength of its public finances in 2011–2012 by the World Economic Forum (with mainly oil-producing states ahead of it) compared to Ireland in 142nd place at the bottom of the league table, could provide a role model. Although New Zealand does not face as grave a recession as Ireland, it has enforced strict cash limits, so that expenditure will be capped for several years. Departments are expected to reallocate resources from lower quality spending to frontline services. This will necessitate significant changes in the ways they operate.[18]

In Ireland, communication with many stakeholders will need to be handled skilfully. Many sceptics need to be won over, and continued opposition, either overt or covert, can be expected, particularly from strong vested interests. Various seminars relating to the Croke Park Agreement changes have been held, but details of the proposed changes must be carefully disseminated throughout the service. Examples of successful role models could be shown on the web, as well as comparative paid elsewhere in Europe, where civil servants generally are less well remunerated, though expecting this must be the equivalent of expecting turkeys to promote Christmas. Early cuts in ministerial transport costs and reduction in politicians' expenses by the new Government have sent out a clear message of intent. The cabinet, political parties and the public need to be informed constantly, as do (most importantly) Ireland's IMF and EU creditors, who have received commitments which they will be monitoring quarterly.

The challenges ahead are daunting for any government attempting to introduce radical change. The Irish Government has certainly tried to create a sense of urgency. Whether or not the guiding coalition has adequate resources and is strong enough to implement change in the face of strong vested interests remains to be seen. A clear vision and strategy is hard to develop, unless both Government coalition parties can unite against backbencher opposition. Communication of an austerity strategy is problematic in times of high unemployment and currency uncertainty. Public sector employees may not wish to be empowered to effect changes, while short-term wins remain few and far between.

The extent of resistance can be gauged by the reactions both from within and outside the public sector. Some senior managers in commercial State organisations sought to pay substantial performance bonuses in 2011 in contravention of explicit Government policy. Strong interest groups lobbied vigorously against many of the changes contained in the December 2011 Budget. With Moody's reduction of Ireland's credit rating to junk status, many anxious parties at home and abroad will be following the Government's achievements with interest. The EU and IMF will be monitoring progress closely, which should help to concentrate minds.

## Conclusions

- Any plan, if poorly executed, is doomed to failure.
- The disciplines of sound project management are applicable to cost reduction.
- Resistance to change is to be expected.
- Managing change successfully requires strong leadership.
- The plan must be skilfully communicated.
- Proper monitoring of the project is critical.

## Management checklist

1. Is the board brief clear and comprehensive?
2. Who needs to be involved, consulted or informed?
3. Has adequate information been collected?
4. Is the timeframe appropriate?
5. Is the proposal realistically costed, and are the risks adequately assessed?
6. What elements of the plan are negotiable?
7. What resistance is anticipated?
8. How will communications be organised?
9. How will the plan be monitored?
10. Will the plan produce sustainable savings and lead to continuous improvement?

# Chapter 20

# Planning the journey

"A journey of a thousand miles starts with a single step."

*Mao Tse Tung*

At the outset of this book, we stated that our target audience was senior management, chief executives and their boards, who want to reduce their costs in a significant way. We have sought to write in a way that is readily intelligible to the practising manager. We will finish with an attempt to provide an overall 'route map' for such managers to devise their own route in the current economic context and to plan their own unique action plan, as follows.

- The current scenario
- The fitness challenge
- Planning the journey
- Getting started

### The current scenario

We outlined in the introduction the economic situation from an Irish perspective. While Ireland may face greater challenges than most, stormy weather lies ahead for many countries. Given that the recession has been deeper than any within the living memory of most people, the shock has been severe.

For many businesses, the aftermath of the financial crash has been challenging in the extreme. Markets have contracted at an alarming rate and competition for the remaining business has intensified, putting further pressure on profit margins. Credit has become scarce and, when it is available, may come at a much higher cost, while sources of equity capital have diminished. Banks themselves have needed to raise further capital to meet more stringent solvency requirements and are facing higher costs of compliance as regulations tighten, so customers can expect higher fees and charges. Unsurprisingly, after an era of relative trading stability, insolvencies have increased at an alarming rate and many businesses are finding working capital management problematic. In 2011, Irish business failures increased by 20% to almost 2,000, with debts of over €1 billion.[1]

While few question the gravity of the situation, there is widespread disagreement globally amongst economists and commentators as to the best way forward. Some favour continued 'quantitative easing' to provide more credit, while others see no alternative to greater austerity. Some analysts question the effectiveness of fiscal policies adopted both in the UK and the US, as it faces a presidential election. In the Eurozone, the outlook for the stronger countries, such as Germany, may be constrained by the problems of the weaker members. In Asia, India's growth is declining, Japan is burdened by the enormous cost of its earthquake and tsunami, while worried pundits forecast the bursting of a property bubble in China, which has provided the engine of world economic growth in recent years.

In such gloomy circumstances, a presumption of renewed growth may be premature and the goal of business survival is often problematic. Few mourned the passing of 2011, with its non-stop crises and deepening economic gloom. Judging by the depressed state of global stock markets, many expect 2012 to bring yet further austerity and uncertainty. In a slowing global economy, the threat of another worldwide recession is rising.[2] Based on the collapse of consumer spending in the EU in the final quarter of 2011, the EU forewarned of a fully-fledged recession.[3] Even if the threat of double dip recession recedes, the world is unlikely to return to the relative stability of the late 20th Century. One influential US economist, Nouriel Roubini, who had forecast the ending of the property bubble, expects a more U-shaped gradual recovery with more shocks on the way.[4] The basic tenets underlying business, particularly the consequences of a weakened financial sector, have altered with consequential instability and insecurity expected by many commentators for some years ahead. It seems likely that turbulent times lie ahead for an economic system less able to absorb shocks than was formerly the case.

Fortunately, managers are not obliged to become armchair economists or to determine how the economic system led to the present crisis. Many, of course, do attempt to provide answers, freely expressing their views. They proffer their advice on how to restore economic growth and lobby politicians accordingly. What they cannot, however, ignore is how the downturn impacts their specific business and the decisions they should make on how best to react to difficulties which have been created by the downturn and its aftermath. The world economy in general seems, at best, to be headed for minimal growth in the short and even medium term. At worst, there could be a severe downturn and prolonged uncertainty. Managers should control their costs accordingly to maximise their chances of survival.

The year 2012 brought increased currency uncertainty. The troubles of the Eurozone are likely to affect all economies in the global marketplace, with renewed fears of a further recession. Few commentators can confidently predict the consequences of a collapse of the Euro, if it were to occur, or the extent of the resultant chaos. The likelihood is that new national currencies will add significantly to the cost base with higher interest rates and a reversal of the exchange rate savings brought about from the introduction of a common currency. Prudent management necessitates a harsh, but realistic approach to ensure survival in challenging times. Such widespread uncertainty has further damaged confidence internationally and has provided yet another reason – as if one were needed – to examine the cost base of both the public and private sectors.

The economic problems globally relate not just to a serious downturn in trade, but also to confidence in the system itself. Prior to 2007, most businesses had become accustomed to an era of constant growth. The era of free market capitalism heralded by Margaret Thatcher in the UK and President Reagan in the US had spread widely around the world. The management of public finances generally was based on the thinking of neo-liberal economists, such as Milton Friedman[5] since the 1980s and followed a 'Washington Consensus', with government intervention in the markets being avoided at all costs. With the advent of the sub-prime bubble in the US and the collapse of banks globally, particularly after the failure of Lehman Brothers, it became evident that the system had failed. The age of the 'Great Moderation,' comprising high economic growth, low interest rates and a plentiful supply of credit is truly over.

In due course, the banking crisis has morphed into a sovereign debt crisis. The possibility of defaults by developed European countries, once considered unthinkable, became a reality once Greece announced a 'voluntary haircut' or discount on the redemption of its bonds. With bond markets in turmoil, many fear the consequences of contagion in world markets and the possibility of further defaults, whether in an orderly or disorderly manner. The cost of trading with these countries in danger of defaulting on their debts increases as risks are magnified and insurance becomes costlier or prohibitive.

As the situation in financial markets has deteriorated, concern has spread for the future of the current capitalist model. In many countries it is alleged that a form of 'crony capitalism' has emerged, where a close group of oligarchs wield the real power. Commentators increasingly question the legitimacy of the current capitalist model, criticising the rising levels of inequality, regulatory failures, rewards for failure and lack of bank credit, together with wider concerns about bank management and high unemployment. However, following the collapse of communism and the decline of Marxism, no alternative economic system to capitalism has been in evidence.

In Europe, less faith was traditionally placed in the pure market model than in the US but, nevertheless, the system faltered and severe problems within the Euro indicated that a new model of regulation was required to support the currency and to reconcile conflicting national aspirations. Serious doubts have also been expressed about whether the neo-liberal approach is a suitable model for less developed countries, where state capitalism, whatever its theoretical disadvantages, holds considerable sway.[6] A new paradigm may emerge in due course, but this is likely to take many years, particularly where strong vested interests exist.[7] In the interim, uncertainty in financial markets and the future of the entire system, as well as the poor outlook for economic growth, has spread fear and damaged confidence globally.

The Irish economic situation is particularly dismal, with high unemployment, minimal growth prospects and lack of international confidence, as evidenced by the high cost of sovereign debt on the bond markets. There is no easy route out of recession, given the particularly weakened banking system and the dire state of our public finances. The policy options are limited, given the country's membership of the Euro, which preclude an independent monetary or exchange rate policy and have become even more constrained since Ireland has to comply with the terms of assistance from the European Financial Stability Fund. After years of growth which accompanied the Celtic Tiger era, it has been difficult to adjust expectations to a sustained period of austerity, and achieving progress in this direction has been slower than advocated by many commentators and well-wishers.[8] The new Government in 2011 faced daunting challenges, but committed itself to public sector reform and cost reduction, appointing a senior cabinet minister to oversee the project. Nevertheless, fears remain that the country could fail to achieve the goals of its austerity programme and face possible default on its sovereign debt.[9]

Arthur Schopenhauer, the German philosopher, famously proclaimed that truth passes through three stages. First, it is ridiculed. Secondly, it is violently opposed. Thirdly, it is accepted as self-evident. The wisdom of financial de-gearing is now entering the third stage. During a time of increased uncertainty, worldwide consumers and businesses alike have adjusted to the recessionary environment. As business risk increases, many have attempted to reduce financial risks which arise from high borrowings. For consumers, this has led to reduced expenditure and increased savings. For businesses, it has generally resulted in lower investment and, where possible, reduced borrowings, despite the low level of interest rates. De-gearing or deleveraging for both consumers and businesses has become the conventional wisdom.

Planning in an uncertain world is not easy, but that does not mean that it should be abandoned. Few people, other perhaps than politicians seeking votes, dare to predict with any degree of confidence how long the present difficulties will persist. Flexibility and agility have become the new watchwords, but both may be imperilled by an excessive cost base. Unfortunately, many businesses enter this new world with much baggage and costs inherited from a more benign environment. It, thus, becomes imperative for businessmen and businesswomen to see if costs can be reduced in an orderly manner, consistent with the survival of the entity in the longer term. Three years after the publication of the first edition of this book in 2009, the need for strategic cost reduction has become even more pressing.

## The fitness challenge

In **Chapter 4**, we used the analogy of a health check. Companies should decide on the level of fitness they wish to achieve and set themselves a target return on invested capital (ROIC). Assuming the current ROIC is significantly less than the target, they will need to reduce costs in a radical way.

Let us assume that the goal is the fitness of an Olympic team.[10] Initially coaches might benchmark the performance of their athletes against global competitors and establish the gap to be filled. Those businesses seeking the highest level of fitness may choose to examine the latest operational tools that are available to them, especially 'lean' to eliminate waste and six sigma to achieve consistency. Naturally, some techniques will not suit them at all. Before deciding on specific treatment, it may be helpful to review the overall strategy and values that the company espouses. The company does not wish to develop anorexia and, therefore, should consider seriously the functional constraints. Thought might also be given to size. Would the company be more likely to succeed if it were substantially bigger or smaller?

The next stage might be to devise a training plan. It may be helpful to break down the skills required by an analysis of the activities involved through a value chain analysis, as outlined in **Chapter 9**. It would then be decided what expertise should be made available in-house and where it would be appropriate to buy in the relevant knowledge. The latest training techniques would be examined and those best suited to the task selected. Care would be taken to ensure that whatever diet is prescribed does not involve the use of banned substances, whatever may be the behaviour suspected of competing teams in this respect. Finally, the individual athletes would need to be properly motivated to try to win their particular events.

Throughout the training period, there would be constant monitoring of performance, benchmarking levels of fitness not only against the athlete's previous performance, but against the remainder of the team and the best in class to be found in other teams. The coach would constantly seek to close the performance gap between his team and those of the top teams. In the case of a team event, the coach would be likely to check that the best balance of skills is achieved when the team is selected. A sports psychologist may be used to help motivation.

It can be seen that a good athletics coach faces the same issues as a CEO. The starting point is the strategy and the constraints imposed by the functional requirements and values. There needs to be an evaluation of overall size of the company for efficiency and a check on the composition of the labour force. The value chain analysis is the starting point of seeing what areas need attention, while certain activities may be outsourced. Fundamental corporate values will not be overlooked in the process. There is constant benchmarking both of overall performance and each single element involved. Particular care will be given to employee motivation to ensure that it is aligned to the strategy through an appropriate remuneration system, which rewards success, rather than failure.

## Planning the journey

Let us take a second analogy, 'crossing the swamp'. Suppose that you are trying to take a group of people over a dark and treacherous swamp. You are competing with other teams, all of which are trying to do the same thing. The winner will be the team that crosses first in a safe and orderly manner. Conditions have deteriorated recently, and it appears that the traditional route, 'budgeting', will not provide a safe crossing. How should you plan your crossing?

### Step 1: Benchmarking

To assess your chances of winning, you must first make some measurements and comparisons. Is your team quicker, sturdier and fitter than the other competitors? Is the team likely to survive intact? This requires a financial analysis and projection into the future. You highlight your relative strengths and weaknesses, discovering the gaps that need to be closed.

## Step 2: Strategic analysis

From the outset, you should have a clear objective and set principles governing your choice of route. Clearly, the less baggage you carry the faster you can travel. But it would be unwise to abandon tents, compasses and protective clothing. You should know the boundaries of the swamp and the rules of the competition by which you must abide. The individual functional skills will act as gatekeepers in setting boundaries beyond which danger lies. You need a clear understanding of the features that make for an effective group. You may have flexibility over the size of the group. If it is too large, there may be organisational problems. If it is too small, each member may need to carry too heavy a load. It is also worth checking in particular the lights and flares of the present information system to ascertain if they are adequate for this task.

## Step 3: Value chain analysis

Before choosing your route, it is sensible to break down the crossing into its main components – the primary activities. These could be the ascent over the rocks, the sharp descent, crossing the river and circumventing the deep quagmire. You might then view the secondary activities: what you need to buy, the policies for managing problems and technological aids and the overall organisation. The more you can benchmark your skills in these areas, the better you will be able to assess your chance of winning and which areas you need to improve.

## Step 4: Outsourcing

An unusual feature of this competition is that you are entitled to get help from outsiders, from wherever you choose. You do not need to have all the skills within the team. You may well decide that your greatest skill is in the river crossing and that you will rely on expert outside help to cover the other main activities. Clearly, this is a major decision and, if the outside expertise is flawed, you ruin your chances of success. You need a tight agreement with such outsiders.

## Step 5: Selecting the optimal route

Having decided that the traditional budgeting route is no longer adequate, you can select from a range of alternatives or a combination of them. There are four major routes with smaller variations on each one. The first is entitled 'lean' and is much favoured by the Japanese, who have earlier also introduced the 'just-in-time (JIT)' route. A second route close by is 'Six Sigma' much favoured by large teams where there are actions repeated a large number of times. A third route, called 're-engineering', involves a detailed look at how the team members liaise with each other, taking advantage of technology aids. The final route, 'labour force re-structuring', is quite different, requiring more human resources skills, rather than operations or engineering. Some competitors may need to avail of all routes simultaneously.

## Step 6: Motivating the team

If the team is to win, it must be properly led and well-motivated. Careless mistakes can damage morale. The initial team selection needs careful handling of those who are omitted. Different members will have different expectations. There are those loyal members who wish to remain with the team after this particular competition, while others will not expect to stay. There are also the porters or casual workers, who know their role well and have no wish to be involved in any decisions. If the members are to be called to make superhuman efforts, they will not wish to find that they have inadequate rations or shoddy equipment. If the team is pared to the bone, it may be unable to overcome unexpected obstacles, which will probably appear along the way. Good communication within the team is of crucial importance.

## Step 7: Monitoring progress

The journey to be undertaken will be lengthy and unlikely to be fully completed in one year. During its course, it is important that no collateral damage is incurred. Obviously, the cost savings should be tracked and the budget aligned to the strategic plan. However, there are at least two crucial areas to watch:

- Quality, customer service and customer satisfaction
- Employee morale and employee satisfaction

If the customers or employees desert the business, there may be no business left to monitor. It is suggested that this can be achieved through monitoring key performance indicators, through the use of a tool such as the 'balanced scorecard'. In this way, cost reduction targets can become a source of continuous improvement in a balanced manner.

## Getting started

It finally remains for the reader to decide what action, if any, he or she will take. The first step of the proposed journey is to assess the current situation, the likely changes arising from the current environment and how the company benchmarks with its peers. If the outcome of such an analysis indicates that no serious situation exists, then it is unlikely that it will be possible to generate the necessary momentum to produce major change. If, on the other hand, a crisis or near crisis is predicted, then there is a basis for action.

Usually, there will be plenty of excuses to avoid serious cost reduction.[11] Often, justifications rely on smugness, cynicism or lethargy, such as: "We have done enough already," or, "The process is unlikely to generate sustainable results," or simply, "We are too busy at present." Others are based on self-protection with an understandable fear of change: "My department does not need it," or, "It should be confined to the purchasing department," or, "We don't need interference from people who do not understand our business." Others again will purport to be concerned with collateral damage: "This will damage our relationships with suppliers," or, "It will have damaging consequences on customer service, quality, innovation or operational risks." If, of course, the project is approached in the strategic manner advocated in this book, the latter critics should be confounded. Where, of course, supplier relations are not conducted on a fully commercial basis, it may be desirable to change the relationship.

Doing nothing is a decision by default. Some people resemble Charles Dickens's famous character in *David Copperfield*, Mr Micawber, who always believed that something would turn up, but ended up being committed to a debtors' prison by his creditors. The result of allowing expenditure to exceed revenue was, as he predicted, misery rather than happiness. Unfortunately, whatever turns up may not be good news, and some businesses, which adopted such a policy of 'masterly inactivity' when the recession arrived, are no longer trading. Unjustified optimism is a hazardous attitude, which may result in misery, if it is not tempered with a measure of realism.

To ascertain the need for cost reduction, the first step of the long journey is a health check, setting out the target, preferably with the assistance of financial benchmarking. A meeting then of the management team, with sufficient time and information to assess the situation, is the next step. If action is required, then the project team can be set up with a brief on how to proceed and when to report back.

There is no ideal starting point for a major cost reduction project. If a serious crisis has already arrived, it may be difficult to plan for the longer term, so that the business has to adopt emergency measures as outlined in **Chapter 5**. Where, on the other hand, the business believes that, while the threat is real its demise is not imminent, there is room for a more measured strategic approach. There are likely to be many demands on managers' time, but allocating time to a realistic analysis of the situation and a search for practical solutions is likely to be time well spent. It can also be that, the longer the wait, the more hazardous the journey will be. Remember the advice of Winston Churchill: "I never worry about action, only about inaction." The current economic scenario is challenging and turbulent times lie ahead. *Bon Voyage!*

## Conclusions

- In any downturn, it makes sense to review the cost base to assess competitiveness.
- Current uncertainties about economic recovery prospects, the credit crunch, currency stability, sovereign debt and the future of capitalism itself make such a review urgent to ensure survival.
- If the business faces serious threats ahead, but its failure is not imminent, there is a strong case to reduce costs in a way that is consistent with long-term survival.

## Management checklist[12]

For our final thoughts we will revert to the health analogy.

1. What is your desired level of fitness (financial benchmarking)?
2. Are you happy with your present size (economies of scale), and what are you currently doing to improve your fitness (role of the functions)?
3. Will normal diet rectify the situation (budgeting and control), and how long will you survive without remedial action (emergency cost reduction)?

4. What are your reasons for being overweight (strategic cost drivers)?
5. What parts of your anatomy need treatment (value chain)?
6. What factors do you need to bear in mind during treatment (strategy and values)?
7. What dangers exist in the treatment (functional considerations)?
8. Is radical major treatment or surgery required (outsourcing, business process re-engineering, labour force restructuring)?
9. Can current operational tools be applied to improve performance ('lean,' Six Sigma, benchmarking)?
10. Are you properly motivated to change (rewards)?
11. How will you monitor the plan to assess progress and avoid undesirable side effects ('balanced scorecard')?
12. What are you going to do, if anything, next? How, when and where will you begin (change management and action plan)?

# Appendix 1

# Companies addressing IMI SCR conferences 23 June 2004, 26 May 2006 and 28 April 2009*

| Company | Industry |
| --- | --- |
| Accenture | IT outsourcing |
| Bausch & Lomb | Lens manufacturing |
| Canada Life | Life assurance |
| Coll & Co* | Financial consultancy |
| Dell Inc | Computer manufacturing |
| DMRI | Food manufacturing consultancy |
| Empower Solutions | HR consultancy |
| Fujitsu* | IT services |
| Glanbia Ingredients | Food manufacturing |
| Guinness Ireland | Brewing |
| Halpin International, Mauritius* | Outsourcing |
| Hibernian Group | Financial services |
| Hollister ULC | Surgical appliances manufacturing |
| Iona Technologies Plc | High technology |
| McStay Luby* | Insolvency practitioners |
| Michael McNamara & Co* | Construction |
| Purchasing Solutions | Purchasing consultancy |
| Right Transitions | HR consultancy |
| Ryanair | Low fares airline |
| Schering Plough* | Pharmaceuticals |
| Softex, Microsol | High technology |
| Tayto | Food manufacturing |
| Thomas Crosbie Holdings* | Newspaper publishing |
| Zara | Clothes retailing |

* The third conference took place after the first edition of this book

# Appendix 2

# Approaching Six Sigma

As in judo, Six Sigma practitioners are awarded belts for levels of proficiency. Here, an experienced green belt leading a project team in a large global business outlines the processes and tools used in a particular call centre project. An outline of the main steps illustrates the rigour applied to an important project.

*Step 1: Define the project*

As in all well-managed projects, the starting point is the project definition. This step establishes the scope of the project. It explains the problem and formulates goals, which need to be measurable, and sets out timelines. It sets out the sponsor, the stakeholders who will be affected, and the members of the project team. It also estimates the benefits which may be realised.

The particular issue being addressed was the need to visit the site to fix technology problems. Computer down time could entail very expensive costs, but site visits were much more expensive than resolving the problem remotely. The metric selected was the 'Repeat Despatch Rate'. The goal was set out in 'SMART' terms:

| | |
|---|---|
| Specific: | Call Centre Support |
| Measurable: | Visit Repeat Despatch Rate |
| Achievable: | Target Rate historically achieved |
| Relevant: | Fits with Corporate Plan |
| Time: | Quarter 2, 2008 to Quarter 1, 2009 |

*Step 2: Establish the focus of the project*

The next step was to identify the focus of the project and what could be ignored. We isolated the department, the technicians, the types of call received and the process which needed changing. This led to a formal 'Problem Statement' and the target reduction, which was to reduce the 'Repeat Despatch Rate' by 36%.

## Step 3: Produce a detailed process definition using COPIS

The next step was to consider the problem for the stakeholders. The process was described in terms of the Customers, Output, Process, Inputs and Suppliers as follows:

The output would be if the technicians had to despatch hardware or service engineers to the location. The customer also had to be satisfied. The processes were flowcharted in detail.

## Step 4: Gather data and create metrics

To assess the effectiveness of the outputs, satisfied customers and reduced despatch rates, it was necessary to gather data and create the relevant metrics. It also entailed a detailed examination of how the technicians performed the diagnostic As-Is.

The data was analysed, showing the impact of incorrect troubleshooting, the problems for technicians, and where procedural errors were occurring. This highlighted such problems as the significance of poor case logging and using incorrect part numbers when booking service calls. It also pointed to the potential benefits to be gained from successful completion of the project.

| Process Definition Sheet ||||||
|---|---|---|---|---|
| Process Name: **Reducing Metric** |||| Process Owner: **Frontline Technician** ||
| Starts With: **Customer Contact** |||| Ends With: **Case Closure** ||
| **C** <br> **Customer** | **O** <br> **Output** | **P** <br> **Process** | **I** <br> **Inputs** | **S** <br> **Suppliers** |
| 1. Management <br> 2. Technical Account Managers <br> 3. Technicians <br> 4. Customers | 1. Technicians Dispatch Service Call <br> 2. Satisfied/Dissatisfied Customer | See Process Map. | 1. Diagnostic Logs <br> 2. Technicians' Knowledge <br> 3. Technicians' Analytical Skills <br> 4. Contact from Customer <br> 5. Relationship Skills | 1. Customers of Call Centre <br> 2. Technicians <br> 3. Vendors <br> 4. Account Managers <br> 5. Call Centre Management |

## Step 5: Brainstorm the problem and analyse results in a cause & effect 'fishbone' diagram

A cross-section of people from all parts of the Call Centre Operations was convened to discuss the reasons for the high repeat despatch rate. This entailed examining the relevant policies and procedures, troubleshooting, logistics and various product issues.

From this analysis it was possible to identify the areas on which attention should be focused. The causes were then screened to establish the likelihood of their occurrence and the ease with which they could be addressed. The conclusion was that most of the issues arose from incorrect troubleshooting.

## Step 6: Selection of improvements

The fishbone diagram helped identify the root causes of the problem. This suggested various remedies. Not all of these could be applied for cost reasons. Detailed consultation took place with all the relevant parties. A system of weighted voting was used to prioritise the causes and to isolate the principle causes of the high despatch rate. The analysis was refined by the use of a Force Field Analysis. The selected improvements were shown in a 'Should-be' process map, which was compared with the 'As-Is' process map.

## Step 7: Action plan

The selected improvements were then translated into an action plan. This set out the details of each action and identified the owner for implementation.

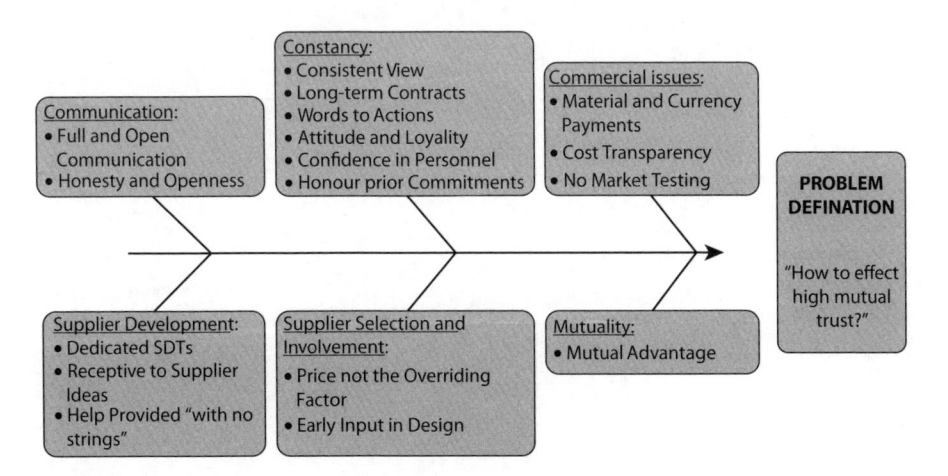

**Communication:**
- Full and Open Communication
- Honesty and Openness

**Constancy:**
- Consistent View
- Long-term Contracts
- Words to Actions
- Attitude and Loyalty
- Confidence in Personnel
- Honour prior Commitments

**Commercial issues:**
- Material and Currency Payments
- Cost Transparency
- No Market Testing

**Supplier Development:**
- Dedicated SDTs
- Receptive to Supplier Ideas
- Help Provided "with no strings"

**Supplier Selection and Involvement:**
- Price not the Overriding Factor
- Early Input in Design

**Mutuality:**
- Mutual Advantage

**PROBLEM DEFINATION**

"How to effect high mutual trust?"

The process ensured that the new troubleshooting procedures were available to, and understood by, the front line technicians.

## Step 8: Monitoring

For the improvements to be effective, the individual technicians needed to be able to monitor the new metrics. Control metrics were put into place.

## Step 9: Approval by management

Before the plan could go live it had to obtain management approval. This highlighted the diagnosis, the As-Is and Should-be processes, Implementation issues and controls, together with a summary of the benefits and estimated savings.

# References

## Introduction

1. Marion O'Connor, Centre for Management Research, Irish Management Institute, 2003.
2. *Action Learning*, Reg Revans, Blond & Briggs, 1980. For application of the technique at the IMI see *Managers, not MBAs*, page 193, Henry Minzberg, Prentice Hall, 2004.
3. *Global Competitiveness Report 2010–11*, World Economic Forum.
4. *National Recovery Plan 2011 to 2014*, 24 November 2010, Government Stationery Office.
5. Ireland was ranked 5th out of 169 countries in a quality-of-life index by a UN Development Programme report and 5th out of 183 countries in the World Bank "Doing Business" rankings published in 2010, quoted in *The Irish Times*, 5 November 2010.
6. PriceRunner.co.uk quoted in *The Irish Times*, 10 December 2008.
7. *Survey of MNCs in Ireland*, IMI and National Irish Bank, October 2008, October 2009, November 2010 and November 2011.
8. "2011 Report of National Competitiveness Council," *The Irish Times*, 12 January 2012.
9. *Global Competitiveness Report 2010–11*, World Economic Forum.

## Chapter 1

1. *Winning*, p189, Jack Welch, Harper Collins, 2005.
2. Behavioural aspects of budgeting are dealt with in most management accounting textbooks, e.g. *Management and Cost Accounting*, Colin Drury, Thomson Business Press, 7th Edition, 2008 or *Cost Accountancy*, Horngren, Foster and Datur, Prentice Hall, 13th Edition, 2010. The particular problems outlined here are based on discussions with practising Irish managers.
3. Zero-based budgeting rose to prominence in the 1970s after its adoption in Texas Instruments by Pyhrr and its subsequent adoption by the Carter administration in the public sector. It was abandoned by the Reagan administration due to its complexity and subsequently waned in popularity.
4. *The Irish Times*, 4 July 2008.

5. See: *Budgeting – an unnecessary evil*, Jan Wallander, Svenska Handelsbanken, 1997.
6. *The Irish Times*, 21 April 2011.
7. For a review of forecasters see: *Future Babble – Why expert predictions fail and why we believe them anyway*, Dan Gardner, Virgin Books, 2010.

## Chapter 2

1. Cost is assumed to be depreciated historic cost, as measured in most sets of accounts. Cost models are discussed in **Chapter 7**.
2. *The Irish Times*, 1 September 2008.
3. *Sunday Business Post*, 27 July 2008.
4. This theme under the title *Short Term Cost Management in the Credit Crunch* formed the basis of an address by Tim McCormick to the annual conference of the Institute of Chartered Accountants in Ireland during May 2009. Subsequently, a condensed version *Can your Budgeting System Cope with the Credit Crunch?* was published in both *Accountancy Ireland* and the journal of the Global Accounting Alliance, February 2010.

## Chapter 3

1. For a short general review of cost-cutting in functional areas see *How to Cut Costs in Business*, John Allan, Kogan Page, 2007.
2. The traditional term, 'Financial Controller' has been used throughout this book. The more modern and proactive role has led to a change in the name to 'Financial Manager,' or 'Business Manager.' See for example *Finanzmeister – Financial Manager and Business Strategist*, Nigel Kendall and Thomas Sheridan, Pitman, 1991 and *CFO Architect of the Corporation's Future*, Price Waterhouse, Wiley, 1997.
3. "CFOs peer into a turbulent future", *Financial Times*, 13 November 2008.
4. *Financial Times*, 25 October 2008.
5. *The Irish Times*, 22 November 2010.
6. See: *Getting More*, Stuart Diamond, Portfolio Penguin, 2011.
7. *Driving Down Cost: How to Manage and Cut Costs Intelligently*, Andrew Wileman, Nicholas Brearley Publishing, 2008. See also "Purchasing Must Become Supply Management", Peter Kraljic, *Harvard Business Review*, Sept–Oct 1983.

8. In Ireland, grants and tax credits are available for certain research and development expenditure. In 2011, a reconstituted Sustainable Energy Authority of Ireland was set up which can make grants to both businesses and householders.
9. *Value Chain Management – Strategy and Excellence in the Supply Chain*, Peter Hines *et al.*, Financial Times Prentice Hall, 2000.
10. *Financial Times*, 18 March 2011 and *The Economist*, 2 April 2011.
11. *FÁS chiefs enjoy a good life*, Shane Ross and Nick Webb, *Sunday Independent*, 23 November 2008.
12. See: *A Dynamic Approach to Management by Objectives*, John Humble, Management Publications, 1965.
13. *Cost Reduction and Control Best Practices*, Institute of Management and Administration, Wiley, 2002.
14. See, for example: *2001 Innovative Ways to Save your Company Thousands by Reducing Costs*, Cheryl L. Russell, Atlantic Publishing Group, 2007.
15. See, for example: *Profit Building: Cutting Costs without Cutting People*, Perry J. Ludy, Berrett-Koehler, 2000.

# Chapter 4

1. *Creating Shareholder Value*, Alfred Rappaport, Free Press, 1998.
2. The cost of equity is a complex technical problem. Just because a company may choose not to pay a dividend does not imply that equity has no cost. The usual approach is through the Capital Asset Pricing Model (CAPM). This is based on the cost of debt + the equity risk premium + the riskiness of the particular stock relative to the market. The equity risk premium is based on stock market returns over a long period. Research is needed to see whether it and the relative stock riskiness relative to the market (or 'BETA') have been affected by recent stock market turmoil, particularly in the financial sector.
3. 'Capital Employed' is normally defined as Shareholders' Funds + Long-term Liabilities. The main difference between it and 'Invested Capital' is the absence of short-term financial borrowings. Where short-term borrowings are small the difference should not be material.
4. Many consulting firms set a target ROIC based on the average cost of capital. This is a mix of debt and equity capital. Shareholder value is created when ROIC exceeds the cost of capital and destroyed when it is less than the cost of capital. Examples of such approaches are Economic Value Added (Stern Stewart & Co), Cashflow Return on Investment (Braxton, Deloitte Touche), Equity Cashflows (Marakon), Free Cashflow (Rappaport/Alcar) and Return on Invested Capital

(McKinsey). While the differences are sometimes stressed, there is much in common between the different methodologies.

## Chapter 5

1. *Sunday Tribune*, 15 September 1996. Chartbusters was placed into liquidation in 2010.
2. *The Irish Times*, Business Agenda, 21 November 2008.
3. *Sunday Independent*, Business, page 3, 14 December 2008.
4. *Financial Times*, 25 October 2008.
5. Ibid., 2 December 2008.
6. "Survey of 600 members of Institute of Credit Managers put figure at 2/3rds," *Financial Times*, page 17, 22 December 2008.
7. *Financial Times*, 17 November, 2008.
8. "Managing in the downturn: Desperately seeking a cash cure", *The Economist*, page 74, 22 November 2008.
9. *The Irish Times*, 30 January 2009.
10. The Irish examinership legislation is broadly similar to the UK administration. One difference is an examiner is appointed by the board and does not replace it. Also it is more closely under the control of the courts, which can give rise to higher costs than administration.

## Chapter 6

1. *Competitive Advantage*, Chapter 1, Michael E. Porter, Free Press, 2004.
2. *The Discipline of Market Leaders*, Michael Tracey and Fred Wiersema, Addison Wesley, 1995.
3. *The Delta Project: Discovering Sources of Profitability in a Networked Economy*, A. Hax and D. Wilde, Palgrave, 2001.
4. See: *The Walmart Effect*, Charles Fishman, Penguin, 2006 and *Tescopoly*, Andrew Simms, Constable, 2007.
5. *Gods of Management*, Charles Handy, Arrow, 1991.
6. IMI Cost Reduction Conferences 2004, 2006, 2009.

## Chapter 7

1. *Blue Ocean Strategy: How to Create Uncontested Market Space and Make Competition Irrelevant*, W. Chan Kim and Renée Mauborgne, Chapter 2, Harvard Business School Press, 2005.

2. See: *Relevance Lost: The Rise and Fall of Management Accounting*, H. Thomas Johnson and Robert S. Kaplan, Harvard Business School Press, 1987.
3. *The Goal*, Eliyahu M. Goldratt & Jeff Cox, Gower, 2004.

## Chapter 8

1. *Competitive Advantage*, Chapter 3, Michael E Porter, Free Press, 2004.
2. *The Fifth Discipline: The Art and Practice of the Learning Organisation*, Peter Senge, Doubleday, 1990.
3. This example was published in "Costs: Understanding Strategic Cost Drivers", Tim McCormick, *Accountancy Ireland*, August 2010.
4. *The Croke Park Agreement*, 1 April 2010, http://www.finance.gov.ie/documents/publications/other/2010/payagree
5. "The 'New Public Management' in the 1980s: Variations on a Theme", C. Hood, *Accounting, Organisation and Society*, Vol. 20, Nos 2/3, 1995.
6. "Briefing: Public-sector workers", *The Economist*, 8 January 2011.
7. "The Abuses of Austerity", *The Economist*, 2 July 2011.
8. "Taming Leviathan", *The Economist*, 19 March 2011.
9. *Wasters*, Shane Ross & Nick Webb, Penguin, 2010.
10. *Managing the Professional Service Firm*, Chaper 3, David Maister, Free Press, 1993.
11. *Back from the Brink*, Michael Edwardes, Pan, 1984.

## Chapter 9

1. *Competitive Advantage*, Chapter 2, Michael E. Porter, Free Press, 2004.
2. *The Southwest Airlines Way*, Jody Hoffer Gittell, McGraw-Hill, 2005.
3. Ryanair Accounts, http://www.ryanair.com/doc/investor/2010/Annual_report_2010
4. Trip Advisor quoted in *The Irish Times* 27 October 2006. In 2010–11 passengers totalled 75 million.
5. *The Irish Times* 27 October 2006.
6. Ibid., 7 May 2011.
7. The substance of this example was published in articles published both by Accountancy Ireland and the journal of the Global Accounting Alliance, entitled *"Understanding Costs Using the Value Chain – a Ryanair example"* by Tim McCormick, October 2010.

8. *The Irish Times*, 29 March 2008.
9. *Ryanair: How a Small Airline Conquered Europe*, page 122, Siobhan Creaton, Aurum, 2005.
10. *Ruinair*, page 13, Paul Kilduff, Gill & Macmillan, 2008.
11. *Michael O'Leary*, pages 302–3, Alan Ruddock, Penguin, 2007.
12. *The Irish Times*, 9 April 2008.
13. *Ruinair*, page 40, Paul Kilduff, Gill & Macmillan, 2008.
14. *The Irish Times*, 27 March 2008.
15. *Ruinair*, page 50, Paul Kilduff, Gill & Macmillan, 2008.
16. *No Frills*, page 194, Simon Calder, Virgin, 2003.
17. *Ruinair*, page 10, Paul Kilduff, Gill & Macmillan, 2008.

## Chapter 10

1. *Economics for Business*, Chapter 5 pages 107–115, Dermot McAleese, FT Prentice Hall, 2004.
2. See: *Small is the New Big*, Seth Godwin, Portfolio, 2006.
3. There is plenty of literature on franchising. See for example: *Running a Successful Franchise*, Kirk Shivell and Kent Banning, McGraw-Hill, 1993 or *The Franchising Paradox*, Stuart Price, Cassell, 1997.
4. The author is indebted to Richard Lyons of Henry Lyons, the Sligo-based department store, for an explanation of this model.
5. "Outsourcing as you sleep", *The Economist*, 21 February 2009.
6. *The World is Flat*, Thomas L. Friedman, Penguin, 2006.
7. *Wikinomics*, Don Tapscott and Anthony D. Williams, Atlantic Books, 2007.
8. *Borderless Economics*, Robert Guest, Palgrave Macmillan, 2011.
9. *The Long Tail*, Chris Anderson, RH Business Books, 2006.
10. "Briefing 3D printing", *The Economist*, 12 February 2011 and "A light-bulb moment", *Financial Times*, 29 December 2011.
11. "The Third Industrial Revolution", page 13, *The Economist*, 21 April 2012.
12. "Small is not beautiful", *The Economist*, 3 March 2012.

## Chapter 11

1. *World Class Manufacturing*, Richard Schonberger, The Free Press, 1986.
2. Based on: *The Toyota Way*, Jeffrey K. Liker, Chapter 1 page 6, McGraw-Hill, 2004.

3. "Learning to Lead at Toyota", Stephen J. Spear, *Harvard Business Review*, May 2004.
4. Based on: *The Toyota Way*, Jeffrey K. Liker, Chapter 3, page 33, McGraw-Hill, 2004.
5. Based on: *The Toyota Way*, Jeffrey K. Liker, Chapter 9, page 176, McGraw-Hill, 2004.
6. *A New American TQM*, Shoji Shiba, David Walden & Alan Graham, Productivity Centre for Quality Management, 1993.
7. Based on: *The Toyota Way*, Jeffrey K. Liker, Chapter 14, page 256, McGraw-Hill, 2004.
8. *Lean Thinking*, James P. Womack & Daniel T. Jones, Simon & Schuster, 2003.
9. *The Toyota Way to Continuous Improvement*, Jeffrey K. Liker & James K. Franz, McGraw-Hill, 2011.
10. *Facing up to the learning organisation challenge*, Vol. 2, Chapter 9, Editors: Barry Nyhan, Michael Kelleher, Peter Cressey & Rob Poell, CEDEFOP, 2003.
11. *How to Implement Lean Manufacturing*, Lonnie Wilson, McGraw-Hill, 2010.
12. In Ireland, manufacturing businesses or eligible internationally-traded services with a five-year history may avail of subsidised consultancy assistance from Enterprise Ireland. Programmes range from LeanStart over 8–10 weeks to a longer LeanPlus over six months or a comprehensive LeanTransform over a period of a year.
13. This case study is a synopsis of "Rational Expense Reduction: Lean Budgeting at Irving Oil", Lawrence Carr, Professor of Management Accounting and William Lawler, Leadership Professor of Strategy & Accounting, both of Babson College and Joseph Reny, Finance Director of Irving Oil Marketing, to be published in the *Journal of Corporate Accounting & Finance*, 2012.

# Chapter 12

1. *Process Innovation*, T.H. Davenport, Harvard Business School Press, 1993.
2. *Toyota under Fire – Lessons for turning crisis into opportunity*, Jeffrey K. Liker & Timothy Ogden, McGraw-Hill, 2011.
3. *The Toyota Way*, Jeffrey K. Liker, McGraw-Hill, 2004.
4. *DMRI Study, Enterprise Ireland study visit*. Unpublished report, 2005.

5. *The Race*, Eli Goldratt, North River Press, 1986.
6. *Kaizan, The Key to Japan's Competitiveness*, Masaaki Imai, McGraw-Hill, 1986.
7. Reuters, 11 June 2011.
8. *Best Practices LLC*, Christopher Bogan and Michael English, McGraw-Hill, 1994.
9. *Lean Six Sigma Pocket Toolbook*, Michael George *et al.*, The George Group, 2005.
10. *Lean Six Sigma: Combining Six Sigma Quality*, Michael George, McGraw-Hill, 2002.
11. *Lean Six Sigma for Service*, Michael George, McGraw-Hill, 2003.
12. Company disguised, unpublished thesis proposal.
13. Company disguised, unpublished thesis proposal.

## Chapter 13

1. *Re-engineering the Corporation*, Michael Hammer and James Champy, Harper Collins, 1994.
2. "Process Re-Engineering", The *Journal of the Strategic Information Systems Management*, pages 71–73, Spring 1994.
3. "Business Re-engineering at CIGNA Corporation, Experiences and Lessons Learned from the first 5 years", Caron M. *et al.*, *MIS Quarterly*, 1994.
4. "Rapid Fire Fulfilment", Kasra Ferdows, *Harvard Business Review*, November 2004.
5. *Ingmar Kamprad and IKEA*, Harvard Business School Publishing, 1996. A more recent, critical and controversial account by an insider is contained in *The Truth About IKEA,* Johan Stenebo, Gibson Square, 2011.
6. *Lean Thinking*, James P. Womack and Daniel T. Jones, Simon & Schuster, 2003.
7. Unpublished thesis.
8. Unpublished thesis.

## Chapter 14

1. *The Search for Industry Best Practices that Lead to Superior Performance*, Robert Camp, ASQC Quality Press, 1989.
2. For further information see the Enterprise Ireland website.

# Chapter 15

1. *The Black Book of Outsourcing*, Douglas Brown and Scott Wilson, Wiley, 2005.
2. *The Outsourcing Revolution, why it makes sense and how to do it right*, Michael F. Corbett, Dearborn, 2004.
3. *Strategic Outsourcing: A Structural Approach*, Maurice Greaver, Amacom, 2005.
4. *New Directions in Finance*, The Economist Intelligence Unit, 1995.
5. This section first appeared as "Outsourcing – Offshoring or Onshoring" by Tim McCormick in *Accountancy Ireland*, April 2011 and subsequently in *GAA Accounting*.
6. *Outsourcing to India, a Legal Handbook*, Bharat Vagadia, Springer, 2007.
7. *No Logo*, Naomi Klein, Flamingo, 2000.
8. For a description of various structures see *The Offshore Nation — Strategies for Success in Global Outsourcing and Offshoring*, Atul Vashistha and Avinash Vashistha, McGraw-Hill, 2006.
9. *The Outsourcing Revolution, why it makes sense and how to do it right*, Michael F. Corbett, Dearborn, 2004.
10. "Time to Rethink Offshoring", Ajay K. Goel, Nazgol Moussavi & Vats N. Srivatsan, *McKinsey on Business Technology*, Winter 2008.
11. *Financial Times*, 7 October 2011.

# Chapter 16

1. *The Age of Unreason*, Chapter 4, Charles Handy, Century Business, 1991.
2. First published as "5 Practical Approaches to Reduce your Labour Costs", *Accountancy Ireland*, February 2011 and reproduced in *GAA Accounting*, February 2011.
3. "South tops North in public pay, welfare", *The Irish Times*, 23 November 2010.
4. 74% of companies reported a pay freeze in 2011 and 76% intended to either freeze or reduce pay in 2012, IBEC Survey, reported in *The Irish Times*, 9 January 2012.
5. There were 37,300 official redundancies notified in 2008, up 57% on an annual basis. "Jobless rate jumps to 7.8% in November", *The Irish Times*, 4 December 2008.
6. "Desperately Seeking a Cash Cure", *The Economist*, page 74, 22 November 2008.

7. *The Telegraph*, 14 November 2008.
8. We are indebted to our former IMI colleague, Martin Farrelly, for this example.
9. See: "The folly of rewarding A, while hoping for B", Steven Kerr, *Academy of Management Journal 18*, 1975.
10. There are many journalistic accounts of the financial crisis caused by the collapse of the subprime market. From the UK are: *Fool's Gold*, Gillian Tett (of the *Financial Times*), Abacus, 2009 and *Meltdown*, Paul Mason (of the BBC), Verso, 2009. A different perspective from the US is *The Big Short*, Michael Lewis, Allen Lane, 2010.
11. *The Greed Merchants*, Philip Augar, Penguin, 2006.
12. Examples include:
    *Binge Trading – the real inside story of cash, cocaine and corruption in the City*, Seth Freedman, Penguin 2009.
    *How I Caused the Credit Crunch*, Tetsuya Ishikawa, Icon Books, 2009.
    *Cityboy*, Geraint Andersen, Headline, 2008.
    *The Accidental Investment Banker – Inside the decade that transformed Wall Street*, Jonathan Knee, Oxford, 2006.
    *F.I.A.S.C.O.*, Frank Parthnoy, Profile Books, 1997 (updated 2009).
13. *Liars Poker*, Michael Lewis, Hodder & Stoughton, 1989.
14. *Good Strategy/Bad Strategy*, Chapter 20, Richard Rumelt, Profile Books, 2011
15. *The Tipping Point*, Malcolm Gladwell, Abacus, 2006.
16. *Infectious Greed – how deceit and risk corrupted the financial markets*, Frank Partnoy, Henry Holt, 2003.
17. See: *Bad Money*, Kevin Phillips, Penguin, 2008.
18. *The Age of Turbulence*, Alan Greenspan, Penguin, 2008.
19. Evidence to Congress, 24 October 2008.
20. *The Bangalore Tiger*, Steve Hamm, McGraw-Hill, 2006.

## Chapter 17

1. *Strategies and Styles, the Role of the Centre in Managing Diversified Corporations*, Michael Goold and Andrew Campbell, Blackwell Business, 1989.
2. *The Irish Times*, 30 April 2008.
3. *Built to Last*, Chapter 3, James Collins and Jerry Porras, Random House, 2000.
   *In Search of Excellence*, Chapter 4, Tom Peters and Robert Waterman, Harper & Row, 1982.

4. "Creating Shared Value", Michael E. Porter and Mark R. Kramer, *Harvard Business Review*, January–February 2011.
5. "Using the Balanced Scorecard as a Management System", Robert Kaplan and David Norton, *Harvard Business Review*, Jan–Feb 1996. Also *The Balanced Scorecard*, Robert S. Kaplan and David P. Norton, Harvard Business School Press, 1996.
6. *Strategy Maps*, Robert Kaplan and David Norton, Harvard University Press, pages 99–102, 2004.
7. Much of this material has appeared in articles by Tim McCormick in *Accountancy Ireland*: "Responding to the Irish Banking Disgrace" in June 2010, "Banking – the Road to Recovery" in December 2010 and "Irish Banking after Nyberg" in June 2011. A fuller account is set out by him in "Ethical Banking: Reasonable Expectation or Impossible Oxymoron?", *The Business Compass: Perspectives on Business Ethics*, Chartered Accountants Ireland, 2012. His views were first expressed in "Banks have only themselves to blame for crisis", *The Sunday Tribune*, 21 September 2008.
8. *The Irish Banking Crisis – Regulatory and Financial Stability Policy*, A Report to the Minister for Finance by the Governor of the Central Bank, 31 May 2010.
9. *The Irish Times*, 20 January 2011.
10. "The Irish Credit Bubble", Morgan Kelly, *Understanding Ireland's Economic Crisis – Prospects for Recovery*, Eds: Stephen Kinsella and Anthony Leddin, Blackhall, 2010.
11. *The Irish Times*, 9 July 2010.
12. For the principles of credit see "The 20 'Cs' of Credit – Basic Considerations the Banks Overlooked", Tim McCormick, *Accountancy Ireland*, August 2009.
13. *Sunday Business Post*, 13 March 2011.
14. *The Irish Times*, 20 May 2011.
15. *Misjudging Risk: Causes of the Systemic Banking Crisis in Ireland*, Report of the Commission of Investigation into the Banking Sector in Ireland, March 2011.
16. 'Groupthink' is not a new discovery. It was identified as a cause of the banking crisis in "Restoring Confidence in the Irish Banks", Tim McCormick, *Accountancy Ireland*, June 2009.
17. *Ireland's House Party*, Derek Brawn, Gill & Macmillan, 2009.
18. *The Bankers – how the banks brought Ireland to its knees*, Shane Ross, Penguin Ireland, 2009.
19. Taoiseach Bertie Ahern in 2006, quoted in *The Economist*, 17 February 2011 and speech to ICTU on 4 July 2007.

20. *Open Dissent,* Mike Soden, Blackhall, 2010.
21. *The Irish Times,* 2 September 2011.
22. *The Irish Times,* 12 November 2010.
23. *The Irish Times,* 1 April 2011.

## Chapter 18

1. Research by A.T. Kearney management consultants, reported at the Supplierforce conference in *The Irish Times,* page 19, 24 November 2008.
2. First published as "Business Failure – the Seven Deadly Sins", Tim McCormick, *Accountancy Ireland,* December 2009.
3. *Corporate Collapse: The Causes and Symptoms,* J. Argenti, McGraw-Hill, 1976. Also *Corporate Financial Distress and Bankruptcy,* Edward Altman, 2nd Edition, Wiley, 1993.
4. *Corporate Financial Crisis in Ireland,* Edward Cahill, Gill & Macmillan, 1997.
5. *How the Mighty Fail,* Jim Collins, R.H. Business Books, 2009. He identifies five stages on the route to failure. The first stage is hubris, born of success, which corresponds to pride and neglect of change. The second is undisciplined pursuit of more, which resembles over-trading. The third is denial of risk and peril, which usually leads to over-borrowing. The fourth is grasping for salvation or taking the big risk. The last is irrelevance or death, where an attempt can be made to restore controls.
6. *Shepherd's Pie,* George Mordaunt, Mercier, 2011.
7. *Greed and Glory on Wall Street – the fall of the house of Lehman,* Ken Auletta, Penguin, 1986, recounts this collapse.
8. *Liar's Poker,* Michael Lewis, Hodder & Stoughton, 1989.
9. *A Colossal Failure of Common Sense – the incredible story of the collapse of Lehman Brothers,* Larry McDonald, Ebury Press, 2009.
10. *Too Big to Fail – Inside the Battle to Save Wall Street,* Andrew Ross Sorkin, Penguin 2010.
11. *The Irish Banking Crisis – Regulatory and Financial Stability Policy,* A Report to the Minister for Finance by the Governor of the Central Bank, 31 May 2010.
12. *The Irish Times,* 6 August 2010.
13. *The FitzPatrick Tapes – the Rise and Fall of One Man, One Bank and One Country,* Tom Lyons and Brian Carey, Penguin Ireland, 2011.
14. *Banksters – How a powerful elite squandered Ireland's wealth,* David Murphy & Martina Devlin, Hachette Books Ireland, 2009.

15. *The Bankers – How the Banks brought Ireland to its Knees*, Shane Ross, Penguin Ireland, 2009.
16. *Breakfast with Anglo*, Simon Kelly, Penguin Ireland, 2010.
17. *RTE News*, 19 December 2008.
18. *The Irish Times*, 19 November 2010.
19. This example was given by Tim McCormick in "Have Politicans been guilty of the 7 Deadly Sins Found in Business Failure?", *Accountancy Ireland*, February 2012.
20. *How Ireland Really Went Bust*, Matt Cooper, Penguin Ireland, 2011
21. In the case of Ireland, Gross National Product (GNP) statistics can be misleading, due to the considerable impact of multinational companies which repatriate their profits. Gross Domestic Product (GDP) is considered by many to be a better guide.

# Chapter 19

1. "Defining the 'field at a given time'", Kurt Lewin, *Psychological Review*, 1943. Republished in *Resolving Social Conflicts and Field Theory*, American Psychlogical Association, 1997.
2. *What worked in cost cutting – and what comes next*, McKinsey, 2010.
3. *Leading Change*, John P. Kotter, Harvard Business School Press, 1996. For a profound account of this material told as a fable see:
*Our Iceberg is Melting*, John Kotter & Holger Rathgeber, Macmillan, 2006.
4. Tim Jeans, formerly Sales and Development Manager, Ryanair, quoted in *Easyjet*, Lois Jones, 2007.
5. Most of this material has been published in *Accountancy Ireland*, "Cost Reduction in the Public Sector – Lessons from the Private Sector", Tim McCormick, August 2011.
6. "Amárach Survey", reported in *The Irish Times*, 28 November 2011.
7. "Indecon Survey", reported in *The Sunday Independent*, 31 July 2011.
8. *Irish Independent*, 3 September 2011.
9. *The Implementation of Accruals Accounting in the Irish Public Sector – a Comparative Study of Northern Ireland*, Ciaran Connolly & Noel Hyndman, Chartered Accountants Ireland, 2009.
10. *Report of the Special Group on Public Service Numbers and Expenditure Programmes*, Department of Finance, July 2009.
11. *The Irish Times*, 10 March 2012.
12. *The Sunday Times*, 6 November 2011.
13. "*Dysfunctional culture of Civil Service management*", Eddie Molloy, page 14, *The Irish Times*, 18 April 2012.

14. *The Irish Times,* 24 March 2011.
15. *The Irish Times,* 12 April 2011.
16. "Retired State staff get their jobs back," *The Sunday Times,* page 1, 13 May 2012.
17. *The Irish Times,* 1 February 2012.
18. *Strategic Cost Reduction,* Tim McCormick & Dermot Duff, New Zealand Institute of Chartered Accountants, 2011.

# Chapter 20

1. *Business Barometer Weekly Gazette,* 6 January 2012.
2. *Financial Times,* 31 December 2011.
3. *The Irish Times,* 7 March 2012.
4. *Crisis Economics – A Crash Course in the Future of Finance,* Roubini Nouriel & Mihm Stephen, Penguin, 2010.
5. *Free to Choose,* Milton and Rose Friedman, Pelican Books, 1980.
6. *23 Things They Don't Tell You about Capitalism,* Ha-Joon Chang, Penguin Books, 2011 and "The Rise of State Capitalism", *The Economist,* 21 January 2012.
   Also *How the West Was Lost,* Dambisa Moyo, Penguin, 2012.
7. See: "The Crisis of Capitalism", *Financial Times,* 9–14 January 2012 and *Capitalism 4.0: The Birth of a New Economy,* Anatole Kaletsky, Bloomsbury, 2010.
8. *Understanding Ireland's Economic Crisis – Prospects for Recovery,* Eds: Stephen Kinsella and Anthony Leddin, Blackhall, 2010.
9. *What if Ireland Defaults,* Eds: Brian Lucey, Charles Larkin & Constantin Gurdgiev, Orpen press, 2012.
10. The fitness analogy is described in an article by Tim McCormick, "Achieving Peak Corporate Fitness – Learning from the Olympics", *Accountancy Ireland,* August 2012.
11. For this list of excuses we are indebted to Duane Deason, Director of the National Cost Control Standards Board, USA.
12. This summary is amplified in an article by Tim McCormick, "Strategic Cost Reduction – Steps to Success", *Accountancy Ireland,* April 2010.

# Selected Further Reading

The following books and articles form a short list of available literature for managers wishing to pursue any particular area in greater detail. It is not intended to be comprehensive, but rather to provide pointers for further research. In the spirit of action learning, this brief selection ranges from academic or technical books, articles and reports to memoirs and journalistic contributions, where they illustrate a particular aspect or example. References to other materials on specific matters are contained within the chapters.

### Introduction

IMI and National Irish Bank, *Survey of MNCs in Ireland*, October 2008, October 2009, November 2010 and November 2011.
Minzberg, Henry, *Managers, not MBAs*, Prentice Hall, 2004.
Revans, Reg, *Action Learning*, Blond & Briggs, 1980.
World Economic Forum, *Global Competitiveness Report 2010–11*.

### 1. Budgeting challenges

Drury, Colin, *Management and Cost Accounting*, Chapter 15 "The Budgeting Process", Thomson Business Press, 7th Edition, 2008.
Wallander, Jan, *Budgeting – an unnecessary evil*, Svenska Handelsbanken, 1997.

### 2. Effective control

Drury, Colin, *Management and Cost Accounting: Chapter 16 Management Control Systems*, Thomson Business Press, 7th Edition, 2008.

### 3. The role of the functions in traditional cost reduction

Allan, John, *How to Cut Costs in Business*, Kogan Page, 2007.
Institute of Management and Administration, *Cost Reduction and Control Best Practices*, Wiley, 2002.
Diamond, Stuart, *Getting More*, Portfolio Penguin, 2011.
Wileman, Andrew, *Driving Down Cost: How to Manage and Cut Costs Intelligently*, Nicholas Brearley Publishing, 2008.

## 4. Is there a problem?

Copeland, Tom; Koller, Tim and Murrin, Jack, *Valuation – Measuring and Managing the Value of Companies,* McKinsey & Co, 1990.
Rappaport, Alfred, *Creating Shareholder Value,* Free Press, 1998.

## 5. Emergency cost reduction

Brearley, Richard; Myers, Stewart and Allen, Franklin, *Principles of Corporate Finance,* 10th Edition, Part 7: "Financial Planning and Working Capital Management", McGraw-Hill, 2010.
Brummer Alex, *The Crunch,* RH Business Books, 2008.

## 6. Preliminary strategic considerations

Handy, Charles, *Gods of Management,* Arrow Books, 1991.
Porter, Michael, *Competitive Advantage,* Chapter 1, Free Press, 2004.
Simms, Andrew, *Tescopoly,* Constable, 2007.

## 7. Critical functional considerations

Kim, Chan and Mauborgne, Renee, *Value Innovation,* Harvard Business Review, 2004.
Kim, Chan and Mauborgne, Renee, *Blue Ocean Strategy,* Harvard Business School Press, 2005.
Johnson, Thomas and Kaplan, Robert S., *Relevance Lost: The Rise and Fall of Management Accounting,* Harvard Business School Press, 1987.
Kaplan, Robert and Cooper, Robin, *Cost and Effect,* Harvard Business School Press, 1998.

## 8. Discovering the strategic drivers of cost

Maister, David, *Managing the Professional Service Firm,* Chapter 3, Free Press, 1993.
Porter, Michael, *Competitive Advantage,* Chapter 3, Free Press, 2004.
Senge, Peter, *The Fifth Discipline: The Art and Practice of the Learning Organisation,* Doubleday, 1990.

## 9. Exploiting the value chain

Creaton, Siobhán, *Ryanair*, Aurum, 2005.
Porter, Michael E., *Competitive Advantage*, Chapter 2, Free Press, 2004.

## 10. Deciding on size

Anderson, Chris, *The Long Tail*, RH Business Books, 2006.
Friedman, Thomas L., *The World is Flat*, Penguin, 2006.
McAleese, Dermot, *Economics for Business*, Chapter 5, FT Prentice Hall, 2004.
Price, Stuart, *The Franchising Paradox*, Cassell, 1997.

## 11. 'World-Class' and 'Lean Manufacturing'

Schonberger, R.J., *Operations Management – Continuous Improvement*, Irwin, 1994.
Masaaki, Imai, *Gemba Kaizen: A Commonsense, Low-Cost Approach*, McGraw-Hill, 1997.

## 12. Radical improvement

Bill, George, *Lean Six Sigma for Service*, McGraw-Hill, 2006.
Liker, Jeffrey, *The Toyota Way*, McGraw-Hill, 2004.
Womack, J.P. and Jones, D.T, *Lean Thinking*, Simon & Schuster London, 2003.

## 13. Business process re-engineering

Bessant, John *et al.*, *Managing Innovation*, Wiley, 4th Edition, 2005.
Hammer, M. and Champy, J., "Transforming the Corporation", *Harvard Business Review*, 1997.
Hammer, M. and Champy, J., *Reengineering the Corporation*, Harper, 1994.

## 14. Benchmarking

Camp, Robert C., *Business Process Benchmarking*, ASQC, 1995.

## 15. Outsourcing

Brown, Douglas and Wilson Scott, *The Black Book of Outsourcing*, John Wiley & Sons, 2005.
Corbett, Michael F., *The Outsourcing Revolution*, Dearborn Trading Corporation, 2004.
Klein, Naomi, *No Logo*, Flamingo, 2000.
Quinn, James Brian, "Make versus Buy: Strategic Outsourcing", *McKinsey Quarterly*, 1995.
Vashistha, Atul and Vashistha, Avinash, *The Offshore Nation: Strategies for Success in Global Outsourcing and Offshoring*, Mcgraw-Hill, 2006.

## 16. Structuring and rewarding the labour force

Goold, Michael and Campbell, Andrew, *Strategy and Styles, the Role of the Centre in Diversified Corporations*, Blackwell Business, 1989.
Greenspan, Alan, *The Age of Turbulence*, Penguin, 2008.
Hamm, Steve, *Bangalore Tiger*, McGraw-Hill, 2006.
Handy, Charles, *The Age of Unreason*, Century Business, 1991.
Mason, Paul, *Meltdown*, Verso, 2009.
Tett, Gillian, *Fool's Gold*, Abacus, 2009.

## 17. Strategic cost reduction – the critical links

Honohan, Patrick, *The Irish Banking Crisis: Regulatory and Financial Stability Policy*, A Report to the Minister for Finance by the Governor of the Central Bank, 31 May 2010.
Kaplan, Robert and Norton, David, *The Balanced Scorecard*, Harvard Business School Press, 1996.
Nyberg, Peter, *Misjudging Risk: Causes of the Systemic Banking Crisis in Ireland*, Report of the Commission of Investigation into the Banking Sector in Ireland, March 2011.
Ross, Shane, *The Bankers: How the banks brought Ireland to its knees*, Penguin Ireland, 2009.

## 18. Avoiding financial failure

Argenti, J., *Corporate Collapse: The Causes and Symptoms*, McGraw-Hill, 1976.
Cahill, Edward, *Corporate Financial Crisis in Ireland*, Gill & Macmillan, 1997.

Collins, Jim, *How the Mighty Fail*, RH Business Books, 2009.
Lyons, Tom & Carey, Brian, *The FitzPatrick Tapes: The rise and fall of one man, one bank and one country*, Penguin Ireland, 2011.
McDonald, Larry, *A Colossal Failure of Common Sense: The incredible story of the collapse of Lehman Brothers*, Ebury Press, 2009.
Sorkin, Andrew Ross, *Too Big to Fail: Inside the Battle to Save Wall Street*, Penguin 2010.

## 19. Managing the process

Duff, Dermot and Quilliam, John, *Project Management*, Management Briefs, 2010.
Kotter, J.P, *Leading Change*, Harvard Business School Press, 1996.

## 20. Planning the journey

Kaletsky, Anatole, *Capitalism 4.0: The Birth of a New Economy*, Bloomsbury, 2010.
Kinsella, Stephen and Leddin, Anthony (Eds), *Understanding Ireland's Economic Crisis – Prospects for Recovery,* Blackhall, 2010.
Roubini, Nouriel and Mihm, Stephen, *Crisis Economics: A Crash Course in the Future of Finance,* Penguin, 2010.

# Index

3 Es approach 20–23, 24, 217
4 M branches 138
5 S system 152, 160
6 Sigma 133, 153, 154–7, 160, 268, 271, 277–80
7 S model 217–18, 222
7 Steps problem solving 133, 135, 137–9, 158
9/11 attacks 7, 16, 106, 112

absenteeism 32, 158, 198, 259
academic leadership style 71
activity-based budgeting 82, 144–5
activity-based costing (ABC) 81–2, 83, 87, 103
activity-based management (ABM) 81–2
accountability 259–60
accounting periods 14, 214
accounting systems 258–9
Adare group 97–8
administration *see* examinership
advertising 35, 96, 110
agriculture 104–5, 122
Aldi 57
Allied Irish Bank 238
Anglo Irish Bank 224, 226–7, 238–43, 246
Apple 97
assets, sale of 55, 68, 261
auditors 243
autocratic management 232–3, 236, 237, 240–41, 245

bad debts 56, 206, 231
balance of work 150
balanced scorecard 220–21, 230, 254, 262, 271

Bank of Ireland 227, 228, 238
bank relations 58
banking crisis 47, 55–6, 210, 222, 224, 226–30, 235–43, 246–8, 263; *see also* credit crunch
banking finance 43, 55–6
banking industry 32, 204, 206–11, 222–30, 235–43
Barroso, José Manuel 222
Bausch & Lomb 58
benchmarking 44–5, 98, 99, 102, 133, 170–79, 188, 205, 257, 268, 269–70
benefits-in-kind 199–200, 204–5, 212
beyond budgeting 11–12
bonuses *see* rewards
bottlenecks 83, 143, 150
brainstorming 136, 138, 251
brands 84, 96, 97, 110–11, 115, 119, 121–2, 154, 181, 186–7
Branson, Richard 116
brokers 29
budgeting 3–24, 213–14, 230, 233
building *see* construction industry
business failure 231–48, 264–5
business health checks 41, 268
business process re-engineering (BPR) 33, 73, 161–9, 271
business size 116–27, 268
business units 94–5
buying power 22, 28, 119, 122

Camp, Robert 171
capacity utilisation 92–3, 97, 101
capital budgets 4
capital expenditure 54, 97
capital investments 215, 216
capital turnover 42, 46, 47, 49

capitalism 42, 219, 222, 229, 266–7
Carey, Brian 240
Carton Brothers 141
cash generation, short-term 54–5, 58, 60
cashflow forecasts 58
cashflow model 51–2
cashflow statements 243
casual workers 197–8, 211
Central Bank of Ireland 227, 229, 260, 262
centralisation 94–5
change
   failure to respond to 233, 236–7, 241, 245–6
   resistance to 100, 171, 251, 252–3, 257, 263
change management 64, 162, 249–63
changeover times 152–3, 167
chief executive officers (CEOs) 10, 65, 70–72, 75–7
chief financial officers (CFOs) 26–7
club culture 71
Collins, Jim 232, 246
Colorman 141
communication 33, 120, 121, 123, 253–4, 256, 262, 263
construction industry 52, 84, 101, 197
consultants 72–3
continuous improvement 82–3, 136–9, 146–7, 158, 254–5
core competences 183–4
core employees 197–8, 211
core values 66, 69–70, 74, 75–88, 218–19, 222, 225–30
corporate anorexia 9–10, 59
corporate culture 71, 113, 151, 218, 257
corporate social responsibility 69–70, 219
cost accounting 26
cost control 25, 233

cost drivers 89–102
cost leadership strategy 67–8
cost management 25
cost reduction failures 63–4
cost reduction potential 19
cost reduction strategies 63–74
cost reduction targets 38, 46–7
cost significance 19
costing systems 13–14, 76, 80–82, 87, 103, 213–14, 230
costs *see* direct costs; discretionary costs; fixed costs; hidden costs; indirect costs; interest costs; key costs; labour costs; materials costs; opportunity costs; travel costs; variable costs
creative accounting 48, 234, 237, 247
credit control 33, 52–3, 233
credit crunch 55–9, 60, 207; *see also* banking crisis; recession
credit insurance 53
creditors 52, 244
critical path analysis 250
Croke Park Agreement 98–9, 100, 257–8, 262
crony capitalism 229, 266–7
cross-training 151; *see also* multi-skilling
customer service *see* service

debt 43
debtors 52–3
decentralisation 11
Dell Computers 30, 54, 217
derivatives 56, 209, 236, 237
differentiation strategy 67–8, 77–8, 96
direct costs 4, 80
discretionary cost drivers 96–7
discretionary costs 54, 55, 59, 64
diseconomies of scale 90, 117, 120–21, 125–6, 257

distribution *see* logistics
dividends 42, 51, 54
Drucker, Peter 36
Drumm, David 238, 239
duplication 21, 35, 95, 99, 120, 166, 167

early retirement 85, 141, 178, 199, 201
Ebbers, Bernie 18
economic model 72
economic stimuli 65
economies of increased dimension 119
economies of scale 90, 97, 116, 117, 118–19, 124–5, 126, 180
economies of scope 118–19
*Economist* 99, 100, 228, 245
economy 20–21, 22–3
effectiveness 21–3
efficiency 12, 21, 22–3, 76, 262
electronic distribution 124
emergency cost reduction 50–60
employees *see* human resources; labour force
empowerment 32, 83, 134, 144, 145, 156, 158, 167, 256
engineering function 30–31, 86–7
engineering model 72
Enterprise Ireland 171
enterprise resource planning (ERP) systems 14, 76, 120
entertainment 13, 35, 36, 199, 207
equity 43
examinership 59
exchange rates 42, 185
existential culture 71
expenses 9, 36, 199, 207, 246

factoring 184–5
FÁS 23, 36, 260

fashion industry 7, 163
financial benchmarking 170
financial control 26–7, 78–82, 104, 171
financial crisis *see* banking crisis; credit crunch
financial reporting 79–80
firm infrastructure 104, 105, 113
first movers 97
FitzGerald, Niall 228
FitzPatrick, Seán 238, 239, 240–41, 242
five S system 152, 160
fixed costs 76, 80, 119, 145
fixed pay 99, 205
flattening of organisations 200
flexibility 7, 12, 16, 120, 151, 268
focus strategy 67–8
followers 97
force field analysis 251–2, 261
Ford 152
four M branches 138
franchising 121–2, 127
Fuld, Dick 235, 236, 237
functional benchmarking 171
functions
   critical considerations 75–88
   roles in cost reduction 25–39
   separation of 79

gearing 55, 237, 243
General Electric 1, 211
generic strategies 67–8
Gladwell, Malcolm 208
globalisation 92, 121, 122–4, 127, 182, 228
Glucksman, Lew 235
government expenses 9, 36
government spending cuts 20, 98–9, 261
Greenspan, Alan 209, 210

groupthink 208, 226, 228
growth 14, 15–16, 48
growth cost drivers 89–91
Guinness 140–41

Hammer, Michael 161, 162
Handelsbanken 11, 208
Handy, Charles 71, 197
head offices 69, 104, 113, 115, 215–17, 230
health and safety 83–4, 86
health checks for business 41, 268
Health Service Executive (HSE) 28
hedging 79, 237
hidden costs 183, 195–6, 212
holistic approach 37–8
Honohan, Patrick 222, 224–5, 228, 240, 241
hotel industry 22, 92, 122, 181
human behaviour 18
human resources (HR) 31–2, 84–6, 104, 105, 113, 171; *see also* labour force
Humble, John 36

IBM 198
IKEA 163
inbound logistics 34, 103, 104, 108, 109
incentives *see* motivation; rewards
incremental budgeting 8
indirect costs 4, 80; *see also* overheads
indivisible costs *see* fixed costs
industrial action 33, 120, 251
inflation 215
information technology (IT) 33–4, 87, 104–5, 112–13, 121, 123–5, 127, 162, 187
infrastructure 104, 105, 113
innovation 7, 68, 91, 171

insolvency 59, 264–5; *see also* business failure
institutional cost drivers 93
integration 95
Intercontinental group 122
interest costs 4, 245
internal audit departments 35–6
internal controls 79
invoice discounting 56, 185
Irish Life and Permanent 229
Irish Nationwide Building Society 226, 239, 240
Irving Oil 144–5

just-in-time (JIT) 133, 150, 151, 155, 159, 162, 271

kaizen 133, 255
Kelleher, Herb 106
Kelly, Morgan 245
key costs 17–18
key performance indicators (KPIs) 14
Kotter, John 255

labour costs 27, 31–2, 33, 58, 97, 98, 101, 109, 175, 177, 195–6, 198–201, 204–5
labour force 27, 76, 144, 195–212, 271; *see also* human resources
labour force reduction 84–5, 87, 178, 198, 217, 253, 261–2; *see also* redundancies
labour mobility 123
labour turnover 196, 206, 212
leadership 255, 256, 263
leadership styles 70, 71–2, 74
lean operations 82–3, 121, 131–45, 163, 165, 268, 271; *see also* World Class Manufacturing
learning curves 90–91, 118, 123

Lehman Brothers 222, 235–8, 242, 266
Lewin, Kurt 251
limiting factors 14
linkages 93–5
liquidation 59
liquidity 48, 79, 114, 224, 239, 243
Loane, Nelson 97
location 92
logistics 34–5, 103, 104, 108
low fares airlines 31, 103, 105–15; *see also* Ryanair
Lyons, Tom 240

McDonald, Larry 236, 238
McDonalds 151
management accounts 4, 26, 76, 79–80, 233
management by objectives (MBO) 36
management control 120, 121
marketing *see* sales and marketing
master budgets 15
materials costs 27, 97
Maxwell, Robert 232–3
Mazda 152
mentors 73
Metcalfe's Law 119
Microsoft 97, 184
military leadership style 72
mission statements 66, 69, 76, 84, 218
mistake prevention 151
motivation 5, 7, 12, 18, 113, 120–21, 204, 206, 210, 271
motor industry 77–8, 152; *see also* Toyota
Motorola 154
multi-skilling 32, 113, 151
Murphy, Richard 50
music industry 124

National Asset Management Agency (NAMA) 224–5, 226, 239, 247
natural wastage 84, 85, 196, 199, 212
negative equity 223
negotiation 28–9, 112, 119, 254
New Public Management 99–100, 258
newspaper industry 175–9
Nyberg Report 226, 241

objectives 15
offshore outsourcing 123, 124, 182, 185–7, 191
oil industry 95, 144–5
oil prices 7, 17, 106, 111, 123
O'Leary, Michael 105–6, 109, 110, 113, 114
operating margins 43, 46–7
operations 27, 82–4, 103, 104, 108–9, 171
opportunity costs 175
optimal size 116–18, 120–21, 126, 127
organisation and methods departments 35–6
organisational culture 71, 113, 151, 218, 257
organisational learning 90–91
organisational structure benchmarking 171
outbound logistics 34, 103, 104, 109
outplacement 85, 178
outsourcing 76, 111, 114, 121, 123, 133, 180–91, 261, 270
overall cost leadership strategy 67–8
Overall Equipment Effectiveness (OEE) 151
overborrowing 233–4, 235, 246–7
overheads 4, 27, 80–81; *see also* indirect costs
overtrading 48, 233, 237, 241, 246, 247

Paretto, Vilfredo 124
Paulson, Hank 237
payroll costs *see* labour costs
pensions 32, 86, 196, 198, 199, 204, 205, 261
performance benchmarking 170
performance evaluation 5, 16, 32, 40–49, 254–5, 269, 271
performance ratios 243
performance variances 16
permanent employees 197–8, 211
pharmaceutical industry 94, 168
Philips 26
piecemeal approach 37–8
planning 264–73
political model 72
political stimuli 65
Porter, Michael 67, 89, 219
primary activities 94, 103–5
Prince, Chuck 209
printing industry 97–8, 141, 153
prioritisation 18–20
priority-based budgeting 10
problem identification 136
problem solving 136–9, 151
procurement 28–30, 87, 104, 111–12, 144
product benchmarking 171
productivity 32, 140, 171, 198, 205
professional service firms 100–101
profitability 243
profit margins 42
profit sharing 11, 205
project management 64, 162, 165, 188, 249–51, 263
property bubble 56, 207, 223–5, 236–7, 241, 245
property lending 56, 206–11, 222–30, 236–8, 241
public sector 5, 7, 21, 28, 36, 65, 70, 98–100, 117, 185, 200, 205, 244–8, 257–63

purchasing *see* procurement
Pyrrh, Peter 8

qualifications 86
quality 9–10, 219–20, 230

radical improvement 146–60
rating agencies 207, 208, 210, 243
receivership 59
recession 16, 24, 29, 42, 43, 45, 46, 52, 53, 100–101, 122, 125, 153, 198–9, 202, 233, 246, 264–8; *see also* banking crisis; credit crunch
reckless trading 59
recruitment 31–2, 98, 99, 179, 196, 199, 212; *see also* human resources
redundancies 58, 85, 98, 200–202, 212, 213, 235, 253, 261–2
regulation 93, 95, 125, 186, 204, 207, 209, 210, 228, 267
relationship cost drivers 93–5, 98
relocation 201, 202–3
remuneration 23, 32, 64, 93, 101, 153, 177, 196, 197, 198, 199, 200, 204–5, 211, 246, 258, 261–2
repurchase agreements 238
research and development 31, 96, 121, 153
return on capital employed (ROCE) 44, 45
return on invested capital (ROIC) 44–8, 49, 268
rewards 5, 11, 16–17, 18, 23, 32, 54, 115, 159, 196, 198, 200, 203–11, 212, 246
risk management 79, 234, 237, 240, 241–2
role culture 71
rolling budgets 16, 214

Roubini, Nouriel 265
Ryan, Tony 105–6, 114
Ryanair 103, 105–15, 252, 257

safety *see* health and safety
salaries *see* remuneration
sales and marketing 35, 77–8, 103, 104, 109–11, 171
sales forecasting 14, 17
SAP 14, 120
scalability 125
securitisation 207, 208–9, 236
Semco 116
Semler, Ricardo 116
separation of functions 79
service 103–4, 111
service benchmarking 171
service industries 27, 31, 80, 92, 98–101, 105, 121, 142–4, 195, 197–8
set-up times 152–3, 168
seven S model 217–18, 222
Seven Steps problem solving 133, 135, 137–9, 158
'Shamrock Organisations' 182, 196–8, 201
share incentive schemes 113, 204
share prices 42, 47, 66, 243
shareholder value 42–3, 47–8, 49
Shook, John 134–5
short-termism 48
short-time working 58, 85, 200
silo mentality 5, 24, 38
situational cost drivers 92–3
Six Sigma 133, 153, 154–7, 160, 268, 271, 277–80
size of business 116–27, 268
size cost drivers 89–91
Smith, Adam 90, 118
social media 125
social stimuli 65

Social Partnership programme 99, 205
social values 69–70, 219
soft targets 7
software rental 33
Southwest Airlines 105–6
specialisation 118, 120, 126
sponsorship 35
standard costing 214–15
standardisation 150, 155
stock control 27, 33, 53–4, 163
strategic frameworks 64–5
strategy 14, 63–74, 76, 114, 171, 217–18, 230, 270
stretch targets 7, 15
subcontractors 197–8, 211; *see also* outsourcing
sub-prime lending 56, 206–11, 222, 236–7, 266
supermarket industry 17, 28, 54, 70, 119
supplier management 28–30
supply chains 34–5
support activities 94, 103–5
swaps market 236

target costing 215
targets 5, 7, 15, 38, 45, 46–7, 268
task assignment culture 71
taxation 52, 93, 246
team selection 70, 72, 250, 255
technological stimuli 65
technology *see* information technology
temporary workers 197–8, 211
Tesco 28, 57
Texas Instruments 8
three-dimensional printing 124
three Es approach 20–23, 24, 217
timing decisions 97
Tomkins 142–4

Total Productive Maintenance (TPM) 133, 151–2
Total Quality Management (TQM) 133
Toyota 134–5, 140, 147–54
Toyota Production System (TPS) 133, 151, 157–8
tracker mortgages 223, 229
trade credit *see* credit control; creditors
trade unions 32, 72, 86, 93, 109, 111, 120, 157, 198, 252
training 32, 86, 96, 121, 153, 159, 179, 196, 198, 268–9
travel costs 22–3, 34, 35, 36, 175, 199
travel industry 7, 16, 181; *see also* low fares airlines
turnover *see* capital turnover; labour turnover

Unilever 35, 228
UPS 150

value analysis 31
value chain 94, 103–15, 268–9, 270
value engineering 31
values 66, 69–70, 74, 75–88, 198–9, 218–19, 222, 225–30
variable costs 76, 80
variable pay 99, 205
vertical integration 95

Virgin Group 116
vision 256
visual management systems 152, 159
Volcker, Paul 210
voluntary redundancies 85, 98, 199, 201, 253, 261

Wallander, Jan 11
warehousing 134, 163; *see also* logistics; stock control
waste elimination 21, 27, 99, 132, 133, 141, 165–6, 167, 268
WCM *see* World Class Manufacturing
Welch, Jack 1, 211
Wipro 211
working capital 43, 52–4, 59, 97, 180, 233, 243
working conditions 86, 186–7, 204
World Class Manufacturing (WCM) 76, 82–3, 87, 131–45, 146–60; *see also* lean operations
WorldCom 18

Xerox 171
Xtra-vision 50

Zara 163
zero-based budgeting 8–10

"This is an interesting book, providing a useful guide to cost reduction with application throughout Europe."
**Dr Klaus Oesch, Chairman, Orell Füssli Holding Ltd (Swiss Listed Printing and Publishing Group)**

"The authors are to be congratulated on tackling cost reduction in a strategic context with appropriate overall business performance measures."
**Horst Schneider, Chairman, IPAG AG (Engineering Consultancy)**

"The authors have managed to crystallize a broad range of themes and issues in 'Strategic Cost Reduction', which makes for an outstanding reference source on corporate strategic thinking around cost management."
**Mike Soden, Member of the Central Bank Commission and former CEO of Bank of Ireland**

"This book contains excellent practical advice, highly relevant to the public sector, which needs to address the task urgently."
**Shane Ross TD, Independent Irish politician**

"This handbook is timely and offers a range of suggestions for significant and long-lasting cost savings that will support future strategy."
**Terry McLaughlin, Chief Executive, New Zealand Institute of Chartered Accountants**

"Strategic cost reduction is not just for a crisis, it is for life. This book provides a welcome handbook for managers seeking to reduce costs in a focused, strategic manner."
**John McStay, McStay Luby, Chartered Accountants and Corporate Recovery Specialists**

"Success in cost reduction is a function of understanding the customer value embedded in your strategic position and how each element of your delivery system supports this. McCormick and Duff provide a thorough discussion of the various tools and methods that are considered best practice, presenting both clear examples and a framework for those embarking on the quest."
**Bill Lawler, Leadership Professor of Strategy & Accounting, Babson College, Boston, USA**

"This is an excellent guide for practitioners and is strongly recommended reading for MBAs."
**Michael Flynn, MBA Programme Director, Trinity College, Dublin**